# Start Here!™

# Fundamentals of Microsoft®
# .NET Programming

Rod Stephens

Published with the authorization of Microsoft Corporation by:
O'Reilly Media, Inc.
1005 Gravenstein Highway North
Sebastopol, California 95472

ISBN: 978-0-7356-6168-4

1 2 3 4 5 6 7 8 9 LSI 6 5 4 3 2 1

Printed and bound in the United States of America.

Microsoft Press books are available through booksellers and distributors worldwide. If you need support related to this book, email Microsoft Press Book Support at *mspinput@microsoft.com*. Please tell us what you think of this book at *http://www.microsoft.com/learning/booksurvey*.

Microsoft and the trademarks listed at *http://www.microsoft.com/about/legal/en/us/IntellectualProperty/ Trademarks/EN-US.aspx* are trademarks of the Microsoft group of companies. All other marks are property of their respective owners.

The example companies, organizations, products, domain names, email addresses, logos, people, places, and events depicted herein are fictitious. No association with any real company, organization, product, domain name, email address, logo, person, place, or event is intended or should be inferred.

This book expresses the author's views and opinions. The information contained in this book is provided without any express, statutory, or implied warranties. Neither the authors, O'Reilly Media, Inc., Microsoft Corporation, nor its resellers, or distributors will be held liable for any damages caused or alleged to be caused either directly or indirectly by this book.

**Acquisitions and Developmental Editor:** Russell Jones

**Production Editor:** Jasmine Perez

**Editorial Production:** S4Carlisle Publishing Services

**Technical Reviewer:** Debbie Timmins

**Indexer:** WordCo Indexing Services, Inc.

**Cover:** Valerie DeGiulio

# Contents at a Glance

# Contents

**What do you think of this book? We want to hear from you!**

Microsoft is interested in hearing your feedback so we can continually improve our
books and learning resources for you. To participate in a brief online survey, please visit:

**http://microsoft.com/learning/booksurvey**

## Chapter 12   Globalization                                                    183

## Chapter 13   Data Storage                                                     191

---

### What do you think of this book? We want to hear from you!

Microsoft is interested in hearing your feedback so we can continually improve our
books and learning resources for you. To participate in a brief online survey, please visit:

**http://microsoft.com/learning/booksurvey**

# Introduction

Programming languages do one very simple thing: they allow you to write programs that tell the computer what to do. You can tell a computer to read a value from the keyboard, add two numbers, save a result in a file on the hard disk, or draw a smiley face on the screen.

No matter what programming language you use, the underlying commands that the computer can execute are exactly the same. Whether you use Java, C#, Microsoft Visual Basic, COBOL, LISP, or any other language, you can make the computer perform roughly the same tasks. Two languages may have very different syntaxes, and some languages make some tasks easier than others, but the fundamental operations they can perform are the same. All these languages can carry out numeric calculations and manipulate files; unfortunately, none of them can reliably pick lottery winners. (If you write a program that can, let me know!)

At a more conceptual level, programming concepts have been refined over the years until most modern languages share a common set of fundamental concepts, such as variables, classes, objects, forms, menus, files, and multiprocessing. Don't worry if you don't know what these are—the purpose of this book is to provide more information about such terms and concepts.

Because programming languages share so many operations and concepts, programming books tend to cover the same topics as well. Books about databases or graphics cover these specialized topics in great detail. Different authors may place emphasis on different subjects, but there's a lot of overlap, particularly in beginning and general "how to program" books. Every one of these books explains what a variable is, how to create objects, and what a text file contains.

All this means that if you want to learn more than one programming language (a practice that I highly recommend), you're going to encounter much of the same material repeatedly. Even if you skim the familiar sections, you still have to pay for the content. You may start with a 600-page book about Visual Basic programming. Later, when you buy a 500-page C# book, you'll discover that 200 of those pages cover things you already know. Next, when your boss decides you need to learn LISP, you'll find that your new 550-page book contains 100 pages that you already know. (There are a lot of differences between LISP and the other two languages, so there will be less overlap if you shift to that language.)

This edition of the *Start Here!* series changes all that. Rather than making each *Start Here!* book cover the exact same topics, those common topics have been moved into this volume for easy reference. Now if you read *Start Here! Learn Microsoft Visual C# 2010 Programming* or *Start Here! Learn Microsoft Visual Basic Programming*, you won't need to rehash the exact same topics. Instead, those books refer you to this one for background information, such as how disk buffering works, freeing the other books to focus on language-specific issues.

There still will be some overlap between any books about different languages. For example, Visual Basic and C# both let you read and write disk files. Although *Start Here! Fundamentals of .NET Programming* explains in general what disk files are and how programs interact with them, the other books still need to explain the syntax for the code that their respective languages use to read and write files.

Note that this book doesn't necessarily cover every last detail of each background topic. It just gives you the information you need to understand how programs fit into a larger context so that you can get the most out of them. For example, this book explains some important programming issues relating to disk drives, but it doesn't explain in detail how disk drives work.

Moving underlying common topics into this separate book provides several benefits, including the following:

- Other *Start Here!* books can spend less time on the background material covered in this book and more time on language-specific issues. Those books can rely on and refer to this book to provide extra detail as needed.

- This book provides more room for, and spends more time on, basic concepts that beginning programming books often must gloss over to make room for language-specific concepts.

- This book provides a single location for learning about general computer topics, without focusing on a particular language. This is important because it can give you a broader understanding of what you can make computers do easily and what might be difficult to make a computer do, regardless of which programming language you choose.

- This book can act as an enhanced glossary, giving you a place to look for explanations of common computer terms. A normal glossary briefly defines key terms, but in addition, the rest of the book provides much more detail about important concepts.

# Who Should Read This Book

This book is for anyone who wants a basic understanding of computers and the environments in which programs operate. It provides background information that is useful when you are trying to learn to use any programming language. It also provides information that can help you understand how programs work in general. For example, it explains what multithreading is and why multi-core computers may not always perform much better than single-core systems.

## Assumptions

This book does *not* assume that you have any previous programming experience. In fact, it doesn't even assume that you have a computer! Instead, this book is about understanding computers and programs in general, and Microsoft Windows and .NET concepts in particular, not about writing programs in a specific language.

This book is intended for two main audiences: those who want to learn a new programming language, particularly those who are reading one of the other books in the *Start Here!* series, and those who want a better overall understanding of computers.

Although the content of this book is as general as possible, it is not primarily intended as a stand-alone work; instead, it's intended as an accompanying volume for use with other *Start Here!* books, which cover a range of languages and technologies. Most of the information you'll find here applies to computers and programs running Windows, but many of the concepts also apply to other operating systems, such as Unix, Linux, or OS X. Sometimes, however, specificity aids clarity, so in some places this book is targeted toward Windows.

# Who Should Not Read This Book

If you're interested in general programming—particularly non-Windows and non–Microsoft .NET Framework programming—this book is not for you. Much of the information in this book applies to programming in general, but a substantial portion of the information applies to .NET Framework topics, and this book does not make any particular effort to distinguish between general and Windows- or .NET Framework–specific information.

# What You Need to Use This Book

If you want to use this book, all you'll need is this book. No computer, no software, no programming language, and no programming experience is required!

# Organization of This Book

If you just want a better understanding of computers and programming concepts, you can simply read the book.

If you're reading this book along with one of the other *Start Here!* books, you can take a couple of different approaches. First, you can use this book as a reference for the other. When you reach the part of *Start Here! Learn Microsoft Visual C# 2010 Programming* that discusses operators, you may want to read this book's chapter on operators for additional background. *Start Here! Learn Microsoft Visual C# 2010 Programming* may also explicitly refer to places in this book where you can get additional information on a topic.

Another approach to using this book with another *Start Here!* book would be to read this one at odd moments when it's hard to read the other one. For example, I like to use my computer to work through examples and experiment with the code as I'm learning a new language. That makes it hard for me to work through a book like *Start Here! Learn Microsoft Visual C# 2010 Programming* on the bus, waiting at the dentist's office, or while sunning myself on the beach. In contrast, *Start Here! Fundamentals of Microsoft .NET Programming* doesn't require a computer, so it's easy to read just about anywhere (although at the beach, I'd rather play volleyball anyway).

This book is divided into 14 chapters plus a glossary. The chapters are independent, so you can read them in any order. In fact, many of the sections in the chapters are independent, so you can jump around within a chapter to suit your interests and needs.

- **Chapter 1, "Computer Hardware,"** briefly describes the hardware of a computer system. It explains terms such as *computer processing unit (CPU), graphics processing unit (GPU), random access memory (RAM),* and *multi-core,* and explains why those terms are important to programmers. It explains how memory, disk accesses, and other hardware issues can affect a program's performance.

- **Chapter 2, "Multiprocessing,"** summarizes some of the challenges that face programmers writing multiprocessing programs. It explains how the future of programming is likely to be highly parallel and summarizes the Task Parallel Library (TPL) that makes programming for multi-core systems easier.

- **Chapter 3, "Programming Environments,"** explains what a programming environment is and describes some of the features that make Microsoft Visual Studio one of the best programming environments available. It explains how a program's code must be compiled and how a programming environment can make that code transparent to the programmer.

- **Chapter 4, "Windows Program Components,"** describes the pieces of a Windows program from the user's point of view. It describes menus, content menus, accelerators, shortcuts, and dialog boxes. It also mentions several design considerations that beginning programmers should understand if they want to make programs easier to use.

- **Chapter 5, "Controls,"** describes in general terms what controls and components are and how they are used. It also mentions some common properties, such as *Dock* and *Anchor,* which make using many controls easier for the programmer.

- **Chapter 6, "Variables,"** explains the concept of a variable. It explains variable concepts such as data types, conversions, strong and weak type checking, value versus reference types, scope, and accessibility.

- **Chapter 7, "Control Statements,"** describes control statements, such as *If Then* and *For Each,* which a program uses to manage a program's flow. It describes these statements in general terms, provides some examples in pseudocode, and shows a few simple examples in Visual Basic and C# for comparison.

- **Chapter 8, "Operators,"** explains operators. It discusses precedence rules and operator overloading.

- **Chapter 9, "Routines,"** explains what routines are and how they are useful in programming. It describes different kinds of routines, such as methods, subroutines, and functions. It also defines parameters and explains the confusing topic of parameters passed by value or passed by reference.

- **Chapter 10, "Object-Oriented Programming,"** provides an introduction to object-oriented programming. It explains classes, constructors, and destructors. It describes non-deterministic finalization.

- **Chapter 11, "Development Techniques,"** describes basic programming techniques such as using comments, naming conventions, interfaces, and generic classes.

- **Chapter 12, "Globalization,"** explains how to localize a program in Visual Studio so that it works in multiple places. It explains several localization issues, such as different date, number, and currency formats.

- **Chapter 13, "Data Storage,"** describes different methods for storing data such as using the registry, configuration files, and files on disk. It explains different kinds of files, such as Extensible Markup Language (XML) files and databases, and mentions some of the classes that a program would use to work with different kinds of files.

- **Chapter 14, ".NET Libraries,"** summarizes some of the libraries that are most useful in writing NET programs. These libraries let a program encrypt and decrypt information, work with data structures such as stacks and queues, interrogate objects and types to learn about them, and work with multiple threads of execution.

- **The glossary** provides a brief summary of key terms to remind you of their meaning. (In a sense, the whole book acts as a glossary for use by the other *Start Here!* books.) It summarizes key concepts in one or two sentences.

## Conventions and Features in This Book

To help you get the most from the text and keep track of what's happening, I've used several conventions throughout the book.

### Splendid Sidebars

Sidebars such as this one contain additional information and side topics.

**Warning** Boxes with a Warning icon like this one hold important, not-to-be-forgotten information that is directly relevant to the surrounding text.

**Note** The Note icon indicates notes and asides to the current discussion. They are offset and placed in a box like this.

**Tip** The Tip icon indicates tips, bits and pieces of advice on effective programming. They are offset and placed in a box like this.

**More Info** The More Info icon indicates somewhere you can go to learn for more information on a particular topic, such as a webpage. They are offset and placed in a box like this.

As for styles in the text:

- New terms and important words are *italicized* when they are introduced. You can also find many of them in the glossary at the end of the book.

- Keyboard keystrokes look like this: Ctrl+A. The plus sign means that you should hold down the Ctrl key and then press the A key.

- Uniform Resource Locators (URLs), code, and email addresses within the text are shown in italics, as in *http://www.vb-helper.com*, *x = 10*, and *RodStephens@vb-helper.com*.

```
Separate code examples use a monofont type with no highlighting.
Bold  text  emphasizes  code  that's  particularly  important  in  the  current
context.
```

**Note** The code editor in Visual Studio provides a rich color scheme to indicate various parts of code syntax such as variables, comments, and Visual Basic keywords. The code editor and the Intellisense feature of Visual Studio are excellent tools to help you learn language features in the editor and help you prevent mistakes as you code. However, the colors that you can see in Visual Studio don't show up in the code in this book.

# Source Code

Because this book covers concepts that are independent of any particular programming language, it also includes little source code from any particular language. You'll find occasional bits of source code used to contrast the syntaxes of different languages; but more often, this book uses *pseudocode* to demonstrate programming constructs. Pseudocode is an informal high-level "language" that looks sort of like a programming language, but isn't really. It's intended to describe a situation sufficiently so that you *could* implement the actual code in whatever language you are using.

For example, the following code shows a *for* loop in pseudocode, which repeats a particular operation a specific number of times:

```
For <variable> From 1 To 100
    Do something
```

This pseudocode says the program should make a variable (however you create a variable in the language you're using) and then loop starting at value 1 and finishing at value 100. For each trip through the loop, the program should "Do something."

Contrast this with the following C# code:

```
for (int i = 1; i <= 100; i++)
{
    DoSomething();
}
```

This code does the same thing as the previous pseudocode, but its syntax makes understanding the code harder—unless, of course, you know C# (or some related language, such as C++ or Java). If you don't know C#, you may have trouble understanding the point that this code is illustrating.

## Acknowledgments

Thanks to Russell Jones, Diane Kohnen, Dan Fauxsmith, Jasmine Perez, and all the others at O'Reilly Media and Microsoft Press who worked so hard to make this book possible. Also thanks to John Mueller, Evangelos Petroutsos, and authors of the language-centric books in this Start Here! series. Between us I think we've put together a great set of resources!

## Errata & Book Support

We've made every effort to ensure the accuracy of this book and its companion content. Any errors that have been reported since this book was published are listed on our Microsoft Press site at *oreilly.com:*

*http://go.microsoft.com/FWLink/?Linkid=230431*

If you find an error that is not already listed, you can report it to us through the same page.

If you need additional support, email Microsoft Press Book Support at *mspinput@microsoft.com*.

Please note that product support for Microsoft software is *not* offered through the addresses above.

## We Want to Hear from You

At Microsoft Press, your satisfaction is our top priority, and your feedback our most valuable asset. Please tell us what you think of this book at:

*http://www.microsoft.com/learning/booksurvey*

The survey is short, and we read every one of your comments and ideas. Thanks in advance for your input!

## Stay in Touch

Let's keep the conversation going! We're on Twitter: *http://twitter.com/MicrosoftPress*.

## Other Resources

You can find more information about this book at *http://www.vb-helper.com/start_here_fundamentals.html* or at *http://www.CSharpHelper.com/start_here_fundamentals.html*. Both of these pages provide links to updates, addenda, and other information related to this book.

If you're interested, subscribe to one of my Visual Basic newsletters at *www.vb-helper.com/newsletter.html* or visit my C# blog at *blog.CSharpHelper.com*.

If you have questions, comments, or suggestions, please feel free to email me at *RodStephens@vb-helper.com* or *RodStephens@CSharpHelper.com*. I can't promise to solve all your problems, but I do promise to try to help.

# Chapter 1

# Computer Hardware

**In this chapter:**

- What the different kinds of computers are and how the type of computer being used influences the performance of various kinds of programs

- How to assess the speed of a computer and look for potential bottlenecks for different kinds of programs

- The strengths and weaknesses of different data storage devices

- How to ensure that data written to a file is saved and not discarded when a program ends or crashes

- What networks and protocols are

**THE MOST ELEGANTLY WRITTEN PROGRAM IN** the world is pointless (except as an esoteric work of art) if it doesn't eventually run on some sort of physical device. Often, that device is an ordinary desktop or laptop computer. Having identified the target platform, you might think you don't have to worry about hardware.

To some extent that's true, and—depending on your program—you may be able to ignore much of the computer's hardware. If you have a simple, self-contained, single-user desktop application, you also may be able to ignore the computer's power supply, fans, universal serial bus (USB) ports, Blu-ray drive, Wi-Fi antenna, sound card, microphone, and many other pieces of hardware.

Most programming languages provide high-level access to hardware such as the computer's disk drives, memory, keyboard, and mouse, so you don't necessarily need to know exactly how they work. For example, you usually don't need to know how many disk heads a disk drive has or how many revolutions per second its disks turn to read and write files.

Even though you don't always need to know all these hardware details, you should at least have some understanding of what's going on behind the scenes. For example, if you don't understand how memory use relates to paging, poor memory use can drag your entire system to a grinding halt.

This chapter explains fundamental hardware concepts that can help you get the most out of your programs. This information can help you avoid problems that can be difficult to solve after they occur.

# Types of Computers

In the 1960s, computers were warehouse-sized monstrosities costing millions of dollars. The acolytes who worked with these behemoths were engineers who dealt as much with hardware as they did software, so they generally knew what equipment was present.

Today, computers can be small and inexpensive, and they are just about everywhere: on your desk, in your dentist's office, under the hood of your car, and in your phone. Despite being millions of times smaller than the now-ancient computers of 50 years ago, these new devices are millions of times more powerful.

> **Note** The Intel 4004 processor introduced in 1971 could perform 0.07 million instructions per second (MIPS). The fastest processors today are cooled by liquid nitrogen. The IBM z196 processor, which is currently not for sale, reportedly can execute up to 50 billion instructions per second (that is, 50,000 MIPS). The Chinese Tianhe-1A supercomputer can execute 2.57 petaflops (quadrillion floating-point operations per second), although it won't fit on your desktop. See *http://www.top500.org* for the latest information about the world's fastest supercomputers.

When you design a program, you need to consider the device that will run it so you know what kinds of capabilities are likely to be present. The following sections summarize common types of computers that are available today.

## Personal Computers

*Personal computer* (PC) is a general term for a computer intended to be used by a single person at one time, although multiple users may use it at different times. It includes other categories such as desktops, laptops, and personal digital assistants (PDAs).

## Desktops, Towers, and Workstations

A *desktop computer* is intended to sit on or beside your desk and not be portable, although most are small enough these days that you can easily pick one up. Because they are not intended to be portable, they typically don't have batteries and integrated screens or keyboards.

The *all-in-one* style desktop has an integrated screen or, to look at it in another way, the computer is attached to a monitor.

A *tower* is similar to a desktop computer, but in a larger case. Its larger size makes it easier to add new hardware, although it may make it hard to fit on a desk.

A *workstation* is a more powerful desktop or tower that may have extra features, such as extra memory and disk space, multiple screens, and fancy graphics hardware for quickly performing three-dimensional (3-D) rendering.

Desktops, towers, and workstations can be quite powerful. They can have fast processors, lots of memory, big hard drives, and large monitors so they can tackle almost any task. If they are connected to a fast network, they also can provide access to centralized databases and servers. Their main disadvantages are that they are not portable, and they may be needlessly expensive for some applications, such as web browsing.

## Laptops, Notebooks, Netbooks, and Tablets

A *laptop* is a computer that is intended to be portable and is used just about anywhere (except in the swimming pool). You can literally use a laptop on your lap while you are riding a bus or airplane (legroom permitting).

Because they are intended to run anywhere, laptops have integrated screens and keyboards. They often run on batteries, so power use and battery quality is very important. Heavy use of some pieces of hardware such as the graphics processing unit (GPU) and DVD drives can quickly drain the batteries.

Laptop disk and Blu-ray/DVD/CD-ROM drives are often slower and smaller than those in desktop systems, so programs that use disk files heavily may run more slowly on a laptop. Often, a desktop is faster than a laptop with the same clock speed because of the performance of devices such as these.

Laptops usually have a touchpad, pointing stick, trackball, or other pointing device. Many people find these devices harder to use than a mouse, so they add an external mouse connected to the computer.

*Notebooks* are basically stripped-down laptops that trade power for portability. They are thin, have relatively small screens, and are ultra-light. They rarely have DVD or CD-ROM drives, and they have fairly limited graphics capabilities.

Because they have no external media such as DVD drives, they typically have integrated network connection hardware so you can load software onto them. Network hardware also means you can use them to access the Internet.

*Netbooks* are even more stripped down than notebooks. They typically have less powerful processors and are intended primarily for use with networked applications such as web browsers, where most of the processing occurs on a remote server.

> **Note** Other terms for these portable computers include *subnotebook, ultraportable,* and *mini notebook*. Many people use all these terms interchangeably.

A *tablet* computer is a portable computer similar to a laptop that uses a touchscreen or stylus as its primary input device. Tablets may display virtual keyboards on their screens and may use handwriting recognition for text input.

Laptops and tablets can have most of the same features as desktop systems (such as fast processors, lots of memory, and big hard drives) so they can handle many application needs.

Some applications can take advantage of a tablet's touchscreen, and in fact, the lack of a keyboard can be an advantage in some environments, for example at dusty construction sites, where a keyboard might let dirt into the system.

Laptops and tablets tend to be a bit more expensive than desktop systems, and some users don't like their smaller keyboards and lack of a mouse. You can overcome those limitations by adding an external keyboard and mouse if you like, although that adds further to the cost, and of course, reduces portability.

Notebooks and netbooks are often not as powerful as laptops and tablets. They are intended to be both ultra-portable and less expensive. They are often intended for running networked applications, such as web browsers. However, they do include keyboards, making them more suitable than tablets for people who need to type a lot of information.

## Minis, Servers, and Mainframes

*Mainframes* are large centralized computers that can serve hundreds or even thousands of users simultaneously. Each user connects to the mainframe via a "dumb" terminal that has little or no processing power; the terminal simply serves as an input device and displays results generated by the mainframe.

A recent innovation that is similar to mainframe computing is *cloud computing,* where applications, data storage, collaboration services, and other key tools are stored on a centralized server that users access remotely, often through a browser. The users typically connect to the cloud services with a desktop, laptop, or other computer instead of a "dumb" terminal.

The centralized services provided by the mainframe and cloud computing allow a business to upgrade tools without modifying the users' computers. For example, a business can add more disk space or an upgrade to a centralized application on the central servers with no changes to the users' computers.

A *mini* or *minicomputer* is basically a small mainframe that can serve a dozen to a few hundred users simultaneously. Typically, a mainframe might fill a room, whereas a mini might be the size of a filing cabinet.

*Supercomputer* is a fairly broad term used to describe only the fastest computers. A supercomputer may act as a mainframe and support many simultaneous users, but its focus is on running one program or a few huge programs extremely quickly, rather than on performing many smaller tasks for many users. Typical mainframe applications include massive simulations for weather prediction, fluid dynamics calculations, and nuclear energy research.

Often, a supercomputer uses other computers as "front-ends." Users prepare programs for execution on a second computer. When the program's code and data is ready, it is transferred to the supercomputer for execution. The results are then returned to the secondary computer for analysis.

*Server* is a generic term for any computer that supports multiple users or client applications simultaneously, so supercomputers, mainframes, and minis are all servers. Mainframes are sometimes called *enterprise servers*.

Minis, servers, and mainframes are useful for applications that have large centralized databases and other resources. For example, suppose you have 100 customer service representatives who may need to interact with any customer's records. In that case, it makes sense to store all the customer information on a server. The users can either use desktop systems to access the information and work with it on their local machines, or "dumb" terminals to work directly on a mainframe.

It's worth noting that there are ways to attach dumb terminals to less powerful servers than mainframes as well.

# Handheld Computers

*Handheld computers* are, as the name implies, computers that you can hold in your hand. These range in size from about the size of a brick to the size of a deck of playing cards.

These devices typically have small screens and may use touchscreens alone or touchscreens with a stylus for input. Some even have integrated barcode scanners and printers.

*Palmtops* or *pocket* computers are small handheld devices, usually with limited graphics and computing power. They are typically used to store simple information such as contact information, phone numbers, and appointment calendars.

PDAs are similar to palmtops but typically use a stylus and various forms of handwriting recognition for input.

Smartphones running the Windows Phone 7 operating system, iPhone OS (iOS), or Android are basically very small, general-purpose computers with integrated telephone features.

Some of the more powerful palmtops include other features, such as networking capabilities and may even act as music players and phones. Overall, the division between cell phones and palmtops is becoming blurred because many modern cell phones include all the features previously provided by PDAs—and even more.

Handheld computers are useful when portability is essential. For example, a telephone technician would have trouble juggling a laptop at the top of a telephone pole. They also are handy for carrying information that you want available throughout the day, such as phone numbers and appointment calendars. These devices tend to have tiny screens and keyboards, so tasks such as entering data on large forms or viewing large amounts of data can be difficult. More and more these days, smartphones have surprisingly fast processors and good graphics capabilities, however.

## Comparing Computer Types

A program's use and needs influence the type of computers you should run it on. Consider the program's processing speed, network bandwidth, and screen size requirements and compare them to the features provided by different computer types.

Conversely, a computer's specific hardware can influence the kinds of programs that you can build effectively. For example, if your company has 75 users who all carry only small handheld computers, your program can't display large forms containing dozens of menus.

# Computer Speed

Many people use *clock speed* as a measure of a computer's total computing power, but that term can be very misleading for a couple of reasons. To really understand why this is so, you need to know a little about how the computer processes commands.

The computer keeps all its devices synchronized by using its clock. This isn't a regular clock—it's a "clock in a chip," which keeps highly accurate time and ticks much more rapidly than a wall clock. The faster the computer's clock ticks, the more quickly the device can move on to a new task. The *central processing unit (CPU)*, the computer's main processor, needs a certain number of clock ticks to execute each of its instructions. Therefore, the faster the clock ticks (that is, the "clock speed"), the more instructions the CPU can execute per second.

However, that's not the end of the story. Different processors use different instruction sets, each of which can require a different number of ticks. That means different kinds of processors may execute different numbers of instructions per second, even if they have the same clock speed. You can use clock rate to compare two of the same *kinds of processor* (for example, a 2.93-gigahertz (GHz) Intel Pentium 4 and a 3.0-GHz Intel Pentium 4) but not as an accurate comparison between two processors of different types (for example, a 3.0-GHz Intel Pentium 4 and a 3.0-GHz AMD Athlon II).

Even if you could figure out which processor executes more instructions per second, that figure alone doesn't necessarily tell you which computer will be faster *for your program*. Many programs—most, in fact—are limited by factors other than sheer processor speed, including amount and speed of memory, disk space, network speed, graphics or floating-point processor speeds, and *bus* speed.

> **Note** The *bus* is the part of the computer that transfers data between the computer's different components such as its processor and disk drives. The USB lets a computer connect to all sorts of external devices, such as hard drives, DVD drives, keyboards, mice, graphics tablets, flash drives, cameras, and much more.

Many modern computers have multiple processors or multiple cores (execution areas within a processor), so they can perform more than one task at the same time. Whether the computer gets a significant benefit from multiple cores depends on whether the tasks it is performing can be easily split into separate pieces—and whether the program was written to take advantage of multi-core hardware.

Many programs are limited by disk drive speed. Disk drives spin at anywhere from 3,000 RPM to 15,000 RPM (speeds between 4,200 RPM and 7,200 RPM are most typical), so the time it takes to read and write data can vary dramatically.

Which of these factors is most important for your application depends on what that application does. If your program uses a local database (that is, one stored on a hard disk attached to the computer) heavily, disk speed will be a big factor. If the database is on a remote server accessed via a network, then the speed of the server and the network's speed are probably bigger performance factors for your application than the speed of your local CPU.

The best way to determine how a computer will perform for a given program is to run that program on the computer. Unfortunately, it's often too late to fix problems after you've written the program and bought the computer.

To get an idea of how well the program will run ahead of time, focus on the system's overall performance, running a wide variety of tests rather than looking just at clock speed. To look at one set of tests in the most recent versions of Microsoft Windows, open the computer's Start menu, right-click the Computer entry, and select Properties to see the basic information display shown in Figure 1-1. (You can also right-click the Computer entry in Windows Explorer and select Properties.) The Windows Experience Index gives you a rough idea of the computer's overall performance.

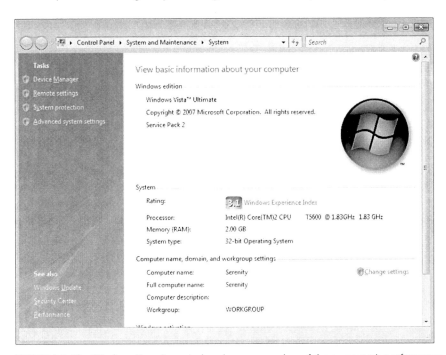

**FIGURE 1-1** The Windows Experience Index gives an overview of the computer's performance.

To get more detail, click the Windows Experience Index link to see the display shown in Figure 1-2. This display shows performance scores for several different system features.

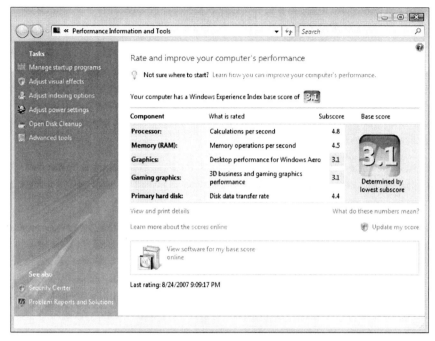

**FIGURE 1-2** This display shows how well the computer performs on various tests.

On the system shown in Figures 1-1 and 1-2, the graphics scores are the lowest, so this system may not give the best performance for high-end graphics programs, such as three-dimensional games. But the processor, random access memory (RAM), and disk scores are higher, so this computer may be just fine for applications that are not graphics-intensive. (In fact, this computer works just fine for me on a wide range of applications.)

The Windows Experience Index still doesn't consider your program's particular needs. For example, it doesn't know what kinds of instructions your program will perform the most (such as integer calculations, floating-point calculations, string operations, and so on) and it doesn't consider network bandwidth, but at least it provides a reasonably consistent value that can help you compare different systems. Start there, and then consider the bottlenecks that your program is likely to encounter.

# Data Storage

A program can store data in several places, including RAM, flash drives, hard drives, Blu-ray, DVDs, and CDs. The following sections describe the advantages and disadvantages of each so you can match them to your program's needs.

# RAM

RAM is extremely fast, but relatively expensive. Moving data between RAM and the processor is lightning-fast, so it's the best place to store frequently used data. Data stored in program variables is generally stored in RAM, which gives them the best performance.

Unfortunately, RAM is also fairly expensive, so computers often have a limited supply. A typical computer might have 2 GB of RAM. That may seem like a lot (and it is), but you need to remember that your program isn't the only one using the RAM. Every program currently running on the system, including the operating system itself, shares it. In fact, the commands that make up the executing programs themselves also take up space in RAM.

Data must move from RAM to the processor and back for anything to occur, so what happens if the programs use up all the RAM? To work around this problem, the computer can page memory to disk.

When *paging* occurs, the computer copies a chunk of its memory onto a hard disk and frees that memory for use by other programs. Later, when a program needs to access the data in the chunk of memory that was copied to the hard disk, the computer pages it back into memory, possibly moving other data to disk to make room in RAM.

Paging lets the computer continue running even if it runs out of RAM—but that capability comes at a heavy performance price. Disk drives are much slower than RAM, so moving data to and from the disk slows the system down greatly.

This is a particular problem with programs that use huge amounts of memory. Suppose you have some complex data analysis program that loads a lot of data into memory. It then jumps around the data, performing comparisons, calculating averages, and so forth. Because the data doesn't all fit in memory at any one time, as the program jumps around in the data, it may cause very frequent paging. (This is sometimes called *thrashing*.) When this happens, you often can hear the disk drive working like crazy, and the computer's performance drops to a crawl.

You can reduce paging and thrashing by buying a computer that has lots of memory (or by adding more memory later). And you can reduce the chances of thrashing by structuring programs so they don't need to jump back and forth across huge amounts of data as often—or at all. If you can redesign a program so it uses the data in chunks, processing one chunk at a time before moving on to the next one, the program may page, but it won't thrash.

Another possibility is to free up chunks of data after using them by disposing of the variables holding the data. That makes their memory available for use by new data. In this case, the program may not page at all.

# Flash Drives

Flash drives store data in solid-state memory. They have no moving parts and are *non-volatile*, meaning they don't require power to retain their data. (In contrast, RAM loses its data if it loses power.)

There are two main varieties of flash drives: USB flash drives and solid-state hard drives.

USB flash drives are small and removable. They can fit easily in your pocket, so they are great for quick backups and transferring data from one computer to another. In many ways, USB flash drives (also called USB keys) have taken the place of older floppy drives. Flash drives may last a long time, but people generally use Blu-ray, DVD, and CD drives for permanent storage instead.

Solid-state flash drives are similar to regular disk drives but use flash memory to store data instead of spinning disks. Because they have no moving parts, they are less vulnerable to vibration and shock.

Flash drives also have faster access times than hard drives. Unfortunately, they're still considerably more expensive per gigabyte than regular disk drives.

## Hard Drives

Normal hard drives store data in spinning magnetic disks. They are generally slower than flash drives, although they may be faster at transferring large blocks of data. They also have *latency,* a period of time that the computer must wait while the drive is positioning itself to read a particular block of data.

Disk drives have the distinct advantage of being significantly cheaper than flash drives on a per-gigabyte basis. For example, a 240-GB solid-state drive might cost more than $500, whereas a 1-TB normal disk drive might cost only $65.

Because these drives are relatively inexpensive and can be quite large (I've seen up to 3-TB drives), they are the most common form of storage in computers today.

## Blu-ray, DVD, and CD Drives

Blu-ray, DVD, and CD devices use removable spinning discs to store data. Although they're less expensive per gigabyte than USB flash drives (typically by a few cents per gigabyte), getting data back from them can be much slower than from either flash drives or hard drives.

The storage capacity of these discs varies depending on the recording format, but typical values are 700 MB for CDs, 4.7 GB for DVDs, and 25 GB for Blu-ray.

Their low cost, high capacity, durability, and removability makes these drive types well suited for backup and long-term storage of large amounts of data.

## Working with Files

Before leaving the topic of data storage, I want to briefly mention an important issue related to working with files.

Disk drives naturally read and write data in large blocks. It takes just as much time to read or write an entire block as it does to read or write a single byte. To improve performance, disk drives buffer their data.

If you tell a program to read a few bytes from a file, the disk drive actually reads an entire block and stores it in a *buffer* (a temporary holding location) in memory. As you request other bytes from the same file, they may already be in memory, so the program doesn't need to fetch the new data from the comparatively slow drive.

Similarly, when you write data into a file, the drive actually stores it in a memory buffer until it has enough data to be worth writing to the physical disk.

Because the drive buffers data, it's not obvious when the drive actually writes the data to the disk. An important consequence of this is that you could lose data if a program ends or crashes before the drive has gotten around to writing the data.

To prevent this kind of data loss, your programs should always close files when you're done writing into them. (Closing input files from which the program is reading data is less critical, but still good practice.)

# Networks

Computer networks—especially the Internet—play a huge role in many computer applications. Even a typical household may have its own small network connecting computers, printers, and scanners. There isn't room to cover computer networking in great depth here, but it is useful to understand some basic computer terminology.

A *computer network* is a series of connected devices that allow computers to communicate. Those devices include:

- **Network interface card (NIC)**   Connects a computer to a network and provides the necessary electronics to send and receive the network's electrical signals. NICs are also called *network interface controllers, network adapters, LAN adapters,* and other similar terms.

- **Hub**   A device with several ports that takes the signals that it receives and rebroadcasts them to all the ports other than the one on which it received the signal. Hubs connect multiple computers in a very simple way.

- **Bridge**   Similar to a two-port hub, but with more intelligence. A bridge inspects incoming information packets from one port and forwards them to its other port only if the destination of the packet is on the other side of the bridge. This reduces unnecessary traffic on the network.

- **Switch**   Similar to a bridge, but with more than two ports. Instead of forwarding signals to every port, they forward signals only to the device that should receive them.

- **Router**   Similar to a switch except it can connect multiple networks, possibly using different protocols. The most common routers connect a home computer with an Internet service provider's network via a cable or modem.

Networks are sometimes categorized by their size. Two of the most common terms used to describe networks are *local area network (LAN)* and *wide area network (WAN)*.

*Wi-Fi* is the trademarked name of a standard for connecting devices wirelessly. *Ethernet* similarly connects devices using wires or cables.

The *Internet* is a global system of connected computer networks. It is the largest WAN, covering the entire world. Often, people use the terms *Internet* and *World Wide Web* (or just *web*) interchangeably, but the World Wide Web (WWW) is only the collection of all hypertext webpages available on the Internet. The Internet contains lots of other information as well, including email, Voice over Internet Protocol (VoIP), and files that are available for download but that are not part of the World Wide Web.

Communication over a network is controlled by various communication protocols. A *communication protocol* is a formal description of the formats and rules for passing information across a network. Protocols often include several layers. The bottommost layers deal with physical signaling and the way the network uses electrical signals to send information. Higher-level layers determine how information is translated to and from electrical signals. Still-higher levels deal with error correction and how to determine whether a message has been received correctly.

The Internet uses the Internet Protocol Suite to define how traffic should work. This suite of protocols is also called TCP/IP, named after the two most important protocols it contains: Transmission Control Protocol (TCP) and Internet Protocol (IP). TCP provides reliable delivery of a stream of bytes from one computer to another. IP provides addressing that lets a network route data packets called *datagrams* to the appropriate destination.

Two of the most common high-level protocols used on the Internet are HTTP and FTP. Hypertext Transfer Protocol (HTTP) is a protocol for hypertext documents that contain links that lead to other documents. This is the protocol that your computer uses when you open a webpage in a browser by using an address that begins with *http://*.

File Transfer Protocol (FTP) is a protocol used to transfer files between computers over a network such as the Internet. This is the protocol that your computer uses when you open a file in a browser by using an address that begins with *ftp://*. Often people use special file transfer programs to upload and download files with the FTP protocol. Addresses that begin with *http://* or *ftp://* are examples of Uniform Resource Locators (URLs).

A Uniform Resource Name (URN) is similar to a URL, but it is intended to be a permanent name for a resource even if the resource is not currently available. The difference between a URL and a URN is minor, and many people use the terms interchangeably.

 **More Info** For more information on networking topics, search online websites such as Wikipedia and About.com, or consult a book on networking.

# Summary

This chapter discussed some of the hardware issues that you should consider when you're designing and building an application. It explained how you can use the Windows Experience Index to compare computers running Windows. It also explained how you should match the needs of an application with the capabilities of a particular kind of computer.

For example, if you need to support many users on a centralized database, you might want to plan to use desktop or laptop systems connected to a server on a high-speed network. In contrast, if you want a small, special-purpose calculator to perform calculations throughout the day, you might be better off using a handheld computer or smartphone.

This chapter also described different kinds of storage hardware and explains their strengths and weaknesses. For example, hard drives are slower than RAM, but they are still reasonably quick and much cheaper, so they are a good choice for storing large amounts of data. DVDs are removable and even less expensive, so they're a good choice for backups and long-term storage.

This chapter explained how disk drives buffer input and output, meaning that to prevent data loss, you should always close files when you are done writing into them.

Finally, this chapter briefly explained some common networking concepts and terminology. It won't make you an expert on networks, but it should help you understand normal network discussions, particularly when you deal with networks from the high-level perspective that programmers usually have when writing computer programs.

This chapter also briefly mentioned multi-core systems: systems with processors that have more than one core capable of executing commands. Multi-core systems have great potential to increase performance without requiring faster processors, something that is becoming increasingly difficult to achieve. The next chapter contains more information about multi-core systems in particular and multiprocessing in general.

# Chapter 2

# Multiprocessing

**In this chapter:**

- What multiprocessing is and how modern computers can provide it

- The difference between multiprocessing and multitasking

- What processes and threads are

- How to design programs that can take advantage of multiprocessing

**MOORE'S LAW, NAMED AFTER INTEL COFOUNDER** Gordon E. Moore, says that the number of transistors that can be placed on a chip roughly doubles every two years, and that leads directly to an increase in computer speed. The law has held up remarkably well for more than 40 years and is predicted to continue to hold for at least a few more years, but chip manufacturers are starting to reach the physical limitations of what's possible using current chip fabrication techniques. This might spell the end to large speed improvements for individual chips, but it doesn't necessarily mean the end of performance gains for computers.

 **Note** For more information on Moore's Law, see *http://en.wikipedia.org/wiki/Moore%27s_law*.

Other techniques, such as writing better code and leaner operating systems, can make a computer faster without changing its underlying hardware. One particularly promising approach to improving computer performance is multiprocessing.

This chapter describes multiprocessing and explains how you can take advantage of it to get the best performance possible.

# Multitasking

Even the slowest computers are much faster than their human users. A typical computer spends practically all its time sitting around twiddling its electronic thumbs waiting for the user to do something. When the user presses a button or clicks the mouse, the computer springs into action, performs a task, and then goes back to waiting.

For example, the world record for fastest typing was set by Barbara Blackburn at 212 words per minute, or about 18 characters per second. Not even the world's fastest typists can keep up with a computer that can execute millions of instructions per second.

To make better use of the computer's blinding speed, modern operating systems multitask. In *multitasking,* the computer runs several tasks (known as *processes*) in turn. The operating system lets one process execute for a while so it can perform calculations, update its display on the screen, respond to user events such as button clicks, and so on. The operating system then pauses that process and lets another one take a turn. It continues rotating through the processes so they each get to execute.

So long as the operating system can switch the processes quickly enough, they appear to the user as if they are all executing simultaneously, although they are really just taking turns. This works well so long as the system doesn't have too many intensive processes, but if some of the processes are performing really heavy-duty calculations, the computer may have trouble maintaining the illusion that it's running simultaneous tasks.

This is where multiprocessing enters the picture. Multitasking fosters the illusion that the computer is performing several tasks at once. In multiprocessing, the computer really is doing several things simultaneously.

# Multiprocessing

In multiprocessing, a computer uses multiple execution elements to perform several tasks at the same time. Those elements could be separate processors running on separate chips or, as is increasingly common these days, they can be separate cores within the same processor. A *core* is the part of a processor that actually executes commands. By putting more than one core on the same chip, a computer can greatly increase its potential computing power.

Today, two or four core computers are common, processors with six or eight cores are also available, and one experimental processor contains more than 1,000 cores! (To learn more about this innovative computer, see *http://www.physorg.com/news/2011-01-scientists-cores-chip.html.*)

With the end of Moore's Law looming over the horizon, these sorts of multi-core systems offer a potential road to increased performance, but multiple cores do not guarantee that applications will run faster. The operating system itself may be able to run different programs on different cores, but a single program could become stuck on a single core and have limited performance. You can allow a single program to run on multiple cores by using multiple threads.

# Multithreading

A *process* is an instance of a program running on a computer. (Note that you could have multiple instances of the same program running. For example, you might have two browsers open or two instances of WordPad running.) A *thread* is a sequence of instructions within a single process that may execute in parallel with other threads. Sometimes you can execute multiple threads within the same process at the same time. Each thread keeps track of its position within the program's code and can move through the code as it needs to without interfering with the other threads. This is called *multithreading*.

For example, suppose you write a program that takes a stock's historical prices, performs some sort of complex statistical calculation, and predicts the stock's future price. (If you can get that last part to work reliably, let me know!) Now suppose you want to perform the same task for several stocks. You could have the program perform the calculations sequentially, one after another. If each calculation takes about 30 seconds and you want to predict prices for 10 stocks, the total time will be around 300 seconds, or 5 minutes.

Another approach would be to start 10 threads, one for each stock. A thread would perform the statistical calculation for its stock and display the result.

A single-CPU system will multitask, switching quickly back and forth between the threads to give the illusion that they are all executing at the same time. There is still only one CPU, however, so the total time will still be around 5 minutes. In fact, there is a little bit of overhead in switching between threads so the total run time may be slightly longer.

In contrast, a computer with multiple cores may truly be able to execute more than one thread at a time. In that case, the total time will be roughly the original total time of 5 minutes divided by the number of cores, plus some overhead for setting up the threads and keeping track of what they are all doing. A two-core system might require about 2.5 minutes, whereas a four-core system might need only around 1.25 minutes to finish the calculations.

Unfortunately this speed improvement isn't automatic or free. In addition to a small (but significant) amount of overhead to set up threads, a program may pay a large performance penalty if the threads interfere with each other. Interference can take the form of several different potential problems with parallelism.

 **Note** Some compilers may be able to detect pieces of code that can always execute safely in parallel and in that case you may gain some benefit from multiple cores without any additional work. To get the full benefit, however, you need to structure your program properly.

# Problems with Parallelism

At a high level, running threads in parallel is easy to understand. When you look closely at specific tasks, however, you can encounter several problems. Some of these include contention for resources, races, and deadlocks.

## Contention for Resources

Sometimes multiple threads need to use the same resources. Consider again the stock calculator example. Suppose the program starts 10 threads to perform calculations for 10 stocks. The first task that each thread must perform is using the Internet to get its stock's price data. If your network bandwidth is limited, this will be a big bottleneck as each thread demands access to the network. Even if your network has plenty of bandwidth, the website that you access to get the stock prices needs to process all the requests and, if it's a slow website, that may cause a bottleneck.

Similarly, multiple threads may need to access the same disk drive, CD or DVD drive, or other limited resource, and performance can be limited as a result. It's bad enough that these sorts of contention can limit performance, but they can also cause incorrect behavior. The most common example of this kind of error is called a *race condition*.

## Race Conditions

A *race condition* occurs when the result of a calculation depends on the exact sequence or timing of execution in multiple threads.

For example, suppose you want to compute the total of 2 million numbers. You could loop through the numbers and add them up one at a time, but you want to save time with multithreading, so you break the task into two pieces and solve each piece in a separate thread. The first thread adds the first million numbers to a value called *total* and the second thread adds the second million numbers to *total*. The basic algorithm for each thread looks like this:

```
For i = start To finish
    Get total
    Calculate result = total + value[i]
    Save result In total
```

This code enters a loop where the looping variable *i* starts at the value start and runs to the value *finish*. In other words, it takes the values *start, start + 1, start + 2, . . ., finish*.

The values *start* and *finish* represent the indices of the values that a thread should process. In this example, the first thread's values for *start* and *finish* would be 1 and 1,000,000, and the values for the second thread would be 1,000,001 and 2,000,000. The two threads run exactly the same code; only the values' *start* and *finish* are different for the two threads.

Inside the loop, each thread reads the current value of the *total* variable, adds the value pointed to by the current value of *i* to *total*, and saves the new result in *total*.

If you're running a single thread to process all the values, this code works perfectly. However, if you use two threads running at the same time, they can enter a race condition. Consider this sequence of events as the two threads execute inside their loops.

```
Thread 1:    Get total
Thread 2:    Get total
Thread 1:    Calculate result = total + value[i]
Thread 1:    Save result In total
Thread 2:    Calculate result = total + value[i]
Thread 2:    Save result In total
```

In this case, both threads start by reading the value *total*. Because thread 1 does this right after thread 2 does it, both threads get the same value.

Next, thread 1 adds a value to *total* and saves the result back in the value *total*. Then thread 2 does the same. Because thread 2 still has the original value for total, it overwrites the new value saved by thread 1.

For a concrete example, suppose *total* starts with the value 100 and the two threads are adding the values 20 and 30, respectively. Both start by reading the value 100. Thread 1 then adds 20 and saves the result 120 in the value *total*. Next, thread 2 adds 30 to the value that it originally read (100), gets the result 130, and saves it in the value *total*. Instead of holding the correct result 150, *total* now holds 130.

> **Warning** Race conditions can be extremely difficult to detect because bugs appear only when events occur in exactly the right order. If the sequence of events that leads to the error is unlikely, you may run a program thousands of times before you encounter the error. When the error does occur, you may be unable to reproduce the exact sequence of events in multiple threads that caused it.

One way to prevent a race condition is to use a lock on the critical section of code.

# Locks

A lock guarantees that a thread has exclusive access to a piece of code, memory, or other item that it needs to prevent a race condition or other bug. In the previous example, a thread could use a lock to gain exclusive access to the variable total while performing its calculation. The new code looks like this:

```
For i = start To finish
   Lock total
       Get total
       Calculate result = total + value[i]
       Save result In total
```

Now, if two threads are running at the same time, one cannot read the value of *total* while the other has it locked so it cannot interfere with the other thread. Instead, it waits until the lock is released, and then it locks the *total* value and performs its own calculation without interference.

Unfortunately, locks add considerable overhead to a program because making multiple threads coordinate in this way makes them much slower. The more locks a program must make and release, the more slowly the program will execute. In this example, the threads must lock and unlock the value *total* for each of the 2 million numbers that should be totaled.

In this particular program, the problem is even worse because each thread performs calculations only while it's running code inside the lock; therefore, no two threads can be doing anything significant at the same time, which eliminates all the benefits of multithreading. The result is that this program really performs its calculations one at a time sequentially, just spread across multiple threads in a complicated way using 2 million locks. All those locks guarantee that this program will be *much* slower than the original single-threaded program, which didn't need to use any locks.

Locks solve one problem but sometimes cause another: deadlocks.

## Deadlocks

A *deadlock* occurs when two threads are waiting for resources held by each other. For example, suppose thread 1 has resource A locked and is waiting for resource B, but thread 2 has resource B locked and is waiting for resource A. Neither thread can get the second lock it needs, so it cannot continue. Because of this, neither thread will release the lock that it already holds, so they're both stuck.

In this example, the deadlock is simple and easy to avoid by making both threads lock resource A before locking resource B. Then, if thread 1 locks resource A, thread 2 cannot lock resource B until it first locks resource A.

Detecting and breaking deadlocks in more general situations can be harder. If a program has many threads that need exclusive access to lots of resources in complex combinations, it can be difficult to prevent deadlocks.

# Looking for Parallelism

Some problems have naturally parallel solutions. For example, consider the Mandelbrot set shown in Figure 2-1. To produce this image, the program considers each pixel in the result separately. For that pixel, it performs a series of calculations that do not involve the other pixels in any way. This program can make as many threads as it wants, and each can work independently to calculate a color for its own pixel.

The only place where the threads need to interact is when they copy their results into the single final image. Even there, the threads don't need to use locks because each thread works with a different pixel and doesn't need to look at or modify the other pixels.

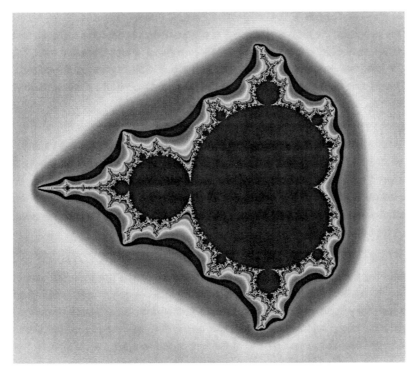

**FIGURE 2-1** Displaying the Mandelbrot set is an embarrassingly parallel task.

This kind of algorithm, which is naturally parallel, is sometimes called *embarrassingly parallel.* Other embarrassingly parallel problems include ray tracing, generating frames for an animated movie (which may also involve ray tracing), some artificial intelligence approaches such as genetic algorithms, and random heuristics where the program picks a random solution and evaluates its effectiveness.

Even if a problem isn't embarrassingly parallel, you may be able to come up with a workable parallel solution. For example, consider the earlier problem of adding up 2 million numbers. The simple solution of making two threads each add up half of the numbers doesn't work because they spend a huge amount of time competing for access to the value *total.*

However, suppose each thread added up its own subtotal and only copied the result into *total* when it was finished. The new thread code looks like this:

```
subtotal = 0
For i = start To finish
    Get subtotal
    Calculate result = subtotal + value[i]
    Save result In subtotal
Lock total
    Get total
    Calculate result = total + subtotal
    Save result In total
```

In this version of the program, the loop where most of the work occurs contains no locks, so the threads can work independently. Only at the end do the threads need to lock the value *total*. The previous version of the program required 2 million locks, and those locks prevented the threads from running in parallel. This version uses only two locks and the threads can execute the vast majority of their calculations in parallel, so this version will be much faster.

**Note** This code was written with the assumption that the threads can access the values they are adding without interfering with each other, and that may not always be the case. If the values are stored on a disk drive, reading one value may move the disk heads, so it takes longer to read other values. If the values are all together on the disk, however, the program can probably read them all into memory at once, and then the threads can work in parallel without disk contention.

This example shows how the approach you use can determine whether a program will benefit from multithreading. The key to making this solution work is avoiding locks. A good multithreaded application doesn't use too many locks, avoids making threads contend for other scarce resources such as disk drives, and generally keeps calculations as separate as possible, as long as possible. Often, a thread's contribution to the overall solution is used at the end of the thread's calculations.

# Distributed Computing

In *distributed computing*, multiple computers linked by a network work together to perform a task. You can think of distributed computing as similar to multithreading except that the "threads" run on different computers.

Although coordination among threads on the same computer can be cumbersome, communication among computers in a distributed application is much slower. That means distributed computing is most useful when the problem is embarrassingly parallel. For example, several computers could be assigned the task of generating separate frames for an animated movie. Those computers could then use multithreaded ray tracing programs to calculate the pixels in each frame.

Other examples of distributed computing are "grid computing" applications, which use idle computers scattered across the Internet to perform CPU-intensive calculations while their users aren't using them. Some of these efforts involve thousands of (or even millions of) computers. Examples include *SETI@home*, which tries to detect alien signals in vast amounts of radio signal data; *Folding@home*, which simulates protein folding and molecular dynamics to study diseases; and the Great Internet Mersenne Prime Search (GIMPS), which tries to find Mersenne primes of the form $2^p - 1$ for some number $p$.

**Note** Currently, only 27 Mersenne primes are known. The largest known prime of any kind is the Mersenne prime $2^{43,112,609} - 1$.

Distributed computing is a specialized subtopic in a specialized field, but some of its basic ideas can be very useful when designing multithreaded (or even single-threaded) programs. One of the most important of those ideas is that each of the cooperating programs should be as independent as possible. If thousands of computers need to communicate frequently with each other or with a central computer, the network's communications needs will quickly outweigh any potential benefits.

Similarly, keeping each thread as separate as possible (avoiding direct communication between them and avoiding locks) makes threads faster, easier to debug, and more scalable so you can easily add more if necessary.

Even if your computer has only a single core, breaking operations up into independent pieces makes writing and debugging the pieces easier. If the pieces are self-contained, then you can debug one without worrying as much about how changes to it will affect other pieces of code.

Keeping the pieces as separate as possible also can help you rewrite the program later if you decide to spread it across multiple threads.

# Task Parallel Library

How you create multiple threads depends on the operating system and language you are using. Microsoft's Task Parallel Library (TPL) is a specific library of tools that makes running parallel threads relatively easy for Microsoft .NET applications.

The following list summarizes the main tools provided by the TPL:

- **Parallel.Invoke**   Executes several pieces of code at the same time.

- **Parallel.For**   Executes the same pieces of code several times in parallel, with different numbers as parameters. For example, it might invoke some code to produce frames in an animated movie where the parameters 1, 2, 3, and so on are passed to the code so it knows which frame number to generate.

- **Parallel.ForEach**  Executes the same pieces of code several times in parallel, with different arbitrary values as parameters. This is similar to *Parallel.For* except that the code receives arbitrary values specified by the program as inputs rather than numbers in a sequence. For example, the program could pass each thread a separate image to manipulate. The threads could then perform image processing techniques on the images, creating embossed images.

These three TPL operations provide a relatively simple way for a program to use multiple threads. These may not handle every scenario that you can imagine, and threads still may run into race, lock, deadlock, and other parallel issues, but these are fairly easy to use.

The TPL is also designed to use multiple cores, if they are available, without imposing too much overhead on single-core systems, so you can run the same program on different computers and expect reasonable performance, whether the computer has 1 core or 16.

# Summary

This chapter discussed multiprocessing and the ways modern computers provide parallel computing, or at least an illusion of it. All modern computers provide multitasking, quickly switching back and forth among applications to make it seem as if they are all running at the same time.

Some computers have more than one element that can execute instructions, and those computers can perform multiprocessing, truly executing multiple tasks at the same time. Those computers may have multiple processors, or they may have multiple cores within the same processor.

Multi-core systems are becoming increasingly common. To get the best performance from your programs, you need to consider parallel programming issues as you write your programs. If you keep the individual parts of a program as separate as possible, you may be able to execute them on different threads running on separate cores, which will improve performance.

Even if you don't plan to run a program across multiple threads, keeping the various elements of your programs as separate as possible makes them easier to write and debug.

Chapter 1, "Computer Hardware," described a range of computer hardware that you might use, such as desktops, laptops, and smartphones. This chapter described topics in parallel programming that you can use to make computer software take advantage of the processors and cores provided by the computer's hardware. The next chapter bridges the gap between the topics of hardware and software, explaining how programming environments translate the software that you write into commands that the hardware can actually execute.

# Chapter 3

# Programming Environments

**In this chapter:**

- How a computer runs a program
- How programs are converted into machine language that a program can understand
- What features typically are included in a development environment
- What features the Microsoft Visual Studio development environment provides

**IN THEORY, YOU COULD WRITE COMPUTER** programs using any text editor, but in practice, that would be difficult. Programming languages are extremely picky, so one missing or misplaced character can make a program useless.

To make it easier to write programs that are at least syntactically correct, programming languages typically come with programming environments that include tools to help you design, write, run, test, and debug programs.

This chapter describes some of the basic tools that typically come with a programming environment. It also briefly describes the Visual Studio programming environment.

## From Software to Hardware

People transfer information using spoken and written languages such as English, Spanish, and even Klingon (at certain gaming conventions, at least). The computer's processor is very different. It reads a series of 0s and 1s and produces a new series of 0s and 1s. For example, the following machine code tells an x86/IA-32 processor to copy the value 01100001 into the AL register (a special memory location for values that the process will later manipulate):

```
1011000001100001
```

**25**

Because this machine code is largely incomprehensible to humans, programmers write programs in higher-level programming languages. Later, another program converts the high-level program into machine code.

Assembly language is a low-level language that uses mnemonics to make machine language more readable. For example, the following assembly statement is equivalent to the previous machine code:

```
MOV AL, 61h    ; Copy the value 61h into AL.
```

A program called an *assembler* translates this assembly code directly into machine code that can execute on the processor. (The text after the semicolon is a *comment*, intended for programmers, that the assembler ignores.)

Assembly language closely mimics the instructions that the processor can understand, so a carefully written assembly program can execute extremely quickly. Unfortunately, the commands are also very basic, so it's quite difficult to write and debug programs in assembly language.

Higher-level programming languages, such as Fortran, Pascal, and C++, include more complex statements that work at a more abstract level than assembly language. A compiler then translates the high-level program into machine language for execution. Figure 3-1 shows the process graphically.

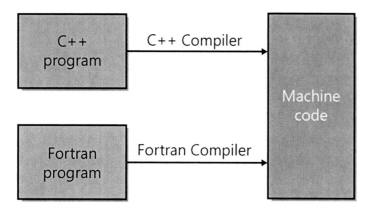

**FIGURE 3-1** A compiler converts high-level languages such as Fortran or C++ into machine code.

Some languages, such as Java, C#, and Microsoft Visual Basic, insert another step in the translation process to make programs more portable. Instead of compiling directly to machine code, these languages' compilers convert the high-level code into an intermediate language sometimes called *bytecode*. Then, at run time, the intermediate code is compiled into machine code for execution. This step from intermediate code to machine code occurs at the last instant before the code is executed, so it is called Just-In-Time (JIT) compilation.

For Microsoft.NET-compatible languages, such as C# and Visual Basic, the intermediate representation is called *Common Intermediate Language* (CIL), and the run-time component that converts it into machine language is called *Common Language Runtime* (CLR).

In Java, the intermediate language is called *Java bytecode,* and the run-time component that converts it into machine language is the *Java Virtual Machine* (JVM).

Figure 3-2 shows the translation from high-level language to intermediate language and then to machine language graphically.

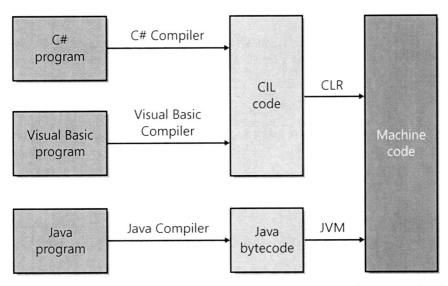

**FIGURE 3-2** Languages such as Visual Basic, C#, and Java compile programs into intermediate languages before eventually converting them into machine code.

> **Note** Actually, the Java specification is somewhat relaxed about exactly how code is executed, so some versions of the JVM may interpret bytecode instructions and carry them out directly rather than compiling the bytecode into machine code.

You might think that adding the extra step of producing intermediate code would slow the process down. That's true, but only to a small extent. The first time you run a piece of code, the CLR or JVM must compile the intermediate code into machine code, so there is a tiny slowdown. However, once compiled, the code stays compiled, so the next time the program needs to run that particular piece of code, it is already in compiled form and doesn't need to be compiled again. In fact, the compiled code is often cached, so it doesn't need to be recompiled even if you close the program and open it again later.

The advantage of using an intermediate language is portability. If you write a program on one computer, then any other computer that has the correct run-time environment (CLR or the JVM) can execute that program, even if that computer uses different machine language instructions. The other computer's CLR or JVM converts the intermediate language code into machine language just in time, and the program runs.

### Design Time and Run Time

*Design time* is the time when you are building a program. *Run time* is the time when the program is running. For example, instructions for building an example may tell you to "Add a text box to the form at design time" or to "Enter the customer's name in the text box at run time."

A few unusual kinds of code may have other less obvious time designations. For example, if you build a new tool to add to a development environment, it is in a special run time while you are using it in the environment that is different from when you built it (though probably in the same environment).

Custom controls, such as special dials and buttons, are an even stranger case. When you build the control, you work with it at design time. When you later add the control to another program, its code may be running in a special *control run time* to provide feedback to the development environment. For example, the control may need to change its appearance when it is enabled and disabled. Finally, when the program containing the control executes, the control's code runs in the end program's run time. The fact that controls may have two different kinds of run time can be confusing.

## Programming Environments

To make writing and debugging programs easier, programming environments include several useful tools. Some of the tools that a given programming environment might include are:

- **Code editor**   A special-purpose text editor that helps you create working code. Typical special features of code editors include automatic text coloring to differentiate kinds of code (such as variables, keywords, literal values, and comments), parenthesis matching (so you can easily see find an open parenthesis' matching closing parenthesis, and vice versa), and syntax error highlighting.

- **Debugger**   Often integrated with the code editor, the debugger lets you step through the program one statement at a time to see what it does while running. Debuggers usually let you stop the program at a particular line of code, follow execution from one piece of code to another, and examine and change variable values. Some even let you change the program code and continue running the program from that point.

- **Compiler**   As described in the previous section, the compiler converts the source code into machine code or intermediate code.

- **Build automation tools**   These tools allow you to customize compilation. For example, a tool might notice that a particular module has been modified, recompile it, and then recompile any other modules that rely on that one so they are all up to date.

- **Testing tools**   These tools let you automatically perform a series of tests on a program to see if a feature works or to see if recent changes to the code have broken existing features (regression testing). Reports tell you if the program failed any of the tests.

- **Source code management tools**   These tools track changes to the source code and keep the code in a safe repository. Many of these tools allow you to compare two versions of the code to see what has changed.

- **Object-oriented tools**   These tools make it easier to understand how classes relate to each other. They may include a class browser, an object inspector, and a class hierarchy editor.

An integrated development environment (IDE) includes tools for performing some or all of these tasks. For example, when you modify a source code file, the IDE may automatically check that file out of a source code management system so that your changes are archived. Later, you can view the differences between old and new versions of the code and remove the changes if they were incorrect.

IDEs typically let you build large projects that may contain dozens or even hundreds of files. A project may include lots of different kinds of files, such as source code files, code files automatically generated by the IDE, image files, and even documentation about the project.

The IDE can include integrated tools for working with these files. For example, some versions of Visual Studio can create new icon files and add them to a project. If you double-click an icon file, the IDE opens an integrated icon editor that lets you create images of different sizes inside the same icon file (so that other applications can display it appropriately at different sizes), modify the icon's pixels, and make parts of the icon transparent.

The IDE also may let you create hierarchical entities at a higher level. Visual Studio lets you create a "solution" that contains related projects. For example, suppose you are writing a client/server application where one program (the client) requests services provided by another program (the server) across a network. In that case, you might build a solution containing the client and server programs, in addition to programs that test the two separately.

# Visual Studio

Visual Studio is an IDE available from Microsoft. Visual Studio provides support for several languages, including C#, Visual Basic, C/C++, and F#. Although it is possible to write and compile programs in those languages without Visual Studio, it's a lot of work without a lot of benefit. If you're using a *Start Here!* book to learn how to use one of these languages, then you will be using Visual Studio extensively.

Visual Studio provides support for building console applications (those that read and write text from a simple text window), Microsoft Windows services that run in the background even if no user is logged in, Windows Forms applications (similar to those you typically see on Windows systems), websites, web applications, and web services (for another program to call across the web). It even supports development for some devices other than typical computers, such as the Xbox 360 game platform and phones running the Windows Phone 7 operating system.

Different versions of Visual Studio include most of the tools listed in the previous section. Every version includes source code editors and a debugger. The compiler and build automation tools are built in so seamlessly that you rarely notice they're present.

Only the more expensive versions of Visual Studio include some advanced items, such as team coordination and testing tools. If you work as part of a large development team, those tools can be useful. If you're working by yourself, as you almost certainly are while you're learning to program, you won't need those tools as much.

Some other specific features that the Visual Studio IDE provides include:

- **Customizable menus and toolbars**   You can rearrange, create, and hide these items easily. You can add and remove commands to make it easier to find the tools that you use the most. For example, if you often edit Extensible Markup Language (XML) data files, you can display the XML Editor toolbar to make editing those files easier. You can even add menu items and toolbar buttons to perform new actions such as opening a web page, sending email, or executing code that you have written.

- **Customizable windows**   You can decide which windows (code editors, toolbars, data views, and so forth) are visible and where they are positioned. You can make windows become tabs in a single window, give each window its own area, or make a window float above others.

- **Auto-hiding windows**   If you want, you can make windows shrink to small headers when you are not using them and then pop back out when you float the mouse over the header. Doing this gives you more space for whatever task you are performing, while hiding windows that you don't need at the moment. You also can "pin" windows so they are always visible if you prefer.

- **IntelliSense**   This is an auto-completion feature provided by the code editor. If you type part of the name of a variable, function, or other program symbol, IntelliSense lists the symbols that might match your choice. For example, if you type "**FirstN**," IntelliSense would list the control name *FirstNameTextBox* (if that control is on the form). When you open a parameter list for a function call, IntelliSense also lists the parameter names and their descriptions so it's easier to see what values you must pass to the function.

- **Call stack**   The call stack window shows the sequence of function calls that lead to the current point of execution.

- **Sequence diagrams and dependency graphs**   These tools, which are available only in Visual Studio Professional and higher, provide information about how functions call each other.

> **Tip** Although you can move windows into completely new arrangements, you might want to leave the most basic windows where they are originally, so others who look at your system are not completely mystified. For example, if you hide all your toolbars, you (or someone else) may have trouble finding them.

# Summary

This chapter described programming environments and some of the features they provide, giving some extra attention to the IDE in Visual Studio. You can use a programming environment to create user interfaces and write the code that lies behind them.

The next chapter discusses common standard types of features that you might want to put in a user interface, such as menus, accelerators, and shortcuts. Such features make your programs faster and easier to learn and use.

# Chapter 4

# Windows Program Components

**In this chapter:**

- What menus are and how to use them

- What context menus are and how to use them

- How to use toolbars and ribbons

- How to use dialog boxes

- General tips on user-interface design

**MICROSOFT WINDOWS PROGRAMS HAVE CERTAIN STANDARD** features that are familiar to users and that users have come to expect. Users feel more comfortable with applications that use those features. They feel safer experimenting with the program, knowing how the features will act.

For example, a menu item's caption ends in an ellipsis (. . .) to indicate that the item displays a dialog box or some other Windows form and does not immediately perform a task. The user can safely click that item without performing any irrevocable action.

This chapter describes these sorts of standard features provided by Windows applications. It explains how to make menus, context menus, and dialog boxes as useful as possible. It also gives some tips about user interface design to make other parts of an application easier to use.

 **Note** The ideas discussed here apply only to Windows applications. The conventions for programs running on other operating systems such as Unix or Macintosh computers may be different. Just because something makes sense to Windows users, that doesn't mean it will make sense to Unix users. Similarly, just because something looks cool on a Macintosh system, that doesn't mean it will help users in a Windows application.

# Menus

Programs have been using menus for a long time, and users have come to expect certain standard behavior from them. For example, the File menu belongs on the left and contains commands to open, close, save, and create files.

The File menu also contains an Exit command, which closes the application. This doesn't really make intuitive sense, but it's been the case for so long that users expect to find the Exit command on the File menu. If you move the Exit command to a different menu, you will confuse and frustrate users. Even after users know where the command is, every time they use it, they will probably think "This is stupid," and you don't want your program to make that impression.

The following sections describe some tips for building usable menu systems.

## Use Ellipses

If a menu item displays a dialog box or other form instead of immediately performing an action, end its caption with an ellipsis. This tells the user that it is safe to select the item and that there won't be irreversible consequences.

For example, the Save As command on the File menu displays a dialog box where the user can select or enter a file name. The user can click the dialog box's Cancel button to cancel the operation, so this command ends with an ellipsis, as shown in Figure 4-1.

In contrast, the Save command immediately saves the file using its current file name. The user has no chance to cancel this operation, so the command doesn't end with an ellipsis.

## Provide Accelerators

Accelerators are keys associated with menu items that let you use the Alt key to navigate the menus quickly. For example, pressing Alt+F opens the File menu for most applications. Experienced users quickly memorize the accelerators for common operations. For example, an experienced user can press Alt+F, A to invoke the Save As command from the File menu immediately.

A menu item indicates its accelerator by displaying an underscore below the character. For example, the File menu is typically displayed as File to indicate that F is its accelerator. (Note that recent versions of Windows don't display the underscore until the user presses Alt.)

> **Note** Different development environments use different methods to let you specify a menu item's accelerator. For example, when you're building a C# or Microsoft Visual Basic application in Microsoft Visual Studio, you precede the accelerator with an ampersand when setting the item's caption. For example, you would set the File menu's caption to *&File*. However, when you build a Windows Presentation Foundation (WPF) application in Visual Studio, you precede the accelerator with an underscore, such as *_File*.

**FIGURE 4-1** If a command displays a dialog box before taking action, end its caption with an ellipsis.

All menu items should have accelerators. No two items in the same menu should have the same accelerator, although two items in different menus can have the same accelerator. For example, the Save As command on the File menu and the Select All command on the Edit menu might both use the accelerator A.

## Provide Shortcuts

Accelerators make it easier to navigate through a menu hierarchy using the keyboard. Shortcuts immediately invoke a menu item that may be far down the menu hierarchy without requiring navigation.

For example, you can use the accelerators Alt+F, Alt+S to save a file. You can also use the shortcut Ctrl+S to save the file without opening the File menu. These two methods for invoking the same command let you find the command in different ways. You can use accelerators to browse through the menus looking for an item, or you can use shortcuts to execute a command immediately if you know its shortcut.

Because shortcuts immediately invoke a command that could be in any menu, no two commands can have the same shortcut, even if they are in different menus.

You should provide accelerators for every menu command, but you should provide shortcuts only for the most frequently used commands. If you provide shortcuts for infrequently used commands, the user is more likely to use the shortcut accidentally.

 **Note** Different development environments use different methods to let you specify a menu item's shortcut keys. The Properties window in Visual Studio provides the shortcut editor shown in Figure 4-2. Use the check boxes to indicate whether the shortcut uses the Ctrl, Shift, or Alt key. Then use the drop-down menu to select the key.

**FIGURE 4-2** In Visual Studio, you set a menu item's shortcut by using an editor.

## Use Standard Menu Items

Use a standard menu structure whenever possible so that users know where to look for standard commands. For example, don't create a Document menu and place commands in it that are usually in the File menu.

Some programs hide menus, display them only with cryptic icons, or change their positions. This makes it hard to find standard commands that should be easily accessible, which frustrates users. For example, Internet Explorer 7 hides its standard menus entirely until you press Alt. (This may be different in other versions of the browser.) This doesn't provide much benefit but can be confusing. A user shouldn't need to use Google to learn how to find the program's version. (This information can be found in the About command on the Help menu, where it is in most programs; it's just not obvious how to display the Help menu.)

You can learn the standard menu structure by looking at almost any popular application, such as Microsoft Word or Notepad.

When you use standard menus and items, give those items standard accelerators and shortcuts whenever possible. Experienced Windows users know the standard accelerators and shortcuts very well, so if you change them in your program, they will probably use them incorrectly. For example, if you use the Ctrl+S shortcut for the Save and Exit command, users will probably close the application by accident when they are just trying to save a file.

The following list shows some standard menus, items, accelerators, and shortcuts. The lines of dashes represent separators in the menus to group related commands.

| File | |
| --- | --- |
| New | Ctrl+N |
| Open... | Ctrl+O |
| Save | Ctrl+S |
| Save As... | Ctrl+A |
| ----- | |
| Page Setup... | |
| Print Preview... | |
| Print | Ctrl+P |
| ----- | |
| Exit | |
| Edit | |
| Undo | Ctrl+Z |
| Redo | Ctrl+Y |
| ----- | |
| Cut | Ctrl+X |
| Copy | Ctrl+C |
| Paste | Ctrl+V |
| Delete | Del |
| ----- | |
| Select All | Ctrl+A |
| ----- | |
| Find | Ctrl+F |
| Find and Replace | Ctrl+H |
| View | |
| Data | |

| Tools | |
|---|---|
| Window | |
| Help | |
|   Search... | |
|   Contents... | F1 |
|   Index... | |
|   ----- | |
|   About... | |

The contents of the View, Data, and Tools menus will depend on your application. For example, a three-dimensional computer-aided design (CAD) program's View menu might include Left, Right, Top, and 3D commands to let the user view a model from different angles.

If your program doesn't need a menu, leave it out.

The About command on the Help menu should display version information about the program. It may also include contact information such as email addresses, phone numbers, and web links so that the user can get information about support and product registration. Alternatively, you can place commands to send email or visit a website in the Help menu.

## Don't Hide Commands

If a command or menu isn't available at a given moment, disable it instead of hiding it. Hiding a menu or command can be disorienting to the user. The user may go looking for the command and be unable to find it, thinking, "I know it's here somewhere," when the command is actually missing. If you leave the command visible but disabled, the user can at least find it and realize that it's not available at that time.

Many programs that have extremely large menu hierarchies violate this rule to save space and make the menus simpler. The idea seems reasonable but can still lead to confusion and wasted effort as the user searches in vain for missing features. A better solution is to move pieces of the menu system into upper-level menus or cascading submenus that the program can then disable.

For example, suppose a program lets you edit customers and orders, and you want the appropriate tools to be available only based on what the user is doing. If the user is editing an order, for example, the program should provide order editing tools, not customer editing tools.

You could put all the tools in the Edit menu and then enable and disable them as needed. But if the two features use a lot of tools, the menu will be uncomfortably large and full of disabled entries.

Another approach is to create upper-level Customer and Order menus and place their respective commands in them. Now, when the user is editing an order, the program can simply disable the Customer menu completely.

# Use Shallow Menu Hierarchies

Shallow menu hierarchies are less confusing than very deep hierarchies. Try to use as few submenus as possible, use sub-submenus only when absolutely necessary, and try not to go any deeper than that.

For example, the menu sequence Data > Sort is ideal. The Data menu contains a Sort command that the user can find easily. The sequence Data > Sort > Sales Figures is a bit more cumbersome but still manageable.

In contrast, the sequence Data > Sort > Sales Figures > Current Year is pushing the limit of easy navigation. So long as the menu and submenu names make logical sense, the user may be able to find a command, but remembering exactly where it is may be tricky. And the sequence Data > Sort > Sales Figures > Current Year > 1st Quarter is getting silly. Even if the user can remember the sequence of menus, navigating that many layers of menus is awkward.

One way to flatten a deep menu hierarchy is to redistribute some of the bottom levels into higher levels. In this example, you could move the bottom level of entries up one level by using the following commands:

- Data > Sort > Sales Figures > Current Year Q 1

- Data > Sort > Sales Figures > Current Year Q 2

- Data > Sort > Sales Figures > Current Year Q 3

- Data > Sort > Sales Figures > Current Year Q 4

If the menu needs to hold commands for several years, this could produce a big, cumbersome submenu.

A better solution in this case is to create a dialog box that lets the user select parameters that encompass all the lower levels of the hierarchy. In this example, the Data > Sort > Sales Figures command could display a dialog box where the user could select the year and quarter and then press OK to generate a report. Instead of using five levels of menus, the new version uses only three levels plus a dialog box.

The dialog box also would be more flexible than a menu hierarchy because the user could select any year available in the database instead of just picking from a few listed in a menu. If the database holds records for 20 years, picking the year from a combo box would be easier than selecting from among 20 menu entries.

# Keep Menus Short

In addition to avoiding deep menu hierarchies, you should avoid making menus too long. The user can find a command easily in a menu containing a half-dozen entries, but a menu containing 100 entries will be practically impossible to use.

You can make it easier to use long menus by adding separators to create some structure. For example, a typical Edit menu might contain a lot of entries, but they generally are grouped naturally into categories such as action (Undo and Redo), clipboard (Copy, Cut, and Paste), selection (Select All), and searching (Find, Find Next, and Replace). The Edit menu design shown earlier in this chapter uses separators to group the commands in each of these categories.

If you need to fit a lot of commands into a menu structure, it can be tricky to strike a balance between creating a deep hierarchy and creating one that has numerous items in each menu. Removing levels of the hierarchy may mean adding more items to the higher-level menus. When a menu hierarchy is too full, consider moving some of the commands to a dialog box, as described in the previous section. Often a dialog box can simplify the menu hierarchy and increase flexibility at the same time.

## A Menu Example

Figure 4-3 shows the Edit menu used by Microsoft Paint 6.0. I opened the menu by pressing Alt+E, so the menu is showing accelerators. It also shows its shortcut keys.

**FIGURE 4-3** The Edit menu in Paint demonstrates many useful concepts, including accelerators, shortcuts, standard menu commands, and disabled commands.

This menu contains standard Edit menu commands, although it has changed the name of the Delete command to Clear Selection.

The menu places ellipses after the Copy To and Paste From commands because they display dialog boxes.

Finally, the menu shown in Figure 4-3 has several commands disabled (not hidden) because they are not currently available. For example, when I took this screenshot, there was no current selection, so the program could not execute the commands Copy, Cut, Clear Selection, Invert Selection, or Copy To. Therefore, those commands are disabled and appear dimmed.

# Context Menus

Context menus appear when the user right-clicks an object in the user interface to provide commands that are appropriate for the object that the user clicked. They are called *context menus* because their commands make sense in the context of the item that is clicked. (They are also sometimes called *pop-up menus*.)

For example, Figure 4-4 shows the context menu displayed by Word 2007 when you right-click a picture. Some of these commands, such as Change Picture... and Format Picture..., make sense only if you are right-clicking a picture.

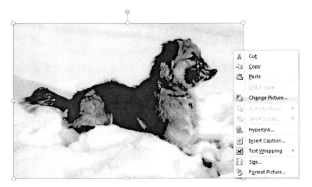

**FIGURE 4-4**  Word 2007 displays this context menu when you right-click a picture.

Compare this to Figure 4-5, which shows the context menu that Word displays when you right-click text. Many of these commands, such as Font... and Paragraph..., make sense only if you are right-clicking text.

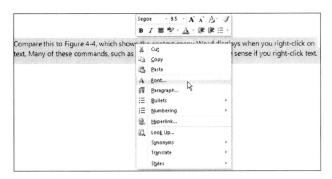

**FIGURE 4-5**  Word 2007 displays this context menu when you right-click text.

The general rules for making context menus are similar to those for making normal top-of-the-form menus. The biggest difference, however, is that context menus don't have upper-level menus. For example, a form might have upper-level menus called File, Edit, View, and so forth. A context menu skips that level and displays commands directly.

As you can see in Figures 4-4 and 4-5, context menus can contain accelerators, cascading submenus, and ellipses to indicate dialog boxes.

Notice, though, that the context menus shown in Figures 4-4 and 4-5 do not contain shortcut keys. Shortcuts go only in main menus, not context menus; but the commands in context menus often duplicate those in main menus, and those commands *can* have shortcuts. For example, a form's Edit menu often contains Copy, Cut, and Paste commands, and those commands can have shortcuts.

# Toolbars and Ribbons

Toolbars let users access the most commonly used commands without opening a menu or context menu. They should contain buttons representing the commands that users will need the most.

Often, toolbar commands aren't amenable to shortcuts for some reason. For example, Figure 4-6 shows the Toolbox window that Visual Studio displays when the Windows Form Designer is open. It's unlikely that you could assign shortcuts for all 67 of these tools that the user could remember.

**FIGURE 4-6** The Toolbox in Visual Studio contains controls that you can put on a form.

The ribbon used by recent versions of some Microsoft products such as Word, Access, Excel, WordPad, and Paint is a combination of a menu and a toolbar. Tabs across the top let you pick a category of tool much as upper-level menus do. When you click a tab, that category's tools appear below it, much as the tools in a toolbox do.

Figure 4-7 shows the ribbon in Word 2007. The tabs include Home, Insert, Page Layout, and so forth. In this screenshot, the Home tab is selected, so the tab's tools include more or less generic ways to modify text, such as choosing the font, changing the color of the text, aligning paragraphs, and making lists.

**FIGURE 4-7** The ribbon in Word provides tabs that display various tools.

**Tip** It's a good idea to give the user many ways to perform the same command. The user should be able to invoke the most commonly used commands through menus, context menus, accelerators, shortcuts, and toolbars or ribbons.

# Dialog Boxes

A *dialog box,* or *dialog,* is a form that is displayed to give information to the user or to get input from the user. Dialog boxes can be either modal or modeless.

A *modal* dialog box keeps the application's focus and won't let the user interact with any other part of the application until it is closed. Many common dialog boxes, such as those that let you select files, fonts, colors, or printers, are modal. Modal dialog boxes are usually displayed for a relatively short time because they prevent the user from doing anything with the rest of the application while they are visible.

A *modeless* dialog box allows the user to interact with other parts of the application while it is still visible. This kind of dialog box may be used as a toolbox or status area. Because the user can interact with other parts of the application while a modeless dialog box is still visible, these dialog boxes may be displayed for long periods of time. For example, a program might use modeless dialog boxes to let the user view and edit several customers, inventories, and other pieces of data at the same time.

Modeless dialog boxes behave more or less like normal forms, and they can have any characteristics that a typical form has. In contrast, modal dialog boxes in Windows applications have certain standard features.

Modal dialog boxes are often not resizable. They perform a single, fairly restricted function, so the program can often size them appropriately. They are usually visible for only a short time, so the user won't want to waste time resizing them anyway.

Modal dialog boxes often have an *Accept button* that automatically fires when the user presses the Enter key. That behavior can change depending on the button that the focus is on, so many dialog boxes appear with the focus initially on the Accept button when Enter is pressed. Often, this button is labeled OK or some other value that indicates the dialog box's primary function, such as Accept, Save, or Open.

Similarly, dialog boxes often have a *Cancel button* that automatically fires when the user presses the Esc key. This button often is labeled Cancel or Close.

Finally, modal dialog boxes can return a result to the code that displays them to indicate which button the user clicked. This value isn't visible to the user, but it is very useful to the program because it allows the program to take appropriate action.

**Tip** In a C# or Visual Basic application, you can use the Properties window to set a form's *AcceptButton* and *CancelButton* properties to the buttons that you want to fire when the user presses Enter or Esc.

You can also set a button's *DialogResult* property to indicate the value that the dialog box should return when the user clicks that button. If the user clicks the button, the form automatically closes, returning the selected result.

# User Interface Design

User interface design is a complex topic, and we won't be getting into detail here. But there are a few basic principles worth mentioning. These ideas can make your programs easier to understand and easier to use, making the user less likely to make errors caused by confusion and missed information.

## Control Order

The most natural arrangement of controls, at least in most Western cultures, is top-to-bottom and left-to-right. You can help the user find information and fill out forms easily and with fewer mistakes by arranging controls in this order. Place the most important controls in the form's upper-left corner and position the fields that the user should read or fill in so they flow down and to the right.

Some types of controls come in natural groups, and keeping them in those groups also will help the user. For example, many forms ask the user to fill out first name, last name, street address, city, state, and postal code. Users expect those fields to be provided in that order, so don't rearrange them. If you switch the order of the Name and Street fields, you're likely to have users entering their names in the Street field and vice versa. Even if the user isn't tripped up by this unusual order, the arrangement will slow the user down and make your application seem strange and annoying.

## Group Related Controls

You can help the user better understand a form by grouping related controls. This helps the user see connections among the fields, and that helps the user fill out fields correctly. For example, if a group of fields contains address information, the user can focus on address concepts such as street and postal code, and that makes filling in the fields easier.

Grouping related controls also helps with form navigation. If you set up the controls' tab order correctly, the user can fill in a field and tab to the next one in the group. After filling in one group of fields (such as the address fields), the user can tab to the next group.

There are several ways you can group controls, including the following:

- Placing related controls inside a group box, frame, or table

- Placing related controls on a background that has a different color

- Aligning controls vertically or horizontally

- Adding blank space, lines, or other separators between groups

- Indenting controls in a group below a heading label

Figure 4-8 shows a badly designed form. The fields are presented in an unexpected order and are not grouped in meaningful ways. In addition, the right edges of the fields don't line up, making a jarring transition as the user's eye moves across the form.

**FIGURE 4-8** This form doesn't let the user's eye flow naturally from top to bottom and left to right.

The lack of grouping in Figure 4-8 also makes the tab order of the fields unnatural. There are two obvious strategies for tab order in this example. First, the tab order can jump from the left fields to the right ones as needed. For example, the tab order might begin with Country, First Name, Last Name, User ID, Password, or Email. In that case, there's no reason to expect the tab to move from Last Name to User ID. When that jump occurs, the user will have to mentally switch gears from name information to user ID and password information. The jump back to Email is just as jarring.

A second approach would be to make the user fill in all the fields in the left column before visiting any of the fields in the right column. This is less jarring but ignores the natural left-to-right flow.

Figure 4-9 shows a better design for this form. Here, fields are grouped with others that have a similar purpose. The tab order moves through the groups in the top-to-bottom, left-to-right order: Login, Address, Other Contact Information, Account. Within each group, the tab order moves top to bottom.

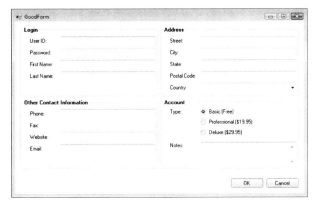

**FIGURE 4-9** This form has much better grouping and flow than the previous version.

This form also makes the following improvements over the previous one:

- The most important information is in the first group and highlighted with a colored background to indicate that it is required.

- The groups are aligned vertically and horizontally, even when one group might contain more fields than another.

- Fields are aligned vertically and horizontally, even across different groups.

- Fields have the same lengths, so they line up nicely even if one field might need to hold a longer value than another.

- Related fields are displayed in their customary order (Country is after Postal Code, and Email is grouped with other electronic contact methods).

- The buttons are in the lower-right corner, as is customary for a dialog box.

- The Account Type option buttons have their select circles aligned.

Many of these changes may seem cosmetic, but they help give the user context while filling out the fields, and that reduces the chance of mistakes.

## The Rule of Seven

Most people can hold about seven items (plus or minus two) in short-term memory at one time. That means if you display too many choices all at once, the user won't be able to keep them all in mind at the same time. This leads to a common user interface design rule that lists of choices should contain no more than seven options.

This may seem like a significant restriction, but it's really about the informational content of the choices rather than the number of choices themselves. For example, suppose you're in the United States and you want to let the user select a state from a list. There are 50 states, so a strict application of the Rule of Seven might say you can't build such a list. In this case, however, the user doesn't need to hold all 50 choices in mind at the same time. The user only needs to pick one choice and doesn't care about the others. Even so, finding the correct choice could be a difficult task if the states are arranged randomly. Fortunately, if you add extra structure by listing the states alphabetically, the user can find the right choice easily.

The reason this example works is that the user needs to make only one selection, understands the choices well, and the list is sorted so that it contains all the structure the user needs to find the desired choice.

If a list doesn't have a simple structure that users can understand easily, you can make things simpler by imposing more structure on it. For example, suppose you want to let a user select one of the 27 cities where your company has offices. A single list containing all those cities would be imposing, even if the choices are sorted alphabetically. Unless the user knew exactly which choice to select, finding the right one would be tricky. For example, to find the closest office, the user would need to look at every choice and decide which was in the nearest city.

You could add structure to this list by grouping the cities geographically instead of alphabetically. For example, the user might first select a state and then see a list of only the cities in that state. Hopefully, after the user has narrowed down the search by state, the resulting list would contain closer to the desired seven items.

## Don't Allow Mistakes

If your application gives users a chance to enter incorrect data, someone eventually will. That means you need to write extra error-handling code to catch errors. It also means that you need to let users know about any mistakes and force them to fix them. That process slows the user data-entry process down and can be frustrating sometimes.

Often, you can prevent errors in the first place by using the right kind of control. For example, instead of letting the user type one of a series of choices, offer users a selection from a drop-down list or a series of option buttons. Similarly, instead of letting users enter a numeric value, let them pick a value from a track bar.

Unfortunately, in some cases it's difficult to provide methods for letting the user pick values instead of filling them in. For example, if a user must provide a number from a huge range (such as 1 to 1,000,000) or a non-integer number (such as 75.317 or $17.34), you can't use a track bar easily. In those cases, you may be stuck letting users type the values and then performing extra error checking.

Figure 4-10 shows two track bars. The first lets the user select a value between 1 and 10 and shows tickmarks below the slider. Track bars handle this situation well.

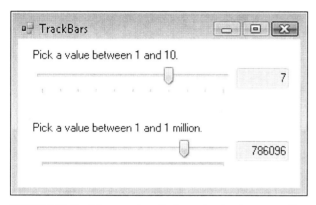

**FIGURE 4-10** Track bars work well when selecting from a small number of choices (top), but not when selecting from a large number of choices (bottom).

The second track bar lets the user select a value between 1 and 1 million. On this control, the tickmarks are so close together that they look like a thick line. The user cannot use the slider to select a specific value easily, making the track bar much harder to use. Also note that track bars cannot handle non-integer values.

## Provide Hints

An application should provide hints to help confused users and to explain what's wrong when an error occurs. Hints should be unobtrusive enough that they don't interfere with or condescend to experienced users but still provide aid to beginners. For example, a tooltip can give users a hint about what is expected in a field. If a user presses F1 while focus is on a field, context-sensitive help can give more information about that field.

Finally, if there's an error, the form can flag the offending field and display an error message indicating what went wrong. Be sure the error message gives the user enough information to fix the problem. Saying "Input string was not in a correct format" doesn't help most users as much as saying "Please enter the number of items purchased."

# Summary

This chapter described some of the standard features of Windows programs. It paid particular attention to menus, context menus, toolbars and ribbons, and dialog boxes. It also briefly described some user interface design recommendations. Unfortunately, user interface design is a major topic, so only a few guidelines have been presented here. For more information on user interface design, consult a book specifically about that topic or search online. For example, the following links provide interesting facts about form design in different scenarios:

- **Best Practices for Form Design:**
  *http://www.lukew.com/resources/articles/WebForms_LukeW.pdf*

- **Web Form Design Guidelines: An Eyetracking Study:**
  *http://www.cxpartners.co.uk/cxinsights/web_forms_design_guidelines_an_eyetracking_study.htm*

- **Sensible Forms: A Form Usability Checklist:**
  *http://www.alistapart.com/articles/sensibleforms*

This chapter mentioned a few kinds of controls that let the user enter values. For example, it briefly mentioned group boxes, drop-down lists, and track bars. The next chapter describes some of the controls that you can use to build a Windows application and explains what they are for. It also explains some of the properties that Windows Forms controls support and tells how you can use them in C# and Visual Basic applications.

# Chapter 5

# Controls

**In this chapter:**

- What controls are and what some common controls are

- What properties are and what some common properties are

- What methods are and what some common methods are

- What events are and what some common events are

A *CONTROL* IS A PROGRAM OBJECT that represents a visible feature in a Microsoft Windows program. The object includes features that let the program manage the control to make it do things (such as making a drop-down menu open) or change the control's appearance (such as changing a label's text or color).

Windows programs are made up of controls. Controls include labels, text boxes, menus, combo boxes, sliders, scroll bars, and everything else you see on a form. In fact, the form itself is a control.

In addition to controls, many programs have components. A *component* is similar to a control except it has no visible presence of its own on the form at run time.

For example, a timer component allows the program to perform some task at regular intervals. (A clock program might use a timer to update its display every second to show the current time.)

Some components do display something at run time under certain circumstances. For example, the *ErrorProvider* component can display an error symbol next to a field, but it does so only if the program marks the field as an error, and it displays the symbol on the form rather than on the *ErrorProvider*. (It's a fairly small distinction, so the line between control and component can be a bit fuzzy. Usually, it's more important to understand what an object does than to know whether it's technically a control or a component.)

This chapter describes some of the most useful controls that you can use to build Windows applications. Different development environments may use different controls or controls with slightly different features, but the general purposes of the controls will be similar. (After all, a text box is for entering text, so how different can it be, even in different programs?)

Microsoft provides two sets of controls: one for use in Windows Forms applications and one for use in Windows Presentation Foundation (WPF) and Silverlight applications.

Windows Forms applications use controls and graphical methods that have been around for years. In contrast, WPF controls use a newer graphical subsystem that has been available since the Microsoft .NET Framework version 3.0 and that is more closely integrated into the DirectX libraries that include high-performance graphics routines. That allows WPF controls to take better advantage of the computer's graphics hardware, giving them a richer appearance and better performance. WPF provides many benefits, including the following:

- More efficient use of graphics hardware

- Property binding to provide property animation

- Property inheritance to promote a consistent appearance

- Styles to give controls a consistent appearance

- Templates to give controls new behaviors

- A richer control-containment model

- Declarative programming

The details about how WPF works is outside the scope of this book, so it isn't covered here. For more information, search online or read a book about WPF programming, such as my book *WPF Programmer's Reference* (Wrox, 2010).

In addition to the controls provided by Microsoft, many third-party vendors make controls that you can buy and add to your applications. These include controls to draw graphs, plot points on maps, display tool ribbons, display hierarchical data in trees, provide editors, and perform many other functions.

This chapter provides only a summary of the most useful controls provided for use with Microsoft Visual Studio and their purposes so that you know what tools are available to you. For more information about a control's specific features, search online for help.

**Tip** You can find Microsoft's web page for a particular Windows Forms control by replacing "textbox" with the control's name in the following link:

*http://msdn.microsoft.com/library/system.windows.forms.textbox.aspx.*

Similarly, you can find the page for a WPF control by replacing "textbox" with the control's name in the following link:

*http://msdn.microsoft.com/library/system.windows.controls.textbox.aspx.*

This chapter concludes by describing some useful properties that you can use to arrange controls on a form.

# Using Controls

At some point, a Windows program must use code to create the controls that make up its user interface. The program's code can then use the control objects to interact with the user.

Fortunately, you usually don't need to worry about the code that creates the controls. Instead, you can use a form editor to build the form interactively. You can use dragging to place controls on the form, resize the controls, move the controls around, and set their properties intuitively at design time. Figure 5-1 shows Visual Studio designing a form.

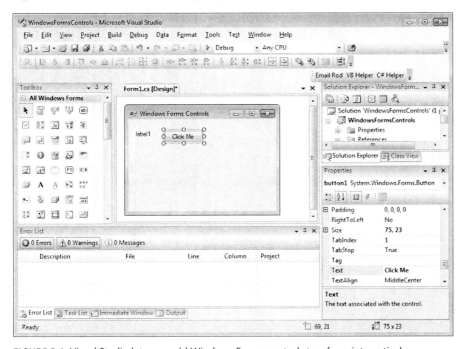

**FIGURE 5-1** Visual Studio lets you add Windows Forms controls to a form interactively.

The Toolbox in the upper-left corner of Figure 5-1 contains controls and components that you can put on the form. You can click one to select it and then click and drag to position a new control on the form.

In Figure 5-1, the button is selected. You can click and drag the grab handles to resize the control, or you can click and drag the control itself to move it. The Properties window on the lower right lets you easily change the control's properties. For example, you can type a new caption for the button to display in its *Text* property.

One particularly important property, which is scrolled off the top of the Properties window in Figure 5-1, is *Name*. If you set a control's *Name* property, your program's code can use that name to refer to the control at run time.

You'll learn much more about how to create and manipulate controls when you read other books such as *Start Here! Learn Microsoft Visual C# 2010 Programming* or *Start Here! Learn Microsoft Visual Basic Programming*. For now, take a look at the following sections to see what kinds of controls are available and to get an idea of what they can do.

## Windows Forms Controls

Table 5-1 summarizes the most useful Windows Forms controls and components. The names of components are followed by asterisks.

**TABLE 5-1** Useful Windows Forms Controls and Components

| Icon | Control/Component | Description |
|------|------------------|-------------|
| | BackgroundWorker * | Lets the program perform an action in the background while doing other things. Notifies the program of the action's progress and completion. |
| | BindingNavigator | Provides a user interface for navigating through bound data. |
| | BindingSource * | Encapsulates a data source, such as a database, for data binding. |
| | Button | Lets the program take action when the user clicks it. |
| | CheckBox | Lets the user select or clear an item. |
| | CheckedListBox | Lets the user select one or more items from a list. |
| | ColorDialog | Displays a color selection dialog box. |
| | ComboBox | Displays a drop-down list from which the user can make a selection. |
| | ContextMenuStrip * | Displays a context menu when the user right-clicks something. |
| | DataGridView | Displays a data source in rows and columns. This control provides features for letting the user navigate through the data if the data source is a database. |
| | DataSet * | An in-memory representation of table-like data. |
| | DateTimePicker | Lets the user select a date and time. |
| | DirectoryEntry * | Represents a node in an Active Directory Domain Services (AD DS) hierarchy. |
| | DirectorySearcher * | Searches an AD DS hierarchy. |

| Icon | Control/Component | Description |
|------|-------------------|-------------|
| | DomainUpDown | Lets the user click up and down arrows to move through a list of choices. |
| | ErrorProvider * | Displays error messages for fields that have errors. |
| | EventLog * | Lets the program interact with event logs. |
| | FileSystemWatcher * | Notifies the program of changes to the file system. |
| | FlowLayoutPanel | Arranges the controls that it contains in rows or columns, wrapping to a new row or column when necessary. |
| | FolderBrowserDialog * | Displays a folder selection dialog box. |
| | FontDialog * | Displays a font selection dialog box. |
| | GroupBox | Displays a caption and a border around other controls. |
| | HelpProvider * | Provides context-sensitive help or online help for other controls. |
| | HScrollBar | Displays a horizontal scrollbar. |
| | ImageList * | Holds images for use by other controls. |
| A | Label | Displays text that the user cannot modify. |
| A | LinkLabel | Displays text with links. When the user clicks a link, the program can act. |
| | ListBox | Displays a list of items that the user can select. Different modes let the user select one or more items. |
| | ListView | Displays a series of items with subitems. The result is similar to the different displays provided by Windows Explorer for files. |
| #_ | MaskedTextBox | A text box that displays a mask to help the user enter formatted values. For example, a 10-digit U.S. phone number might have the mask (___)___-___ so that when a user types in the numbers, it goes into that format automatically. |
| | MenuStrip | Provides a form's main menu. |

| Icon | Control/Component | Description |
|---|---|---|
| | MessageQueue * | Lets the program interact with the message queue system. |
| | MonthCalendar | Displays a calendar where the user can select a date or range of dates. |
| | NotifyIcon * | Displays an icon in the task bar's notification area. The program can change the icon to indicate its status. The icon also can provide a menu to let the user control the application. |
| | NumericUpDown | Lets the user click up and down arrows to select a number. |
| | OpenFileDialog * | Displays a dialog box for opening a file. |
| | PageSetupDialog * | Displays a dialog box that lets the user control the printer's page settings. |
| | Panel | Contains other controls. You can change the appearance of the Panel to group the controls and the Panel can display scroll bars if its contents don't fit its current size. |
| | PerformanceCounter * | Lets the program interact with performance counters. |
| | PictureBox | Displays an image, possibly scaling or stretching it. |
| | PrintDialog | Displays a dialog box that lets the user select a printer. |
| | PrintDocument * | An object that represents a printout. A program uses this object to generate output to send to the printer or to a print preview. |
| | PrintPreviewControl | Displays a preview of a printout in a control that you can integrate into your forms. |
| | PrintPreviewDialog | Displays a dialog box showing a preview of a printout. |
| | Process * | Lets the program control other processes. |
| | ProgressBar | Displays a bar showing the program's progress performing a task. |
| | PropertyGrid | Displays an object's properties in a grid similar to the Properties window shown in Figure 5-1. |
| | RadioButton | Lets the user select exactly one choice from among the RadioButton controls in a group. If the user clicks one RadioButton, the others in the group clear. |

| Icon | Control/Component | Description |
|------|-------------------|-------------|
| | RichTextBox | A text box that can display text in multiple colors, fonts, and styles at the same time, as opposed to a *TextBox*, which displays all text in a single color, font, and style. |
| | SaveFileDialog * | Displays a dialog box for selecting a file to save into. |
| | SerialPort * | Lets the program interact with the computer's serial ports. |
| | ServiceController * | Lets the program interact with Windows services. (A Windows service is a special program that can run when the system is running even if no user is logged in.) |
| | SplitContainer | Holds two child controls and provides a splitter between them. The user can drag the splitter back and forth to make one child bigger and the other smaller. The child controls are often containers, such as *Panel* controls that hold other controls. |
| | StatusStrip | Displays an area, usually at the bottom of the form, where a program can display labels and other status information. (For example, Windows Explorer can display a status strip showing such items as the number of files selected and their total size.) |
| | TabControl | Displays a series of tabs that hold other controls. |
| | TableLayoutPanel | Arranges its child controls into rows and columns, similar to a table. |
| | TextBox | Lets the user enter text. A *TextBox* can use only one color, font, and style at a time. |
| | Timer * | Lets the program take action at periodic intervals. |
| | ToolStrip | Displays a control that functions like a toolbar and can contain buttons, drop-down menus or lists, and other tool controls. |
| | ToolStripContainer | Lets the user move *ToolStrip* controls and dock them on the edges of the form. |
| | ToolTip * | Displays pop-up windows containing help and status information for other controls. |
| | TrackBar | Displays a slider that users can drag back and forth to select an integer value. |
| | VScrollBar | A vertical scrollbar. |
| | WebBrowser | A control that can display web pages. (This is like putting a browser inside your form.) |

Figure 5-2 shows many of the typical Windows Forms controls. Labels give the types of the controls where it's not obvious.

**FIGURE 5-2** This form contains many Windows Forms controls.

Some of the most interesting items in Figure 5-2 are the following:

- *MenuStrip,* which displays the form's main menus at the top of the form.

- *ToolStrip,* below *MenuStrip,* which contains three buttons that hold copy, cut, and paste images.

- *ErrorProvider,* next to the *CheckBox,* which displays an error icon.

- *FlowLayoutPanel,* which contains three buttons. The first two are arranged in a row. The third button didn't fit in the row, so the control moved it to a second row.

- *GroupBox,* which contains a *LinkLabel.* You have to look closely to see the *GroupBox* control's light inset border.

- *StatusStrip,* at the bottom of the form, which contains a label and a progress bar.

# WPF Controls

Just as Windows Forms has a set of controls, WPF does as well. Many of these are functionally similar to Windows Forms controls, but some are new, and many of the controls—even the common ones—are somewhat different, either in appearance, in functionality, or both. Table 5-2 summarizes the most useful WPF controls.

 **Note** The thing you normally call a *form* in a Windows Forms program is called a *window* in a WPF application.

**TABLE 5-2** The Most Useful WPF Controls

| Icon | WPF Control | Description |
|------|-------------|-------------|
| | Border | Displays a border around a child control. |
| | Button | Lets the program act in a defined way when the user clicks the control. |
| | Canvas | Contains other controls positioned by setting left, top, bottom, and right properties. |
| | CheckBox | Lets the user select or clear an item. |
| | ComboBox | Displays a drop-down list from which the user can make a selection. |
| | DockPanel | Lets you dock contained controls to the *DockPanel* control's left, top, right, and bottom edges. |
| | DocumentViewer | Displays a fixed document, which is a document containing contents that the user cannot move. |
| | Ellipse | Draws an ellipse. |
| | Expander | Displays a button that the user can click to expand or hide a content panel. |
| | Frame | Provides page-oriented navigation, somewhat similar to the way a web browser lets you navigate between pages. |
| | Grid | Arranges the controls that it contains into rows and columns. |
| | GridSplitter | Allows the user to resize a *Grid* control's rows or columns. |
| | GroupBox | Displays a caption and a border around other controls. |

| Icon | WPF Control | Description |
|------|-------------|-------------|
| | Image | Displays an image, possibly scaling or stretching it. |
| | Label | Displays text that the user cannot modify. |
| | ListBox | Displays a list of items that the user can select. Different modes let the user select one or more items. |
| | ListView | Displays a series of items with subitems. The result is similar to the different displays provided by Windows Explorer for files. |
| | MediaElement | Plays audio or video. |
| | Menu | Provides a window's main menu. |
| | PasswordBox | A text box that displays a password character for each character typed. |
| | ProgressBar | Displays a bar showing the program's progress at some task. |
| | RadioButton | Lets the user select exactly one choice from among the *RadioButton* controls in a group. If the user clicks one *RadioButton*, the others in the group clear. |
| | Rectangle | Draws a rectangle. |
| | RichTextBox | A text box that can display text in multiple colors, fonts, and styles at the same time, as opposed to a *TextBox*, which displays all text in a single color, font, and style. |
| | ScrollBar | A horizontal or vertical scroll bar. |
| | ScrollViewer | Displays a content control and provides scrolling if that control doesn't fit in the *ScrollViewer* control's current size. |
| | Separator | Displays a separator in a *Menu*, *ToolBar*, or *StatusBar*. |
| | Slider | Displays a slider that the user can drag back and forth to select an integer value. |
| | StackPanel | Arranges contained controls either in a single row or a single column. |
| | StatusBar | Displays an area, usually at the bottom of the window, where a program can display labels and other status information. (For example, Windows Explorer can display a status bar showing such things as the number of files selected and their total size.) |

| Icon | WPF Control | Description |
|---|---|---|
| | TabControl | Displays a series of tabs that hold other controls. |
| | TextBlock | Displays text that can contain segments that use different fonts, colors, styles, and other features. |
| | TextBox | Lets the user enter text. A *TextBox* can use only one color, font, and style at a time. |
| | ToolBar | Displays a toolbar containing buttons, drop-down menus or lists, and other tool controls. |
| | TreeView | Displays hierarchical data in a treelike arrangement that the user can click to open and close branches of the tree. (The result is similar to the way Windows Explorer usually displays folders on the left.) |
| | UniformGrid | Arranges its contents into rows and columns of uniform size. |
| | Viewbox | A control that scales its contents. |
| | WrapPanel | Arranges the controls that it contains into rows or columns, wrapping to a new row or column when necessary. |

Figure 5-3 shows many of the typical WPF controls. Labels give the types of the controls where it's not obvious.

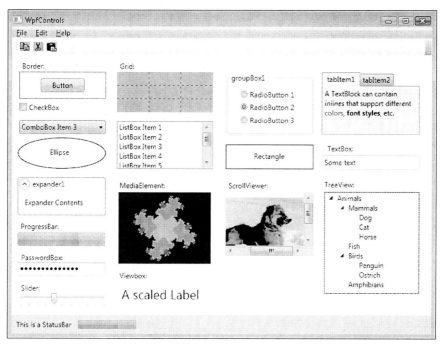

**FIGURE 5-3** This window contains many WPF controls.

The following list mentions some points of interest in Figure 5-3:

- A *Menu* at the top of the window is displaying the window's main menus.

- The *ToolBar* below the *Menu* contains three buttons that hold copy, cut, and paste images.

- The *Border* control contains a *Button*.

- The *Expander* contains a single *Label* that says "Expander Contents." If you click the button in the *Expander* control's upper-left corner, the content area disappears, leaving just the *Expander* control's button and header.

- The *MediaElement* is in the middle is playing a video file.

- The *TabControl*'s first tab page contains a *TextBlock*.

- The *StatusStrip*, at the bottom of the window, contains a *Label* and a *ProgressBar*.

If you compare the lists of Windows Forms controls and WPF controls, you'll find some overlap. You can see a summary of Windows Forms controls and their rough WPF equivalents at *http://msdn .microsoft.com/library/ms750559.aspx*.

# Properties

Typically, programs interact with controls by using the controls' properties, methods, and events. These are described more generally and more completely in Chapter 10, "Object-Oriented Programming."

This chapter doesn't explain in detail how you can *use* properties, methods, and events because the details depend on the programming language you are using. Different controls also provide a wide variety of features, so an exhaustive description of them all in this book is simply impossible. The following sections do describe properties, methods, and events generally to give you an idea about what is possible in your programs. You can also find much more detail and examples of using controls in the companion books *Start Here! Learn Microsoft Visual Basic Programming* and *Start Here! Learn Microsoft Visual C# 2010 Programming*, or by searching MSDN for the particular control you're interested in.

## Windows Forms Properties

Properties are attributes that determine a control's appearance or behavior. For example, a *Label* control's *Text* property determines the text displayed by the control. For an example of a property determining a control's behavior, the *ListBox* control's *Sorted* property determines whether the control sorts its items.

Windows Forms and WPF controls support thousands of properties, so this chapter can't describe them all here. Some are so control-specific that you won't care what they do unless you are using a particular control for a specific purpose.

However, many properties are shared by lots of controls, so it's worth listing a few of the most common ones so that you have an idea about what they do.

There are some big differences between Windows Forms and WPF properties, so they are summarized separately here. Table 5-3 summarizes some of the most useful Windows Forms control properties.

**TABLE 5-3** Useful Windows Forms Control Properties

| Property | Description |
| --- | --- |
| Anchor | Determines whether a control's left, right, top, and bottom edges are attached to those of the control containing it. |
| AutoSize | Determines whether a control resizes to fit its content. (This is particularly useful for *Labels*.) |
| BackColor | Determines a control's background color. |
| BackgroundImage | Determines the image displayed by a control. |
| BorderStyle | Determines the type of border (if any) that a control displays. |
| ContextMenu | Determines the *ContextMenuStrip* that is automatically displayed when the user right-clicks a control. |
| Cursor | Determines the cursor that a control displays. |
| Checked | Determines whether a control is selected, for controls such as *CheckBox* and *RadioButton*. |
| Dock | Determines whether a control docks itself to one of the edges of the control that contains it. |
| Enabled | Determines whether a control will interact with the user. For example, if a *Button* control's *Enabled* property has the value *False*, then the user can see the *Button*, but it is dimmed and the user cannot click it. |
| Font | Determines the font that a control uses to draw text. |
| ForeColor | Determines a control's foreground color. |
| Image | Determines the image displayed by a control. |
| Items | For lists, determines the items displayed by a control. |
| Location | Determines the position of a control within the control that contains it. |
| MaximumSize | Determines the largest size a control will be even if its *Anchor* or *Dock* property tries to make it bigger. |
| MinimumSize | Determines the smallest size a control will be even if its *Anchor* or *Dock* property tries to make it smaller. |
| MultiColumn | For lists, determines whether a control displays items in multiple columns. |
| MultiLine | For *TextBox* and *RichTextBox* controls, indicates whether the control accepts multiline input. |
| ScrollBars | For *TextBox* and *RichTextBox* controls, determines which scroll bars (horizontal or vertical), if any, are visible. |
| SelectionMode | For lists, determines whether the user can select one item or multiple items. |
| SelectedIndex | For lists, determines the index of the currently selected item. |
| Size | Determines a control's size. The final actual size may also depend on the *Anchor*, *AutoSize*, *Dock*, *MinimumSize*, and *MaximumSize* properties. |

| Property | Description |
|---|---|
| TabIndex | Determines the position of a control in the tab order. |
| Tag | This property can hold anything you want. For example, a program could store a text value here to indicate the name of the picture in a *PictureBox* control. |
| Text | Determines the text displayed by a control. Many Windows Forms controls, such as *TextBox*, *Button*, and *Label*, display simple text (and sometimes images) and this property sets that text. |
| Value | Determines the value of a numeric control, such as a *HScrollBar*, *VScrollBar*, *ProgressBar*, *TrackBar*, or *NumericUpDown* control. |
| Visible | Determines whether a control is visible. |

In Windows Forms, the *Anchor* and *Dock* properties play key roles in arranging controls. The *Dock* property keeps a control attached to one of the edges of the control that contains it. For example, a *MenuStrip* typically docks to the top edge of a form and a *StatusStrip* typically docks to the bottom edge. Other controls fill the center of the form.

The *Anchor* property determines which of the control's edges remain a fixed distance from the corresponding edges of the control that contains it. A "normal" control that doesn't move or resize when its container resizes is attached to the top and left of the container. In other words, its top and left edges remain a fixed distance from the container's top and left edges.

A common strategy is to anchor *TextBox* controls that should stretch horizontally on the top, left, and right. You also can place one control that can usefully stretch vertically at the bottom of a form and anchor it on the top, left, right, and bottom.

Figure 5-4 shows a form with *TextBox* controls for First Name, Last Name, and Email anchored on the top, left, and right. When the form's size changes horizontally, those controls stretch to take advantage of the available space. The multiline *TextBox* at the bottom of the form is anchored on the top, left, right, and bottom, so it stretches horizontally and vertically to use any available space.

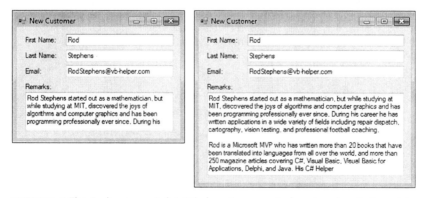

**FIGURE 5-4** The *Anchor* property lets Windows Forms controls resize when their containers resize.

# WPF Properties

Table 5-4 summarizes the most useful properties provided by WPF controls.

**TABLE 5-4** WPF Control Properties

| Property | Description |
|---|---|
| Background | The brush that a control uses to draw its background. (A brush defines the drawing characteristics of a filled area, such as its color, tile pattern, or color gradient.) |
| BorderBrush | The brush that a control uses to draw its border. |
| BorderThickness | The thickness of a control's border. |
| Content | Determines a control's content. |
| FontFamily | The name of a control's font family, such as Seqoe UI or Times New Roman. |
| FontSize | The size of a control's font. |
| FontStyle | Determines whether a font is italicized. |
| FontWeight | Determines whether a font is bold. |
| Foreground | The brush that a control uses to draw foreground elements such as text. |
| Height | Determines a control's height. |
| LayoutTransform | A transformation that rotates, translates, or scales a control before the control is arranged by the program. |
| Margin | The distances between a control's edges and those of its parents. For example, the value 10, 8, 6, 0 would make the control remain 10 pixels from its parent's left edge, 8 pixels from its parent's top edge, 6 pixels from its parent's right edge, and 0 pixels from its parent's bottom edge. |
| MaxHeight | The tallest size a control can be. |
| MaxWidth | The widest size a control can be. |
| MinHeight | The shortest size a control can be. |
| MinWidth | The narrowest size a control can be. |
| RenderTransform | A transformation that rotates, translates, or scales a control after the control is arranged by the program but before it is displayed. |
| Visibility | Determines whether a control is visible. |
| Width | Determines a control's width. |

There are many differences between Windows Forms controls and WPF controls, the most important of which are described in the following paragraphs.

WPF controls use brushes to determine their appearance. Those brushes can be simple solid colors such as red or blue, or they can be more complex objects, such as gradients that shade from one color to another or repeated patterns.

For example, Figure 5-5 shows a window filled with an *ImageBrush* that repeats a diamond pattern. The window contains a *Label* that draws its text with a *LinearGradientBrush* control that shades from lime green at the top to dark green at the bottom.

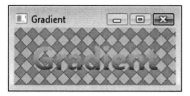

**FIGURE 5-5** WPF controls use brushes to determine their colors.

As is the case with Windows Forms controls, the actual size of a WPF control depends on several properties. For WPF controls, those properties include *Height*, *Width*, and *Margin*. Often, the *Height* or *Width* property is set to *Auto* to make the control pick the size that is most appropriate. Depending on the specific control, this may be the minimum size needed to hold the control's contents (for example, with a *Label*), or it may be the largest size possible within the control's container (for example, with a *StackPanel*).

WPF programs rely heavily on *container controls* to arrange the controls that they contain. Container controls include *DockPanel*, *Grid*, *StackPanel*, *UniformGrid*, and *WrapPanel*. To control the layout of other controls on the form, WPF programs use these container controls more often than they use control properties, such as the properties that are similar to the Windows Forms controls' *Anchor* and *Dock* properties.

WPF properties are different from Windows Forms properties in several respects, one of which is that a WPF control can provide *attached properties* for the controls that it contains. For example, a *Grid* control divides the area that it occupies into rows and columns. When you place child controls into the *Grid*, it attaches *Grid.Row* and *Grid.Column* properties so that those controls can indicate their positions.

Figure 5-6 shows a *Grid* control containing two *Button* controls whose *Grid.Row* and *Grid.Column* properties determine where the *Button* controls are positioned.

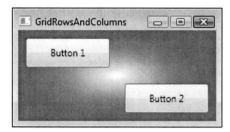

**FIGURE 5-6** The *Button* controls' *Grid.Row* and *Grid.Column* attached properties determine the controls' rows and columns.

Many WPF controls use a *Content* property instead of a simple *Text* property so that they can display much more complex content than Windows Forms controls. For example, a Windows Forms *Button* can display only text and an image, but a WPF *Button* can display practically anything. For instance, a *Grid* contains *Label*, *ComboBox*, and *Image* controls, and even *MediaElement* controls playing videos.

The last difference between Windows Forms and WPF programs described here is the way that the two approaches define controls. When you build a Windows Forms application, you use a form editor, and Visual Studio generates code behind the scenes to create the controls.

In contrast, when you build a WPF application, Visual Studio builds an Extensible Application Markup Language (XAML) file that declares the controls and their properties. In addition to using the Visual Studio editor to modify the WPF controls, you can edit the WPF text directly. The following XAML code defines the window shown in Figure 5-6.

```
<Window x:Class="GridRowsAndColumns.Window1"
    xmlns="http://schemas.microsoft.com/winfx/2006/xaml/presentation"
    xmlns:x="http://schemas.microsoft.com/winfx/2006/xaml"
    Title="GridRowsAndColumns" Height="150" Width="250">
    <Window.Background>
        <RadialGradientBrush>
            <GradientStop Offset="0" Color="White"/>
            <GradientStop Offset="1" Color="Red"/>
        </RadialGradientBrush>
    </Window.Background>
    <Grid>
        <Grid.RowDefinitions>
            <RowDefinition Height="*"/>
            <RowDefinition Height="*"/>
        </Grid.RowDefinitions>
        <Grid.ColumnDefinitions>
            <ColumnDefinition Width="*"/>
            <ColumnDefinition Width="*"/>
        </Grid.ColumnDefinitions>
        <Button Margin="10" Grid.Row="0" Grid.Column="0" Content="Button 1"/>
        <Button Margin="10" Grid.Row="1" Grid.Column="1" Content="Button 2"/>
    </Grid>
</Window>
```

Don't worry too much about how the preceding code works. If you decide to study WPF, you'll learn a lot more about XAML code, but for now, some features of this XAML code that are worth mentioning include the following:

- The window's background is a *RadialGradientBrush* control that shades from white in the center to red at the edges.

- The *Grid* control defines two rows of equal height and two columns of equal width.

- The *Button* controls use *Grid.Row* and *Grid.Column* attached properties to indicate their rows and columns.

- The *Button* controls have a *Margin* property equal to 10, so they adjust their edges to be 10 pixels from the edges of the *Grid* cells that hold them.

- The *Button* controls have *Content* properties set to simple strings.

This section barely scratches the surface of all the possible properties that Windows Forms and WPF controls might provide. Some are specific to particular controls, and you won't need them except under very particular circumstances. However, at this point, you should have some idea of the range of available possibilities.

# Methods

A *method* is a piece of code that you can call to make a control do something. A simple example is the *TextBox* control's *Clear* method, which makes the control clear its contents. The exact syntax for calling these methods depends on the programming language you're using.

Methods tend to be more closely related to particular controls than properties. For example, most controls expose *Location* and *Size* properties that determine their size and positioning; however, only those that allow users to select data (such as controls that contain text) can reasonably provide *Copy*, *Cut*, and *Paste* methods.

Still, it's worth mentioning a few of the most frequently used methods so that you have an idea of the sorts of things that are possible. Table 5-5 lists and describes some common methods provided by Windows Forms controls.

TABLE 5-5 Common Windows Forms Control Methods

| Method | Description |
| --- | --- |
| AppendText | Adds text to the end of a *TextBox*. |
| Clear | Clears a *TextBox*. |
| Copy | Copies the current selection in a *TextBox*. |
| Cut | Cuts the current selection in a *TextBox*. |
| DrawToBitmap | Makes the control draw itself onto a bitmap. |
| Focus | Sets focus to the control. |
| Invalidate | Flags the control's image as invalid so that it is redrawn during the next paint operation. |
| Paste | Pastes the clipboard's contents into the current selection in a *TextBox*. |
| PointToClient | Converts a point from screen coordinates to the control's coordinate system. |
| PointToScreen | Converts a point from the control's coordinate system to screen coordinates. |
| Redo | Redoes the last undone change in a *TextBox*. |
| Refresh | Makes the control redraw itself immediately. |
| ScrollToCaret | Scrolls a *TextBox* so that the current insertion position is visible. |
| Select | Selects some of the text in a *TextBox*. |
| SelectAll | Selects all the text in a *TextBox*. |
| Undo | Undoes the last change in a *TextBox*. |

WPF controls support many of the same methods. In particular, the WPF *TextBox* provides many of the same methods as the Windows Forms version.

Many components also provide methods that let you make the component perform an action. These methods tend to be very specific to particular components. For example, the *ErrorProvider* component's *SetError* method sets an error for a control. The *ErrorProvider* is the only component that sets errors for controls, so it makes sense that other components don't provide a *SetError* method.

Table 5-6 summarizes a few useful component methods.

**TABLE 5-6** Useful Component Methods

| Method | Description |
|---|---|
| *FindAll* | Makes a *DirectorySearcher* perform a search. |
| *FindOne* | Makes a *DirectorySearcher* perform a search and return the first result it finds. |
| *GetError* | Makes an *ErrorProvider* return the error associated with a control. |
| *GetToolTip* | Returns the tooltip that a *ToolTip* has associated with a control. |
| *Kill* | Makes a *Process* component immediately terminate its process. |
| *RunWorkerAsync* | Makes a *BackgroundWorker* start running asynchronously. |
| *SetError* | Makes an *ErrorProvider* associate an error with a control. |
| *SetToolTip* | Makes a *ToolTip* associate a tooltip with a control. |
| *Start* | Makes a *Process* component run a process. |
| *Start* | Starts a *Timer*. |
| *Stop* | Stops a *Timer*. |
| *WaitForExit* | Makes a *Process* component wait until its process exits. |

Although these lists don't describe every method that the Windows Forms and WPF controls provide, they do give you an idea of the sorts of things you can do with methods. When you start writing programs and are working with a particular control or component, you can learn about that object's methods and use them in your code.

# Events

A program uses properties to determine a control's appearance and behavior and uses methods to make it perform some action. A third way that a program can interact with a control is by using events. An *event* is a mechanism that lets a control tell the program that something interesting has occurred.

When something interesting occurs, a control *raises* the event. The program can *catch* or *handle* the event and take whatever action is appropriate. It might display new output to the user, start performing some task, or close the application. The code that processes the event is called an *event handler*.

Probably the most common event is the *Click* event, which is raised by buttons and menu items when the user clicks them. For example, when the user clicks the Exit item on the File menu, the menu item control raises a *Click* event. The program catches the event and exits, possibly saving changes and closing files in the process.

Windows Forms and WPF controls provide a huge number of events, most of which you will never need to use. For example, most controls provide a whole slew of mouse events, including *MouseCaptureChanged*, *MouseClick*, *MouseDown*, *MouseEnter*, *MouseHover*, *MouseLeave*, *MouseMove*, and *MouseUp* to let the program know exactly what the mouse is doing with the control. These events may be useful for a drawing application, but it's unusual for a program to catch these messages for simple controls such as *Label* and *Button*.

The following list summarizes some of the most useful events provided by Windows Forms controls.

**TABLE 5-7**  Useful Windows Forms Events

| Event | Description |
| --- | --- |
| *Click* | The user clicked the control. |
| *DoubleClick* | The user double-clicked the control. |
| *DragDrop* | A drag operation has ended in a drop on the control. |
| *DragEnter* | A drag operation has entered the control. |
| *DragLeave* | A drag operation has left the control. |
| *DragOver* | A drag operation is moving over the control. |
| *Enter* | The control received the input focus. |
| *FormClosed* | A form has closed. |
| *FormClosing* | A form is about to close. Code in the event handler can still cancel the close. |
| *KeyDown* | The user pressed a key down while the control had focus. |
| *KeyPress* | The user pressed and released a key while the control had focus. |
| *KeyUp* | The user released a key while the control had focus. |
| *Leave* | The control lost the input focus. |
| *Load* | A form is loaded and ready for display but is not yet visible. |
| *MouseClick* | The user clicked the mouse over the control. This is similar to *Click*, but it includes the mouse's *X* and *Y* position. |
| *MouseDown* | The user pressed the mouse down over the control. |
| *MouseEnter* | The mouse moved over the control. |
| *MouseHover* | The mouse is sitting still over the control. |
| *MouseLeave* | The mouse left the control. |
| *MouseMove* | The user moved the mouse over the control. |
| *MouseUp* | The user released the mouse over the control. |
| *Paint* | Indicates that the program should draw something. For example, a program might draw something in a *Form* or *PictureBox* control's *Paint* event. |

| Event | Description |
| --- | --- |
| *Resize* | The control has resized. |
| *ResizeBegin* | The control is starting to resize. |
| *ResizeEnd* | The control has finished resizing. |
| *Scroll* | For value selection controls such as *TrackBar* and *ScrollBar*, the control's slider moved. |
| *SelectedIndexChanged* | For selection controls such as *ListBox* and *TabControl*, the current selection changed. |
| *TextChanged* | The text in a control, such as a *TextBox*, has changed. |
| *ValueChanged* | For value selection controls such as *TrackBar* and *ScrollBar*, the control's value changed. |

WPF controls support many of the same (or similar) events provided by Windows Forms controls.

# Summary

This chapter provided a brief summary of controls. It explained that controls are the components that make up the user interface in a Windows Forms or WPF application. It also explained that components are similar to controls, except that there is no visible piece on the form.

This chapter's main purpose was to give you an idea about some of the things that controls and components can do. It listed some of the most common Windows Forms and WPF controls and summarized their purposes. It also summarized the most common properties, methods, and events that those controls and components provide to let programs interact with them. When you study Windows Forms or WPF application development in detail, you'll learn a lot more about controls and how to use them in your programs.

Controls and components define a program's user interface. In addition to a user interface, most programs have extensive code behind the scenes to provide the program's functionality. For example, a simple drawing program would need code to save and load files, change drawing tools, modify the current drawing, and ensure that changes are saved before closing.

The next chapter describes a simple but very important part of the code that sits behind the user interface: variables. A variable holds data that the program can manipulate. The next chapter explains what a variable is and describes fundamental variables concepts, such as data type, type checking, scope, and accessibility.

# Chapter 6

# Variables

**In this chapter:**

- What data types are and what the fundamental data types are
- How strings are implemented in .NET
- What program-defined data types are
- How value and reference types differ
- How a program can convert data from one type to another
- How scope, accessibility, and lifetime affect what code can use a variable

**TO MOST USERS, A PROGRAM IS** a collection of buttons, labels, and text boxes stuck on a form. Behind the scenes, however, programs are all about data. Pieces of data hold the text displayed on the labels, the text entered by the user, the numeric values used to make calculations, and the size and positions of controls. Even the programs themselves are data at some level. If you open an executable program in an editor such as WordPad, you can see the data that represents the program (although it looks like gibberish to human eyes).

A *variable* is a named piece of memory that can hold a piece of data so that the program can manipulate it. This chapter describes variables at a high level. It explains how programs can use variables, what kinds of data they can contain, and programming concepts that make using variables easier to use and less error-prone.

## Fundamental Data Types

Users and programmers think of data values in high-level terms. They think of strings of text, pictures, video files, and numbers. At its lowest level, however, the computer represents everything as 0s and 1s. It's only when you interpret a collection of 0s and 1s in a particular way that you can give it higher-level meaning.

**Note** Each 0 or 1 is called a *bit*. A *byte* is a group of 8 bits. Bytes are grouped into *words*. The number of bytes in a word is chosen so that a particular computer and operating system can manipulate words efficiently. For example, there may be 4 or 8 bytes in a word.

For instance, a piece of memory that holds the binary value 1000001 might represent the character *A* if you know that that piece of memory holds character data. If the memory holds something else, such as a number or a piece of an image, the value 1000001 might represent something else entirely. For example, as a number, this value represents 65; and as an image, it might represent the red component of a single pixel.

A variable is a named piece of memory that can hold data of a specific type so the program can manipulate it. The variable's *data type* tells the program how to interpret the data. In this example, it indicates whether 10000001 is a character, a number, or something else.

Typically, a program declares the variable's data type when it declares the variable. The program can put values only with that data type in the variable. For example, if a program declares a variable to hold an integer, it cannot put a string such as "hello" in it.

**Note** There are ways to convert from one data type to another, however. For example, you might want to convert the number 13 into a string containing the characters *13*, or vice versa. "Type Conversion," discusses conversion in more detail.

You can think of a variable as an envelope of a certain size and shape that can hold only values that have the matching size and shape. You can't fit a long, skinny string in an envelope that is sized to hold short, fat integers.

The following statement shows how a Microsoft Visual Basic .NET program would declare a variable named *customers* that can hold an integer.

```
Dim customers As Integer
```

Here, the keyword *Dim* stands for *dimension* and indicates that the statement is declaring a variable. The next word, *customers*, gives the name of the variable. The final piece of the statement, *As Integer*, means that the variable should be able to hold an integer value. In Visual Basic .NET, an integer uses 4 bytes and can hold values between -2,147,483,648 and 2,147,483,647.

The following code shows the equivalent declaration for a variable in C#:

```
int customers;
```

This does exactly the same thing as the previous code, just using a different programming language.

Table 6-1 summarizes the most common data types in .NET programming. The size indicates the number of bytes that a variable of the type occupies in memory.

**TABLE 6-1**  .NET Programming Data Types

| Type | Size | Range |
|---|---|---|
| Boolean | 2 | True or False |
| Byte | 1 | 0 to 255 |
| Char | 2 | A Unicode character |
| Date | 8 | 0:00:00 on January 1, 0001 through 11:59:59 PM on December 31, 9999. |
| Decimal | 16 | Numbers with roughly 29 digits of precision |
| Double | 8 | Roughly -1.8e308 to 1.8e308, with 17 digits of precision |
| Integer | 4 | -2,147,483,648 to 2,147,483,647 |
| Long | 8 | -9,223,372,036,854,775,808 to 9,223,372,036,854,775,807 |
| Object | 4 | Can hold any data type |
| SByte | 1 | -128 to 127 |
| Short | 2 | -32,768 to 32,767 |
| Single | 4 | Roughly −3.4e38 to 3.4e38, with 8 digits of precision |
| String | Varies | A string with 0 to roughly 2 billion Unicode characters |
| UInteger | 4 | 0 to 4,294,967,295 |
| ULong | 8 | 0 to 18,446,744,073,709,551,615 |
| UShort | 2 | 0 to 65,535 |

**Note** An *e* or *E* in the notation for the *Single, Double*, and *Decimal* data types means that an exponent follows. For example, 1.2e4 means $1.2 \times 10^4$, which is equivalent to 12,000.

The signed integer data types *SByte, Short, Integer,* and *Long* have unsigned versions *Byte, UShort, UInteger,* and *ULong*.

The floating point types *Single* and *Double* store a certain number of significant digits and an exponent. For example, a *Single* can store positive values between 1.401298e-45 and 3.4028235e38. For values close to 0, the significant digits are far to the left of the decimal point. For large numbers, the significant digits are far to the right.

No data type can store digits very far to the left and right of the decimal point accurately at the same time. For example, if you add the *Single* values 1e30 and 1e-40, the result will drop the least significant digits, resulting in 1e30.

The *Decimal* data type stores a total of 29 digits to the left and right of the decimal point so it can store values as large as roughly 7.9e28 and as close to 0 as 1e-28. This gives *Decimal* a more restricted range than *Single* and *Double,* but it has more digits of precision. That makes *Decimal* the preferred choice for working with currency values where precision is important and values are unlikely to exceed they data type's range.

Strings are an odd special case that deserve a section of their own, so let's get to it.

# Strings

Different programming languages handle strings in very different ways. In some languages such as C++, a string is a null-terminated series of characters. In other words, it's a byte array with each byte holding the code for a single character plus a final byte holding the value 0 to mark the end of the string.

In the .NET languages Visual Basic and C#, a string is more complicated. In those languages, a string includes some header information describing the string, plus a reference pointing to a buffer that holds the actual null-terminated string somewhere else in memory.

The characters in a string are stored as Unicode, a system that uses 2 bytes to represent each character. Only 1 byte is necessary to store the characters on a standard Western keyboard (*A*, *B*, *3*, *&*, and so forth) but 2 bytes are needed to represent characters from other alphabets such as Arabic, Chinese, and Cyrillic.

To make matters more confusing, strings in .NET are *immutable*. That means once a string is defined, its value can never change. When a program modifies a string, such as by appending a letter to it, the string is actually replaced by a completely new string holding the new value.

One consequence of string immutability is that it is relatively inefficient to build large strings incrementally. For example, suppose you wanted to build a string containing the names of thousands of customers concatenated together. You could make the program loop through the names, adding each one to an ever-growing string. Unfortunately, each time you added a new name, the program would create a new string, copy the old value plus the new name into it, and discard the old string.

For relatively small strings where the program is only concatenating a few dozen pieces, you probably won't experience serious performance problems. If you need to combine many more pieces, you can use .NET's *StringBuilder* class. This class allocates a buffer and lets its string grow into it. If the string grows too big, the class allocates a bigger buffer with empty space so that the string can grow some more. This is more efficient than creating entirely new strings every time you add a new piece to the string.

Strings share an *intern pool* that holds all the string values that are currently in use. If two strings contain the same value, their buffers actually point to the same location in the intern pool.

This may all seem fairly confusing. Fortunately, you can usually ignore most of the details and treat *String* as a simple data type similar to *Integer* or *Decimal*. You'll need to worry about the details only if your program does a lot of string manipulation.

# Program-Defined Data Types

In addition to using the "simple" data types described earlier in this chapter, such as *Integer*, *Decimal*, and *Boolean*, a program can define new data types. The most common kinds of data types that a program can define are arrays, enumerations, structures, and classes.

# Arrays

An *array* is a series of values with the same data type stored in a single chunk of memory. When a variable is an array, its name refers to the array as a whole, and an integer called *index* in the array lets the program select a particular value inside it.

As an analogy, you can think of an array as similar to the mailboxes in an apartment building. The building has a street address (the array's name) that all the mailboxes share. Each mailbox has a different apartment number (the index) that differentiates them.

In Visual Basic and C#, arrays always have 0 as the smallest index, so if an array contains 10 items, the indexes are 0 through 9.

The syntax for declaring and using arrays varies greatly among different languages. The following C# code declares an array named *salaries* holding 100 *Decimal* values. It sets the first entry's value to 10,000 and then sets the second entry equal to the first.

```
double[] salaries = new decimal[100];
salaries[0] = 10000;
salaries[1] = salaries[0];
```

The following code shows comparable Visual Basic code:

```
Dim salaries(99) As Decimal
salaries(0) = 10000
salaries(1) = salaries(0)
```

Arrays can have more than one dimension. For example, you could declare a two-dimensional array and use two indexes to address the items it contained. As a concrete example, you could use a two-dimensional array to store information about which piece is occupying the squares on a chessboard.

An array can contain items that are of the fundamental data types such as *Integer* or *String*, or it can contain items from some other program-defined data type, such as enumerations or classes (described next). An array can even contain items that are themselves arrays, or structures containing arrays as fields.

# Enumerations

An *enumeration* is a type that defines a list of allowed values. A variable of this type can take only one of the defined values.

For example, a program could define a *MealType* data type that allowed the values *Breakfast*, *Lunch*, and *Dinner*. The following code shows how a Visual Basic program could define this data type:

```
Enum MealType
    Breakfast
    Lunch
    Dinner
End Enum
```

Having defined the enumeration, the program can declare variables of that type. The following Visual Basic code declares a variable of type *MealType* and then sets it equal to the value *Breakfast:*

```
Dim meal As MealType
meal = MealType.Breakfast
```

Internally, variables of the enumeration's type are stored using an integral data type such as *Integer* or *Long*. Different languages may provide ways to specify which integer is used to represent some or all the values, and a language may allow more than one value to represent the same integer.

For example, the following C# code also defines a *MealType* enumeration:

```
enum MealType
{
    None = -1,
    Breakfast = 1,
    Lunch,
    Dinner,
    Supper = Dinner
}
```

This code explicitly sets the numeric value of *None* to -1 and the value of *Breakfast* to 1. The *Lunch* and *Dinner* values take default numeric values equal to 1 more than the previous values, so they are stored as 2 and 3, respectively. The final line in the enumeration defines the value *Supper* and sets it equal to *Dinner* so that the program can use the two values interchangeably.

You could use *Integers* to store values instead of using an enumeration and then just remember that -1 means no meal, 1 means breakfast, and so forth, but the enumeration makes the code much easier to read. It also allows the programming environment to check values so that the code can't make nonsensical assignments accidentally, such as setting a meal type to 10, a meal type that doesn't exist.

**Note** You can still mess up enumeration assignments if you use explicit data type conversion to convert an integral value into an enumerated value. The section "Explicit Conversion," later in this chapter, says more about data type conversion.

## Structures

A *structure* is a named group of related fields. For example, if a program frequently needs to manipulate customer address data, it could define an *Address* structure that includes fields for *Street*, *City*, *State*, and *Zip*. Then the program could declare a variable of type *Address* and set the individual fields within that variable.

The following code shows how a C# program could define the *Address* data type. In this example, the *Street*, *City*, *State*, and *Zip* fields are all strings:

```
struct Address
{
    string Street, City, State, Zip;
}
```

The following code shows one way a C# program could declare a variable of type *Address* and initialize its fields:

```
Address customerAddress;
customerAddress.Street = "1337 Leet St";
customerAddress.City = "Bugsville";
customerAddress.State = "MA";
customerAddress.Zip = "02167";
```

A structure makes it easy to keep related pieces of data together. For example, an *Address* object can hold the address information for a particular customer and routines can pass the information back and forth. (Chapter 9, "Routines," has more to say about routines.)

In another example, an array of structures can hold information about a group of customers. The program could let the user select a customer's name from a list. It could then use the corresponding array entry to get that customer's address information.

In some languages, including Visual Basic and C#, a structure can also define methods to perform actions related to the data. For example, an *Address* structure might have a *PrintEnvelope* method that a program could invoke to print an envelope for the address.

## Classes

A *class* is very similar to a structure (at least in languages that allow structures to define methods). It defines a package that can contain fields and methods that represent some kind of object.

The syntax for declaring and using structures and classes is also very similar. The following code shows how a C# program might define an *Address* class:

```
class Address
{
    public string Street, City, State, Zip;
}
```

The only difference between this code and the previous code is that this version uses the keyword *class* instead of *struct*.

After you create a variable of type *Address*, you can use the same code shown earlier to initialize the variable's fields:

```
customerAddress.Street = "1337 Leet St";
customerAddress.City = "Bugsville";
customerAddress.State = "MA";
customerAddress.Zip = "02167";
```

There are two main differences between structures and classes.

The first difference is philosophical. Some developers think of a structure as a relatively simple piece of data that doesn't really perform any actions of its own. A structure's values may not change much while it exists, and it may have a limited lifetime.

In contrast, a class defines something more complicated that may need to perform complex actions. An object defined by a class may have a long lifetime, perhaps even being stored in a database so that it can be re-created the next time the program runs, and may change frequently during its lifetime.

At *http://msdn.microsoft.com/library/ms229017.aspx*, Microsoft recommends that you use a structure when instances typically have short lifetimes and satisfy all the following conditions:

- It represents a single logical value.

- It is smaller than 16 bytes.

- It is immutable.

- The program will seldom need to convert the instance to and from another object type.

These requirements are rather hard to satisfy, particularly the size restriction. After all, a single *String* variable uses more than 16 bytes to store its header information, even if it contains only a blank string.

The immutability requirement also seems strange. What difference can it make if you change the value of a structure after it has been defined?

Both of these requirements make some sense after you understand the difference between value types and reference types. This is an important and confusing enough topic that it is explained in the following section.

# Value and Reference Types

A *value type* is a data type where a variable stores the actual value of the data. For example, an *Integer* uses 4 bytes to hold the value of a number. When you define a variable of type *Integer*, the variable's memory location holds the value.

In contrast, a *reference type* is a data type where a variable holds a reference pointing to some other location in memory that holds the actual data. *String* is a reference type because a *String* variable doesn't actually hold the characters in the string. Instead, it holds a reference to a position in memory that holds the characters.

Classes are also reference types. That means a variable with a class type actually holds only a reference to a piece of memory that holds the object's data.

Structures, in contrast, are value types. When you declare a variable of a structure type, that variable actually contains the structure's field values themselves.

Figure 6-1 shows the difference graphically. The structure variable on the left (a value type) contains the structure's fields. The class variable on the right (a reference type) contains a reference that points to another piece of memory that holds the data.

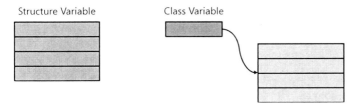

Structure Variable      Class Variable

**FIGURE 6-1** Class variables store a reference to data that is in some other part of memory.

The difference between value and reference types has several important consequences.

First, when you declare a value variable, the program allocates memory for it as soon as the variable exists. For example, if the variable holds an *Address* structure, that variable's *Street, City, State,* and *Zip* fields all exist as soon as the variable exists. Initially, those fields all hold blank strings, but they exist. The following code shows how a C# program might create an *Address* structure:

```
Address customerAddress;
```

However, when a program declares a reference variable, the variable only allocates the reference (the single rectangle under the words "Class Variable" in Figure 6-1). The piece of memory that holds the actual data (represented by the stack of four rectangles on the right) isn't yet allocated.

A Visual Basic or C# program needs to use the *New* or *new* keyword, respectively, to allocate the memory to hold the data. For example, the following code shows how a C# program might create an *Address* object:

```
Address customerAddress = new Address();
```

A second important consequence of the nature of value and reference types involves assignment. If you set one value type variable equal to a second one, the first variable contains a copy of the values in the second.

In contrast, if you assign one reference type variable to a second, the first now points to the same data as the second. The two variables now point to the same data, not to separate copies that happen to hold the same values.

Figure 6-2 shows the difference graphically.

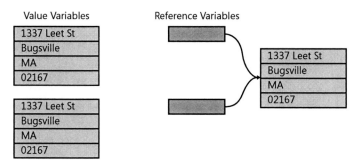

**FIGURE 6-2** Assigning one reference variable to another makes them both point to the same data.

This can cause confusion to programmers who are inexperienced with reference types. For example, suppose that a program has two variables named *customer1* and *customer2*. They represent people who live in the same household, so they would have the same address and phone number. For this example, they even have the same last name. In that case, you might like to set *customer2* equal to *customer1* and then change the *FirstName* field for *customer2*. The following code shows how a Visual Basic program could do this:

```
customer2 = customer1
customer2.FirstName = "Amy"
```

Here's where the confusion occurs. If the *Customer* data type is a structure, then these are value type variables, so setting *customer2* equal to *customer1* makes *customer2* contain a copy of the data, as shown on the left in Figure 6-2. Changing the *FirstName* field in *customer2* works as expected, and everything's fine.

Now, suppose that *Customer* is a class (a reference type) instead of a structure. In that case, setting *customer2* equal to *customer1* makes the two variables point to the same piece of memory, as shown on the right in Figure 6-2. Now, when the code changes the *FirstName* field in *customer2*, it changes the name in the only copy of the data around, so the change also appears in *customer1*.

This is probably not what a beginning programmer expects. To make matters worse, the code will run just fine, and the programmer can even inspect the new values in *customer2* without noticing anything wrong. The error may only surface sometime in the future, in a piece of code far away from the code that did the copying.

To understand further the difference between structures and classes, suppose that you want to store employee information that includes name, contact information, next of kin, a full resume, biography, and senior thesis. If you store the data in a structure, then anytime you declare a variable of that type, you allocate a lot of memory. Declaring one or two such structures won't be a problem, but what if you want to make an array containing an entry for each of your 10,000 employees? In that case, the amount of memory required would be huge.

Copying that much memory around could also be time-consuming. Using structures makes it easy to copy values by setting one variable equal to another. That may be what you want to do, but using structures also makes it easier to do this accidentally. If a program uses a lot of structure variables, frequently setting one equal to another or passing them back and forth between different pieces of code, it may end up spending a lot of time copying values from one structure to another.

Now, suppose that you store the information in a class instead of a structure. In that case, variables of the class occupy very little memory themselves. It's the data to which they point that takes up a lot of memory. (See Figure 6-1 again.)

An array containing 10,000 entries of this type occupies only about 40,000 bytes (4 bytes per entry). The array isn't very big, so allocating it is relatively fast. It's only when you initialize all the values in the array that you allocate big chunks of memory, and that may take a while. If you need to use only a few of the entries, then you may be able to load only those entries and save a lot of time and memory. (If you need to use every entry, then you're stuck loading them all, whether you use a structure or a class.)

Classes also make it easier to pass objects around without copying them. For example, suppose that you need to schedule a tennis tournament and you have an array of *Player* objects representing the participants. The program could perform some sort of calculation and come up with pairs of *Player* objects representing players who should play against each other. The variables representing the players in a match would reference the same data as the array, so the program would not need to copy the players' data or move it around as it performs its calculations.

Now that you have a better understanding of the difference between value and reference types, it's worth revisiting some of the rules Microsoft proposed for using a structure instead of a class. Two of the rules said you should use a structure in the following situations:

- It is smaller than 16 bytes.

- It is immutable.

The first rule makes some sense because value types carry their data around with them. If a structure is large, then setting one variable equal to another or passing the data around to different pieces of code can be slow and use a lot of memory. If you store the data in a class, only a reference to the data moves.

The second rule makes some sense if you think of the variable rather than the data it represents. Suppose that you have a *Player* variable named *opponent* and *Player* is a structure. If the program sets *opponent* once and leaves it alone, there's no problem. However, suppose that in calculating the next opponent for a match, the program must set and reset *opponent* many times. Because *Player* is a structure, each of those modifications makes a new copy of all the data contained in a *Player* structure, and that can be time-consuming. Now, suppose that *Player* is a class. In that case, the program can reassign *opponent* as often as necessary without shuffling large amounts of data back and forth.

The bottom line is that structures and classes are both useful so long as you keep their differences in mind. Sometimes a structure is handy because declaring a structure variable automatically allocates the variable's fields and it's easy to copy one variable's values to another. Other times, it's handy to use a class so that a program can move references to the data without moving the data itself.

> **Tip** To make a copy of a structure, you can simply set one variable equal to another, but that doesn't work for classes. Sometimes, however, a program must make a copy of a class variable's data.
>
> In that case, the program must create a new instance of the class using the *New* (Visual Basic) or *new* (C#) keyword and then copy each of the object's fields.
>
> To make copying objects easier, many classes define a *Clone* method, which makes an object create a copy of itself. For example, the following Visual Basic code shows how a program might make a copy of a *Customer* object, assuming that the *Customer* class provides a *Clone* method:
>
> ```
> customer2 = customer1.Clone()
> ```

In addition to the fundamental differences between value and reference types, programming languages place practical restrictions on structures and classes. For example, in C# and Visual Basic, structures cannot inherit, but classes can. These kinds of restrictions are described further in Chapter 10, "Object-Oriented Programming."

# Type Conversion

Programs often need to convert values from one type to another. For example, if the user types the value **10** into a text box, the program might want to convert that string value into the number 10. Although the string value *10* is obviously a number to a human, the difference between the string *10* and the number 10 is critical to a computer program. The program cannot perform arithmetic operations, such as addition and multiplication, on the value unless it has a numeric type.

Similarly, a program cannot treat a numeric value as if it were a string. For example, it could not extract the last character in the number 1337 because 1337 is not a string. The program would first need to convert the value from a number into a string before it tried to apply string operations such as finding a substring.

Programming languages let you perform conversions in two ways: explicitly or implicitly.

## Explicit Conversion

In an *explicit conversion*, you use programming language syntax or a function call to convert a value from one data type to another. For example, suppose *input* is a variable holding a textual value entered by the user and *total* is an integer variable. The following code shows how a Visual Basic program might convert the value from text to *Integer:*

```
total = CInt(input)
```

In this example, the code uses Visual Basic's *CInt* function to convert the string into an *Integer*.

The following code shows another way that a Visual Basic program could convert the string into an integer:

```
total = Integer.Parse(input)
```

This code uses the *Integer* class's *Parse* method to read the string value and return an integer result.

The following code shows the C# equivalent of the previous code:

```
total = int.Parse(input);
```

Explicit conversions make it clear exactly what your code is doing. In contrast, implicit conversions can happen automatically and, unless you are paying close attention, it may not be clear when they occur.

**Note** Explicitly converting a value from one data type to another is sometimes called *coercion*.

## Implicit Conversion

Many programming languages, including C# and Visual Basic, perform automatic type conversion under certain circumstances. Generally, a program will try to perform implicit conversion if it is combining data of different types or if the result variable has a different type than the arguments of the calculation.

For example, suppose *quantity* is an *Integer,* and *unitPrice* and *subtotal* are *Decimals*. Now consider the following C# calculation:

```
subtotal = quantity * unitPrice;
```

The program cannot multiply *quantity* by *unitPrice* because they have different data types. To solve this problem, it promotes *quantity* to a *Decimal*. Now it can multiply the two values to get a *Decimal* result and save it in the *Decimal* variable *subtotal*.

In another example, suppose that *numPlayers* is an *Integer* and *totalTime* is a *Double*. Then consider the following Visual Basic statement:

```
totalTime = numPlayers
```

In this example, the program implicitly converts the *Integer* value *numPlayers* into a *Double* before saving it in the variable *totalTime*.

Implicit type conversion also can occur when the result of a calculation requires a new data type. For example, suppose *totalSickDays* and *numEmployees* are both *Integers*. If you divide two integers, the result is not always an integer (for example, 1 / 4 = 0.25) so the program cannot store the result *totalSickDays / numEmployees* in an *Integer*. To handle this problem, the program automatically promotes the result to a *Double*, which the program could then store in a *Double* variable.

Whether an implicit type conversion can succeed depends on whether the conversion is a widening or narrowing conversion. In a *widening conversion*, a value is converted from one data type to another data type that is guaranteed to be able to hold the value without losing any precision.

For example, any *Integer* value can fit in a *Decimal*, so converting an *Integer* into a *Decimal* is a widening conversion. That's why the earlier statement `subtotal = quantity * unitPrice` works.

In a narrowing conversion, a value is converted from one data type to another data type that may not be able to hold the value without losing precision.

> **Tip** If you think of variables as envelopes of different sizes, you can use the terms *widening* and *narrowing* literally. A narrow value will fit inside a wide envelope, so the value can fit in a widening conversion without losing precision. In contrast, a wide value will not fit in a narrow envelope, so the value cannot fit in a narrowing conversion without losing precision.

For example, suppose that *totalSickDays* and *numEmployees* are both *Integers,* so, as was explained earlier, *totalSickDays / numEmployees* is a *Double*. Now, suppose that *averageSickDays* is an *Integer*. When it executes the following statement, the program tries to implicitly convert the *Double* result into an *Integer* to store it in the variable *averageSickDays*:

```
averageSickDays = totalSickDays / numEmployees
```

This is a narrowing conversion, so it may fail depending on the programming language. By default, Visual Basic will refuse to compile this code because it performs an implicit narrowing conversion. In contrast, C# will compile this code. At run time, it performs the calculation and then truncates the result to fit in an *Integer*. For example, if *totalSickDays* is 7 and *numEmployees* is 4, the value *totalSickDays / numEmployees* is 1.75, which the program truncates to 1.

Note that a program can use an explicit conversion to performing narrowing conversions even in languages such as Visual Basic that won't perform them implicitly. For example, the following Visual Basic code divides *totalSickDays* by *numEmployees* and then uses the *CInt* conversion function to explicitly convert the result into an *Integer:*

```
averageSickDays = CInt(totalSickDays / numEmployees)
```

This code is not exactly the same as the C# version because *CInt* rounds to the nearest *Integer* instead of truncating. The *Int* function in Visual Basic truncates, but it returns a *Double* rather than an *Integer*. Therefore, the code would need an explicit conversion, as in the following:

```
averageSickDays = CInt(Int(totalSickDays / numEmployees))
```

# Scope, Accessibility, and Lifetime

Scope, accessibility, and lifetime are closely related topics that deal with the situation when a variable (or routine, program-defined type or other programming item) exists and is usable by the program's other pieces of code.

## Scope

An item's *scope* includes the code that can use the item. To make programs manageable, code can be divided in several ways. For example, different structures or classes can contain methods that contain code. In Visual Basic, at least, a code module also can contain routines that exist outside of any structure or class.

The scope of a program item (variable, routine, method, and so forth) is generally determined by the level at which it is defined. For example, if a variable is declared inside a routine, then its scope is the routine and only code inside that routine after the variable's declaration can use the variable. This is called *routine scope* (or *method scope, procedure scope,* and so on, depending on what term you use to name a routine).

Inside a routine, certain code constructions may create their own scopes. For example, a *for* loop makes a program repeat a series of statements a specified number of times. If the program declares a variable inside the loop, only code inside the loop can access it. This is called *block scope*. This kind of block may be nested so that one block might contain another one that defines its own block scope.

At a higher level, a program can define routines, variables, types, and other items inside a structure, class, or code module, but not inside any routine. In that case, all the code in the structure, class, or code module can use the item. This is called *structure scope, class scope*, or *module scope*. For example, the *Person* class might define a *FirstName* field that sits outside any of the class's methods. In that case, all the code inside the class can use the *FirstName* field.

For example, the following code shows a simple but complete *Employee* class written in C#. Don't worry about exactly how the code works or how the main program would create and use *Employee* objects. Just focus on scope:

```
using System;

namespace SalesFigures
{
    class Employee
    {
        public string FirstName, LastName;
        public string[] Years;
        public decimal[] Sales;
        private decimal Bonuses;

        // Return the Employee's name.
        public override string ToString()
```

```
        {
            string result = FirstName + " " + LastName;
            return result;
        }

        // Display the employee's sales figures in the output window.
        private void ShowSales()
        {
            for (int i = 0; i < Sales.Length; i++)
            {
                string entry = Years[i] + ": " + Sales[i].ToString();
                Console.WriteLine(entry);
            }
        }
    }
}
```

The class begins by declaring several fields: *FirstName, LastName, Years, Sales,* and *Bonuses*. These are all declared inside the class but outside of any method, so they have class scope.

The methods *ToString* and *ShowSales* are also declared outside of any method (C# doesn't let you define a method inside another method), so they also have a class scope.

All the class scope items are usable by any code inside the class. They also may be usable by code outside the class, depending on their accessibility (described shortly).

The *ToString* method declares a string variable named *result*. This variable is declared inside the *ToString* method, so it has method scope. It is visible to code inside the method, but not to any other code.

The *ShowSales* method use a *for* loop. The loop itself declares a looping variable named *i* and uses it to control the loop. That variable is considered to be inside the loop, so it has block scope and is usable only to code inside the loop.

Inside the loop, the code also declares a string variable named *entry*. That variable also has block scope, so it is visible only to code inside the loop.

A language may or may not allow two items with overlapping scope to have the same name. For example, classes in C# and Visual Basic can declare variables with the same name at the class and method level. For example, in the previous code, the *ToString* method could declare a new variable named *FirstName*. If the code does nothing to differentiate between the two names (in C#, the code could use *this.FirstName* to indicate the class-scope version), it uses the more tightly scoped variable.

Neither Visual Basic nor C# allows two variables to have the same name inside a routine if their scopes overlap. For example, a routine cannot declare a routines-scoped variable named *number* and then create another variable with the same name inside a block within the routine. The code could create two variables with the same name inside different blocks within the same routine if neither block contains the other.

# Accessibility

A code item's *accessibility* determines what code (if any) outside the item's scope can access the item. For example, a public method declared inside a class can be called by code outside the class.

Items with structure, class, and code module scope can have accessibilities that provide access to pieces of code outside their scope. A programming language lets the code use accessibility keywords to determine how accessible the code is.

Routine and block scope items always have accessibility limited to their scope. In other words, code outside of a block can never use a variable declared inside the block. Because those items always have limited accessibility, the program does not need to use an accessibility keyword to determine what code can use them.

Table 6-2 summarizes the accessibility keywords used by C# and Visual Basic.

**TABLE 6-2** Accessibility Keywords

| C# Keyword | Visual Basic Keyword | Meaning |
|---|---|---|
| *public* | *Public* | The item is usable by any code. |
| *private* | *Private* | The item is usable only by code in the same structure, class, or code module. |
| *protected* | *Protected* | The item is usable only by code in the same structure or class, or in a derived class. (Chapter 10 explains derived classes.) |
| *internal* | *Friend* | The item is usable only by code in the same assembly. |
| *protected internal* | *Protected Friend* | The item is both *protected* (usable only by code in the same structure or class, or a derived class) and *internal/ friend* (usable only in the same assembly). |

The *internal* (or *Protected*) keyword makes an item usable only to code in the same assembly. In .NET applications, an assembly is the smallest self-contained unit of compiled code. An assembly can be a complete application or a library that can be called by other applications.

For example, if the *Employee* class is defined in a library and its *ShowSales* method is declared with the *internal* (or *Protected*) keyword, then the code in a main program that uses the library could not call the *ShowSales* method.

> **Note**  Private accessibility means that only code in the same structure, class, or code module can use the item, but it does not mean that the code must be running in the same instance of the structure or class. For example, suppose that the *Employee* class's *ShowSales* method has private accessibility. Then, any instance of the *Employee* class can call the *ShowSales* method for any instance of the *Employee* class. In other words, if *alice* and *bob* are *Employee* objects, then code running in the *alice* object can call *bob's ShowSales* method.

# Lifetime

A variable's *lifetime* is the time during which it is available for use. A variable's lifetime is usually closely related to its scope. Table 6-3 summarizes the lifetimes for typical variables.

**TABLE 6-3** Variable Lifetimes

| Scope | Lifetime |
| --- | --- |
| *block* | While the block is executing after the variable has been declared |
| *routine* | While the block is executing after the variable has been declared |
| *structure, class* | While the instance of the structure or class exists |
| *code module* | While the program is running |

When a variable's lifetime ends, the variable is no longer available to the program and the variable may be destroyed. (The program doesn't necessarily free the variable's memory right away, however. It can do that whenever it is convenient, but the variable is no longer accessible to the program.)

If the variable's lifetime occurs again, a new instance of the variable is created. For example, when a routine executes, it creates instances of the routine-scope variables that it defines. When the routine exits, those variables are no longer accessible. If the routine executes again, it creates new instances of the variables.

There are two exceptions to these lifetime rules. First, a program can make all instances of a structure or class share the same variable. For example, the *Employee* class might define a *SalesGoal* variable to store the company's total sales goal. That value would be the same for all employees, so the class can make all instances of the *Employee* class share the same value. That means if any instance of the class changes the value, it changes for all instances. It also means the value's lifetime includes all the time that the program is running.

> **Note** C# programs make instances share a code item in this way by using the *static* keyword. Visual Basic uses the *Shared* keyword.

The second lifetime exception allows a routine to declare a persistent variable that retains its value between calls to the routine. For example, suppose that the *LogMessage* routine displays an incrementing message number and a message in the console window. The routine could declare a persistent variable named *messageNumber*. During each call, the routine would increment *messageNumber* and display a message. The persistent variable *messageNumber* would keep its values between calls to *LogMessage* so that the numbers would not reset every time the method was called.

The following code shows how this routine might work in Visual Basic:

```
' Display a message with an incrementing message number.
Private Sub LogMessage(ByVal message As String)
```

```
        Static messageNumber As Integer = 0
        messageNumber += 1
        Console.WriteLine(messageNumber & ": " & message)
    End Sub
```

 **Note** C# does not allow a routine to declare persistent variables. To get a similar effect, you can simply make the routine store its information in a variable with structure or class scope.

## Summary

This chapter explained variables. A variable is a named section of memory that can hold data of a specific data type. It also summarized the most common data types used by .NET applications, which include fundamental data types, strings, and program-defined types such as enumerations, structures, and classes. Chapter 10 discusses structures and classes in more detail.

This chapter also discussed the difference between value and reference types. Not understanding this difference can lead to some very confusing behavior and bugs in intermediate and advanced applications.

Finally, this chapter listed the three features that determine when and where a program can access code items such as variables, structures, and classes: scope, accessibility, and lifetime.

The block scope described in this chapter is created by a code block within a routine. For example, a *for* loop creates a block. Variables declared within that block are inaccessible outside of the loop. The next chapter explains other control statements, such as the *for* loop that manages a program's flow of execution. Such statements let a program repeat groups of statements or take different actions depending on program conditions.

# Chapter 7

# Control Statements

**In this chapter:**

- What pseudocode is

- Statements that a program can use to execute code repeatedly

- Statements that a program can use to take different actions depending on circumstances

- Statements that a program can use to jump to new lines of code

YOU CAN WRITE COMPUTER PROGRAMS TO do all sorts of things. A simple billing application might add up charges for each customer, print monthly invoices, list the customers with the largest outstanding balances, and disconnect service for customers who haven't paid their bills in several months.

To do all those things, the program must manage its flow of execution. It cannot simply step through a series of commands one at a time, from start to finish. For example, a billing program can't use a separate line of code to print an invoice for each customer. If it did, it would take 100,000 lines of code to print invoices for 100,000 customers. That would be hard to write, debug, and maintain, particularly as new customers signed up for service and old ones left.

To make this kind of processing possible, a program needs a way to execute the same pieces of code repeatedly in slightly different ways. It needs to contain a single chunk of code that can print an invoice and then use that same code for every customer.

A program also needs the ability to take different actions depending on the circumstances. For example, in addition to printing invoices, the program might need to examine each customer and decide whether that customer's account should be suspended for nonpayment.

This chapter describes statements that let a program control its flow of execution. It explains looping statements that the program can use to repeat a group of statements. It also describes conditional statements that let a program perform different actions depending on the circumstances.

Before you learn about looping and conditional statements, however, you should learn a bit about pseudocode.

# Pseudocode

*Pseudocode* uses English-like words to describe computer algorithms without relying on any particular programming language. The statements are similar to those used in a real programming language, but the syntax is more flexible and intuitive so that developers using any programming language can understand what they mean.

So far in this book, you've seen occasional code snippets in Microsoft Visual Basic and C# that illustrate or clarify the ideas in the text, but in general, the exact details of the code weren't important. This chapter deals more directly with program statements, so it's worth using pseudocode to make the concepts easy to understand, whether you'll eventually be using Visual Basic, C#, C++, or some other programming language.

For example, the following code shows a simple *For* loop in Visual Basic:

```
For i As Integer = 1 To 10
    Do something...
Next i
```

The following code shows the equivalent C# code:

```
for (int i = 1; i <= 10; i++)
{
    Do something...
}
```

These pieces of code do the same thing, but their syntax differs sufficiently to be confusing. The following code shows the equivalent pseudocode:

```
For i From 1 to 10
    Do something...
```

In this example, a variable i starts at the value 1 and increments each time through the loop until it reaches the value 10. Indentation indicates the statements that should be executed for each trip through the For loop. These statements would create a scope block in a real programming language.

Pseudocode is informal, so the exact syntax doesn't matter so long as it's easy to understand the meaning, although when writing pseudocode yourself, you should try to be as consistent with the syntax as possible.

Depending on the level of detail you want in a particular piece of pseudocode, the code might include English statements that describe what the code should do at a high level. For example, the following pseudocode explains how a program might print invoices for customers with ID numbers 1 through 10:

```
For i From 1 to 10
    Print an invoice for customer i
```

This overview level of pseudocode probably isn't refined enough to let a programmer implement the pseudocode directly in a programming language, so you may need to create a more detailed version later.

The following sections describe program control statements using pseudocode, with occasional examples in C# or Visual Basic so you can get a feel for what they might look like in a real programming language.

# Looping Statements

To allow you to use a series of statements repeatedly, programming languages provide looping statements. Usually a variable or some other factor changes as the loop progresses so that the statements inside the loop don't do *exactly* the same thing every time the loop repeats. For example, a loop to print 100,000 copies of a single customer's invoice would be a lot less useful than a loop that prints different invoices for each of 100,000 customers.

Once in a while, you might want a program to enter a loop that never ends (for example, a program that runs continuously while the computer is running), but usually a loop should stop at some point. To ensure that a program doesn't get stuck in an infinite loop, you should examine the code carefully and make sure it eventually reaches a stopping condition.

The four kinds of loops described here are *For* loops, *For Each* loops, *Do While* loops, and *While Do* loops.

## *For* Loops

A *For* loop repeats a series of steps a given number of times. The basic pseudocode looks like this:

```
For <variable> From <first value> To <last value> By <increment>
    Do something...
```

This code initializes the control variable indicated by *<variable>* to the value *<first value>*. It then executes the code in the indented code block. Each time it finishes the code block, it adds the value *<increment>* to the variable. When the variable's value equals *<last value>*, the block executes one final time and then exits.

Note that the looping variable may never reach *<last value>* if *<increment>* is set incorrectly. For example, the following loop never ends because *<increment>* causes the value of *<variable>* to move away from *<last value>*.

```
For i From 1 To 10 By -5
    Do something...
```

In this example, the variable *i* starts at the value 1. Each subsequent pass through the loop subtracts 5 from *i*, so in the second through fourth passes through the loop, *i* holds the values -4, -9, -13, and so on, and will never reach the stopping value *10*.

Usually a *For* loop uses simple numeric values to control its loop, but that need not always be the case. In some programming languages, the syntax that initializes the control variable, increments the variable, and checks for the loop's ending condition can contain all sorts of code. For example, the following code shows a simple *For* loop in C#:

```
for (int i = 1; i <= 10; i++)
{
    Do something...
}
```

The following code shows a less typical example:

```
for (int x = 0, y = 1; x < y; x += y, y += x)
{
    Do something...
}
```

This loop initializes two variables *x* and *y* to the values 0 and 1, respectively. The loop then continues as long as *x < y* is true. After each trip through the loop's code block, the loop modifies both *x* and *y* by adding *y* to *x* and then adding the new value of *x* to *y*.

This loop is so different from a typical *For* loop that it may be confusing to programmers who try to read and debug it later. It might make more sense to use a different kind of loop to avoid confusion. We will do that now.

## *For Each* Loops

A *For* loop executes a block of code while a control variable ranges over a set of values defined by `<first value>`, `<last value>`, and `<increment>`. A *For Each* loop executes a block of code while a control variable ranges over the values in an array, list, or some other group of values.

The pseudocode for a *For Each* loop is the following:

```
For Each <variable> In <values>
    Do something...
```

For example, suppose that *Customers* is an array containing information about all your company's customers. The following pseudocode describes how a program might print customer invoices:

```
For Each customer In Customers
    Print an invoice for customer
```

A programming language may not guarantee the order in which the items in the `<values>` group are visited, although in practice, the items are typically visited in their natural order from first to last in the group. To ensure that the items are visited in order, you can use the items' indexes in the array or list, as in the following pseudocode:

```
For i From 1 To <number of customers> By 1
    Print an invoice for customer i
```

## *Do While* Loops

A *Do While* loop does something as long as a condition is true. The following shows the pseudocode for a *Do While* loop:

```
Do
    Do something...
While <condition>
```

This loop executes its code block. Then, as long as `<condition>` is true, it executes the code block again. Note that this code always executes its code block at least once because its stopping test occurs at the end of the loop.

## *While* Loops

A *While* loop is similar to a *Do While* loop except it performs its stopping test before it executes its loop. The following shows the pseudocode for a *While Do* loop:

```
While <condition>
    Do something...
```

This loop starts by checking its stopping condition. As long as `<condition>` is true, it executes its code block and repeats.

Note that this loop does not execute its code block even once if `<condition>` is initially false.

## *Until* Loops

Some programming languages also provide *Until* loops. These loops are variations on *While* and *Do While* loops that execute *until* a condition is true (or while a condition is false, if you prefer) rather than *while* a condition is true.

The following shows the pseudocode for a *Do Until* loop:

```
Do
    Do something...
Until <condition>
```

The following shows the pseudocode for an *Until* loop:

```
Until <condition>
    Do something...
```

An *Until* loop is equivalent to a *While* loop with a negated stopping condition. For example, the following two loops are equivalent:

```
While (x < 7)
    Do something...

Until (x >= 7)
    Do something...
```

Similarly, a *Do Until* loop is equivalent to a *Do While* loop with a negated stopping condition, so the following two loops are equivalent:

```
Do
    Do something...
While (x < 7)

Do
    Do something...
Until (x >= 7)
```

# Conditional Statements

Conditional statements let a program take different actions depending on the circumstances. These statements include several versions of *If* statements. Most languages also include a *Case* statement, which is a simpler way of writing a series of *If* statements.

## *If*

The simple *If* statement executes a code block only if some condition is true. The following shows the *If* statement's pseudocode:

```
If <condition>
    Do something...
```

If *<condition>* is true, the program executes the code block. If *<condition>* is false, the program skips the code block and executes the code that follows.

## If Else

The *If Else* statement executes one of two code blocks depending on a condition's value. The following shows the *If Else* statement's pseudocode:

```
If <condition>
    Do something...
Else
    Do something else ...
```

If *<condition>* is true, the program executes the first code block. If *<condition>* is false, the program executes the second code block.

## Else If

The *Else If* statement is really a new *If* statement following an *If Else* statement. A program can use any number of *Else If* statements to make the code follow many different paths of execution depending on the values of several conditions.

The following pseudocode shows an example that uses two *Else If* statements:

```
If <condition 1>
    Do something 1...
Else If <condition 2>
    Do something 2...
Else If <condition 3>
    Do something 3...
Else
    Do something else...
```

If *<condition 1>* is true, the program executes the first code block. If *<condition 1>* is false but *<condition 2>* is true, the program executes the second code block.

The program continues evaluating conditions until it finds one that is true, and then it executes the corresponding code block. If none of the conditions are true, the program executes the *Else* block.

> **Note** The *Else* block is optional. If it is missing and none of the conditions is true, the program skips to the end of the last *Else If* block and executes the code that follows.

## Case

A *Case* statement, which is sometimes called a *multi-way branch*, lets the program take one of several actions based on the value of an expression. The following shows the pseudocode for a *Case* statement:

```
Case <variable>
    Value <value 1>
        Do something 1...
    Value <value 2>
        Do something 2...
    Value <value 3>
        Do something 3...
    Else
        Do something else...
```

The *Case* statement is followed by several *Value* statements that provide comparison values. The program compares *<variable>* with each value. When it finds a match, the program executes the corresponding code block and then either continues with the next comparison value or skips to the end of the *Case* statement, depending on the particular language in use. If the program doesn't match any of the comparison values, it executes the *Else* code block.

 **Note** The *Else* code block is optional. If it is missing and the variable matches none of the values, the program does not execute any of the code blocks.

The syntax for the *Case* statement varies more between languages than the syntax for other conditional statements. For example, suppose a program has defined a *UserType* enumeration. The following code shows a *Case* statement in Visual Basic to take action depending on the value of the *user* variable:

```
Select Case (user)
    Case UserType.Customer
        MessageBox.Show("Sorry, you are not authorized to use this feature")
    Case UserType.SalesClerk, UserType.Supervisor
        MessageBox.Show("You are authorized to use this feature")
    Case Else
        MessageBox.Show("Unknown user type")
End Select
```

The following code shows a C# version:

```
switch (user)
{
    case UserType.Customer:
        MessageBox.Show("Sorry, you are not authorized to use this feature");
        break;
    case UserType.SalesClerk:
    case UserType.Supervisor:
        MessageBox.Show("You are authorized to use this feature");
        break;
    default:
```

```
        MessageBox.Show("Unknown user type");
        break;
}
```

Different languages provide different features for listing the comparison values. Visual Basic has a flexible syntax that lets you list values separated by commas, use a range of values, or indicate that the tested value must be greater than or less than another value. For example, the following statement tests for the values 1 and 5, any value between 10 and 20, and any value greater than 100:

```
Case 1, 5, 10 To 20, Is > 100
```

> **Tip** You can always rewrite a *Case* statement as a series of *If* and *Else If* statements. You should pick the version that makes the code easiest to read.

# Jumping Statements

The control statements described so far make a program jump to various pieces of code. Depending on conditions, the program may jump to a particular code block or jump over other code blocks.

The statements are intuitive, so the jumps are easy to understand—and in fact, it's easy to understand a *While* loop without even thinking about the fact that the loop makes the program jump from the end of the loop to the beginning.

Many programming languages provide a few less structured ways to let a program jump from one place to another. The least structured of these is the *Go To* statement.

## Go To

The *Go To* statement makes the program immediately jump to an arbitrary line of code. The pseudocode for a *Go To* statement looks like the following:

```
    Go To <label>
        Do something...
<label>:
        Do something else...
```

Here, I've added an extra level of indentation so that labels can stand out on the left.

When the program reaches the *Go To* statement, it jumps to the line of code identified by *<label>* and continues execution from there.

This example is a bit unrealistic because there's no way for the program to execute the code in the first code block—in other words, the first *Do something...* code would never execute. The following code shows a more realistic example:

```
If <condition>
    Go To label1
Go To label2
label1:
    Do something...
    Go To label3
label2:
    Do something else...
label3:
```

If <condition> is true, the code jumps to label1. If <condition> is false, the code continues reaches the next *Go To* statement and jumps to label2.

If it goes to label1, the program executes a code block and then jumps to label3, skipping the second code block.

If it goes to label2, the program executes a second code block and then continues executing the code after label3.

This code does the same thing as a simple *If Else* statement, but it's a lot messier. Figuring out exactly where the program goes and when can be tricky, particularly if the code blocks are long.

Even still, matters could be much worse. A program could use *Go To* statements to make the code jump all over the place, including backward to earlier code. (A loop does that implicitly.)

> **Note** In practice, languages do place some restrictions on the *Go To* statement. For example, a language may not allow the program to jump into a *For* loop because that would bypass the code that initializes the loop's control variable. Languages also typically don't let you jump from inside one routine to the middle of another, or from a method in one class to a method in another class.

Unrestricted use of *Go To* can lead to something called "spaghetti code"—code that's so convoluted it's extremely difficult to figure out how it works. To prevent confusion, the vast majority of programmers use the *Go To* statement as little as possible. Many even prohibit its use entirely. You can always rewrite code so that it uses conditional and looping statements instead, so you don't really need the *Go To* statement anyway. (I've seen examples that programmers have created to show that the *Go To* statement is sometimes simpler, but I've never really been convinced.)

Even if you don't use the *Go To* statement, there are times when it's useful to break the normal rules for *If*, *If Else*, *While*, and the other control statements. To make programs more flexible without requiring the use of the overly flexible *Go To* statement, some languages provide *Continue*, *Exit*, and *Return* statements.

## Exit

An *Exit* statement makes the code break out of an enclosing loop and continue executing after the loop's code block. It provides a way to end a loop early.

> **Note** In Visual Basic, the *Exit* statement is followed by the kind of loop that you want to exit, such as *Exit For*. This allows the program to exit a specific loop if the code contains multiple nested loops. If the nested loops include more than one loop of the same kind, the program exits the innermost loop—the one closest to the *Exit* statement.
>
> In C#, the equivalent keyword is *break*.

The following pseudocode searches the *Employees* array for an employee that can handle a certain job. When the code finds an employee that can do the job, it assigns the job to the employee and ends the loop:

```
For Each employee In Employees
    If employee can handle the problem
        Assign the job to employee
        Exit
```

## Continue

The *Continue* statement makes the program skip the rest of a code block inside the surrounding loop and continue with the next iteration of the loop. *For* and *For Each* loops update their control variables before starting the next trip through the code block.

> **Note** In Visual Basic, the *Continue* statement is followed by the kind of loop that you want to continue, such as *Continue For*. This allows the program to continue a specific loop if the code contains multiple nested loops. If the nested loops include more than one loop of the same kind, the program continues the innermost loop—the one closest to the *Continue* statement.

For example, the following pseudocode checks customers and disconnects those who owe $100 or more:

```
For Each customer In Customers
    If customer balance < $100
        Continue
    Disconnect the customer
    Send a disconnect notice email
    Print a disconnect notice letter
```

The code uses a *For Each* loop to examine each customer in the *Customers* array. If the customer has a balance under $100, the code uses a *Continue* statement to skip the rest of the loop's code block and continue the loop with the next customer. Otherwise, the code continues to disconnect the customer and send email and letter notifications.

 **Note** It would be easy to rewrite this example without the *Continue* statement by using an *If* statement that disconnects the customer only if the balance is at least $100. You may want to take a moment to figure out how you would do that.

## Return

The *Return* statement makes the program immediately exit the routine that it is currently executing. If the routine returns a value, the *Return* statement takes a parameter that indicates which value to return.

 **Note** Visual Basic also has *Exit Sub* and *Exit Function* statements that let a program exit subroutines and functions early. Using the *Return* statement seems more consistent to me, but which you decide to use is a matter of personal programming style.

# Jumping Guidelines

All jumping statements break the normal flow of an application, so they make the code harder to understand. To avoid confusion, you should use them as little as possible.

Of these statements, the *Return* statement seems the least confusing. It exits a routine so that a programmer reading the code doesn't need to look at that routine anymore.

Despite its relative simplicity, some developers never use *Return*. Instead, they write code that always exits a routine by executing the last line of code. The thought is that having a single exit point makes it easier to figure out where the routine is exiting.

The *Exit* and *Continue* statements are the next least confusing. Their general ideas aren't too complicated, but a programmer reading them must figure out which enclosing loop is affected and find its start or end.

The *Go To* statement can create unreadable code that's nearly impossible to debug, so many developers never use it. (I've never needed one in many years of experience programming in several languages.)

# Error Handling

No matter how well-designed and implemented a program is, errors will occur eventually. These may be caused by incorrect code or by circumstances outside the program's control, such as the user entering incorrect values or a printer not being connected to the network.

Different languages handle errors in different ways, but Visual Basic, C#, C++, and Java use a similar approach. The basic syntax in pseudocode is as follows:

```
Try
    statements...
Catch <exception>
    statements...
Finally
    statements...
```

The statements after the *Try* keyword are the ones that might cause an error.

If an error occurs, the program executes the statements after the *Catch* keyword. (If no error occurs, the program skips those statements.) The variable *<exception>* gives the program information about the error. For example, this might include an error code, detailed information about the error, and a message describing the error. The program can use this information to try to fix the problem or at least tell the user what has gone wrong.

After the *Try* and *Catch* blocks have finished, the program executes the statements after the *Finally* keyword. It executes those statements no matter how the code exits the error handling code, whether or not it executes the statements in the *Catch* block. It even executes the *Finally* block if the code jumps out of the error handling code by using an *Exit*, *Continue*, or *Return* statement. Often, programs place code in this block to perform cleanup actions that should occur whether or not the code succeeded, such as closing files or disconnecting from databases.

**Note** Handling an error by using a *Try Catch Finally* block is called *catching* the error. Because you catch an error, causing an error to happen is called *throwing* an error.

# Summary

Programming languages provide several statements to let you control the flow of execution. Looping statements, such as the *For Each* and *While* statements, cause a program to execute the same code many times. Conditional statements, such as the *If* and *Case* statements, let a program take different actions depending on the circumstances.

Many languages also provide other statements that let you break the normal flow of control provided by the standard control statements. Examples include the *Return* statement, which causes execution to exit a routine early, and the *Exit* and *Continue* statements, which end or repeat a loop early. Very few programmers use the *Go To* statement regularly.

This chapter described each of these statements using pseudocode, an English-like way to describe algorithms without assuming that you are using a specific programming language.

The looping statements described in this chapter let programs reuse code blocks. For example, a *For* loop can let a program execute the same piece of code many times in a single block.

Another way to reuse code is to place it in a routine and let other pieces of code call the routine as needed. Placing code in a loop lets you call the code repeatedly from one location in the program. Placing it in a routine lets you call code as many times as necessary from other locations in the program.

The next chapter describes routines. It explains the different kinds of routines a program can define and explains how to call a routine. A routine not only allows different parts of the program to invoke the same piece of code, but it breaks the code up into chunks of manageable size.

# Chapter 8

# Operators

**In this chapter:**

- Precedence and how it determines the order of evaluation in mathematical expressions

- What operators are and what the most common operators are in C# and Microsoft Visual Basic

- How you can overload operators to define new actions for them

**COMPUTERS ARE EXTREMELY GOOD AT PERFORMING** mathematical calculations. A typical computer can perform millions of calculations per second without ever getting bored or making mistakes.

As you probably remember from math classes in school, an *operator* is a symbol that a program uses to tell the computer how to combine values to produce a result. An *operand* is one of the values combined by an operator.

A programming language could use any symbols to represent operators, but fortunately, mathematics has a very long history, so many of the basic symbols are determined by common usage, the same in most programming languages, and generally intuitively obvious. For example, the + symbol means addition, and the – symbol means subtraction.

This chapter describes the most common operators provided by programming languages. It explains what they do and the syntax for using them in languages such as C#, Microsoft Visual Basic, C++, and Java.

It also explains precedence rules that tell a program which operators to apply first. Finally, this chapter explains operator overloading, which lets you redefine operators so that they can perform new operations, such as combining two non-numeric objects.

# Precedence

When faced with a statement such as 1 + 2 * 3 - 4, a program must determine the order in which it should evaluate the +, -, and * (which means multiplication) operators. For example, it could evaluate the operators in left-to-right order to get the following:

```
1 + 2 * 3 - 4 =
    3 * 3 - 4 =
        9 - 4 =
            5
```

Alternatively, the program could evaluate the operators in right-to-left order to get the following:

```
1 + 2 * 3 - 4 =
1 + 2 *   - 1 =
1 +       - 2 =
          - 1
```

As you can see, different orders of evaluation can give very different results.

Programming languages use precedence to make it clear how to evaluate expressions. *Precedence* determines which operators are evaluated before others.

For example, multiplication and division (* and /) have a higher precedence than addition and subtraction (+ and -), so they are evaluated first. Operators with the same precedence, such as addition and subtraction, are applied in left-to-right order.

Applying those rules means the previous equation is correctly evaluated as follows:

```
1 + 2 * 3 - 4 =
1 +     6 - 4 =
        7 - 4 =
            3
```

The following sections contain tables listing various operators in their order of precedence. Operators shown in one row in each table are evaluated before those that come in later rows. Operators on the same row in a table have the same precedence and are evaluated from left to right in an expression.

# Operators

Almost all programming languages use the same symbols for the most common operators. For example, + means addition, - means subtraction, and / means division.

A few differences, however, and different languages may also give slightly different precedence to the various operators. The following section explains how you can use parentheses to override the normal precedence and change the evaluation order. The sections after that summarize the most common operators used in C# and Visual Basic.

# Parentheses

After you study the precedence tables that follow, you can come up with some interesting puzzles in figuring out how to evaluate expressions. For example, you can try to figure out the value of the following expression:

```
1 + 2 ^ 3 * 4 / 2
```

 **Tip** The answer actually depends on the language that you are using because the ^ operator means different things in C# and Visual Basic.

Although this sort of puzzle can be entertaining, it has no place in an actual program. In real code, clarity is essential, so if an equation is at all confusing, you should rewrite it to prevent mistakes.

You can use parentheses to change the order in which operators are evaluated in an expression. The program will evaluate the operators inside a matched set of parentheses and then use the result in whatever operators lie outside of the parentheses.

For example, the previous equation is normally evaluated in Visual Basic in the following order:

```
1 + (((2 ^ 3) * 4) / 2)
```

First, Visual Basic evaluates the expression within the innermost parentheses: 2 ^ 3. In Visual Basic, the ^ operator means exponentiation, so this results in 2^3 = $2^3$ = 8.

Next, that result is multiplied by the value 4 (the next matched pair of parentheses), yielding 8 * 4 = 32.

This result is then divided by 2, resulting in 32 / 2 = 16.

Finally, that result is added to 1, which results in a final answer of 1 + 16 = 17.

Contrast that result with the result of the following equation, which uses parentheses to change the order in which the operators are evaluated:

```
((1 + 2) ^ (3 * 4)) / 2
```

In this version, the innermost expressions are 1 + 2 = 3 and 3 * 4 = 12, so they are evaluated first. The next level of parentheses combines those two results with the ^ operator, giving 3 ^ 12 = $3^{12}$ = 531,441. Finally, the equation divides by 2, yielding 531,441 / 2 = 265,720.5, a result considerably different from the previous one.

Unless an expression's value is completely obvious, use parentheses to make it easy to figure out.

# Operator Precedence

The precedence of basic arithmetic operators is similar in all the programming languages I've encountered, but there are slight differences. Some languages also provide operators that others don't. For example, Visual Basic uses the ^ symbol to represent exponentiation, but C# doesn't have an exponentiation symbol.

Table 8-1 summarizes the precedence of the most common operators in C# and Visual Basic, with differences between the two languages noted. Several of these operators are rather confusing, so they are described further after the table.

**TABLE 8-1** Operator Precedence in C# and Visual Basic

| Category | Operator | Meaning |
|----------|----------|---------|
| Primary | A.B | Accessing an object member |
| | F(x) | Method call |
| | A[i] | Array access [C#] |
| | A(i) | Array access [VB] |
| | x++ | Post-increment [C#,1] |
| | x-- | Post-decrement [C#,1] |
| Unary | + | Positive (identity) |
| | - | Negative |
| | ! | Logical negation [C#] |
| | ~ | Bitwise negation [C#] |
| | Not | Bitwise or logical negation [VB] |
| | ++x | Pre-increment [C#, 1] |
| | --x | Pre-decrement [C#, 1] |
| Multiplicative | * | Multiplication |
| | / | Floating-point or integer division [C#] |
| | / | Floating-point division [VB] |
| | % | Modulus [C#] |
| Integer division | \ | Integer division [VB] |

| | | |
|---|---|---|
| Modulus | Mod | Modulus [VB] |
| Additive | + | Addition |
| | – | Subtraction |
| | + | String concatenation |
| Concatenation | & | String concatenation [VB] |
| Bit shift | << | Left-shift |
| | >> | Right-shift |
| Comparison | < | Is less than |
| | <= | Is less than or equal to |
| | > | Is greater than |
| | >= | Is greater than or equal to |
| Equality | == | Equals [C#] |
| | = | Equals [VB] |
| | != | Does not equal [C#] |
| | <> | Does not equal [VB] |
| Logical | & | Logical And [C#] |
| | && | Conditional logical And [C#] |
| | And | Logical And [VB] |
| | AndAlso | Conditional logical And [VB] |
| | ^ | Logical Xor [C#] |
| | Xor | Logical Xor [VB] |
| | \| | Logical Or [C#] |
| | \|\| | Conditional logical Or [C#] |
| | Or | Logical Or [VB] |
| | OrElse | Conditional logical Or [VB] |
| Conditional | ?: | For detailed information on this, see the section "Conditional," later in this chapter. |

| Assignment | = | Equals |
|---|---|---|
| | += | Add and assign |
| | -= | Subtract and assign |
| | *= | Multiply and assign |
| | /= | Divide and assign |
| | \= | Integer divide and assign [VB] |
| | %= | Modulus and assign [C#,1] |
| | &= | And and assign [C#] |
| | &= | Concatenate and assign [VB] |
| | \|= | Or and assign [C#] |
| | ^= | Xor and assign [C#] |
| | ^= | Exponentiation and assign [VB] |
| | <<= | Left shift and assign |
| | >>= | Right shift and assign |

[C#] - This operator is available only in C#.

[VB] - This operator is available only in Visual Basic.

[1] - Visual Basic has no operators for ++x, --x, x++, x--, |=, or %=.

The following sections give further information about some of the more confusing operators.

## Post- and Pre-Increment and Decrement

These operators add or subtract 1 from a variable and return a result. The "pre" operators update the variable before returning the result, whereas the "post" operators return the variable's value first, and then update the variable. Both of these operators have very high precedence, so they take effect before the other arithmetic operators.

For example, suppose that the variable x holds the value 5. In that case, the expression ++x adds 1 to x and returns the result 6. In contrast, the expression x++ returns the value 5 and then updates x so that it contains the new value, 6.

For a more complete example, consider the following statements:

```
x = 5;
result = 3 * x++;
```

The first line initializes *x* to 5. In the next line, the post-increment operator returns the value of *x* (which is 5) and then adds 1 to *x*. The statement multiplies the returned value (5) by 3 to get 15. After the statements are done, *x* is 6 and *result* is 15.

Now consider the following statements:

```
x = 5;
result = 3 * ++x;
```

As before, the first line initializes *x* to 5. This time, the second line increments *x* before returning its value so the equation multiplies 3 by 6 instead of 5. After the statements are done, *x* is 6 and *result* is 18.

Table 8-2 shows the results returned by these operators and the new values for *x*, assuming *x* starts with the value 5.

**TABLE 8-2** Results and Values for x

| Operator | Returns | New Value for *x* |
| --- | --- | --- |
| ++x | 6 | 6 |
| x++ | 5 | 6 |
| --x | 4 | 4 |
| x-- | 5 | 4 |

**Note** You can always rewrite a statement to avoid using these operators if you find them confusing. For example, you can rewrite the statement `result = 3 * ++x` by using the following two lines of code:

```
x = x + 1;
result = 3 * x;
```

## Bitwise Operators

The bitwise operators ^, ~, <<, >>, |, and & operate on an integral variable's bits. For example, suppose the byte variable *x* holds the value 90, which is represented as 01011010 in binary code. The ~ operators negates (switches) the bits in its operand, so ~x is 10100101, which is -91 in binary.

Table 8-3 summarizes the bitwise operators.

**TABLE 8-3** Bitwise Operators

| Operator | Meaning | Example |
| --- | --- | --- |
| ~ | Complement. Switches 1 to 0 and vice versa. | ~11110000 = <br> 00001111 |
| ^ | Exclusive or. A bit is 1 if one but not both of the operands have a 1 in that position. | 10101010 ^ <br> 11110000 = <br> 01011010 |

| | | |
|---|---|---|
| << | Bit shift left. Bits are shifted to the left by the indicated number of positions. New bits on the right are 0. | 11110000 << 2 = 11000000 |
| >> | Bit shift right. Bits are shifted to the right by the indicated number of positions. If the value is signed, new bits on the left duplicate the sign bit, the leftmost bit that indicates the number's sign. If the value is unsigned, new bits are 0. | 00001111 >> 2 = 00000011 |
| \| | Or. A bit is set in the result if the corresponding bit is set in either of the two operands. | 10101010 \| 11110000 = 11111010 |
| & | And. A bit is set in the result if the corresponding bit is set in both of the two operands. | 10101010 \| 11110000 = 10100000 |

## Modulus and Division

The modulus operator % returns the remainder after division. For example, 20 % 3 is 2 because 20 = 3 * 6 + 2.

When you divide two integers in C#, the program treats it as integer division, truncates the result, and discards any remainder. For example, 20 / 3 gives the value 6. Together, the two operators modulus and integer division give you all the information about how two integers divide.

If either of the operands in a division is of a floating-point type, the other is promoted to the same type and the division is performed on floating-point values. For example, to evaluate the expression 20 / 3.0, the program promotes 20 to the floating-point value 20.0, performs floating-point division, and gets the result 6.67 (approximately).

## Conditional And and Or

The conditional logical operators, also called *short-circuit* or *shortcut operators*, perform the same functions as their nonconditional counterparts, but they evaluate operands only when necessary.

For example, consider the following expression using the *Or* operator:

```
result = A | B;
```

This statement evaluates A and B, and makes *result* true if either A or B is true.

The following statement performs a similar calculation, but using the conditional *Or* operator:

```
result = A || B;
```

This statement evaluates A. If A is true, then the result A || B must be true, whether or not B is true. In that case, the program assigns the value true to *result* and doesn't bother evaluating B.

In this example, the difference in performance is small, but suppose that instead of simple variables A and B, the values being combined were returned by functions that took a long time to evaluate. In the following statement, for instance, suppose that A and B are functions that can take several seconds to execute:

```
result = A() || B();
```

In this case, the conditional operator can save the program several seconds by not evaluating B.

There is one drawback to the conditional operators, however. If the function B performs a task that has an effect outside its own code, then you cannot tell after the statement is executed whether the task was performed. For example, suppose that the function B opens a connection to a database and leaves it open. After the previous statement executes, you cannot tell whether the connection is open because you don't know whether function B was executed.

An unexpected effect, such as this one that lasts outside a routine, is called a *side effect* of the routine. Side effects are often confusing and lead to subtle bugs, so it's best if you make every routine perform a well-defined task without side effects.

The conditional *Or* operator doesn't need to evaluate its second operand if the first has the value *true*. The conditional *And* operator doesn't need to evaluate its second operand if the first has the value *false*. Because the *And* operator returns *false* if either operand is false, the operators already knows that the result will be *false* if the first operand is *false*.

## Conditional

The conditional operator *?:*, also sometimes called the *ternary operator*, takes three operands. It evaluates the first and then returns the second or third, depending on whether the first is true or false.

For example, the following code sets the value of the variable *greeting* to "Good morning" if time < noon and sets it equal to "Good afternoon" otherwise:

```
greeting = time < noon ? "Good morning" : "Good afternoon";
```

The conditional operator can be confusing, so many programmers use *If* statements instead. For example, the following code is equivalent to the previous statement:

```
if (time < noon)
{
    greeting = "Good morning";
}
else
{
    greeting = "Good afternoon";
}
```

This version is longer but easier to read.

**Note** The *IIF* function in Visual Basic is similar to the conditional *?:* operator in C#.

## Compound Assignment Operators

The operators +=, -=, *=, /=, %=, &=, |=, ^=, <<=, and >>= take the place of an equal sign. They take a variable on the left, modify it using the appropriate operation and the value on the right, and save the result in the variable on the left.

For example, the following simple statement adds 10 to the value *x* and saves the result in *x*:

```
x += 10;
```

The other compound assignment operators work similarly using their underlying operators.

## Concatenation Operators

C# has a single concatenation operator, +, that combines two strings. Visual Basic can use either the + or & operator to concatenate strings.

In both languages, the + operator combines its operands using whatever data type it thinks appropriate, but the two languages sometimes differ on what they consider appropriate. If a program is adding two integers, the result is an integer. If the program is combining two strings, the result is a string. So far, that makes sense.

If one of the operands of the + operator is a string and the other is numeric; however, the result can be confusing. In this case, Visual Basic converts the string into a numeric value (if possible) and adds the result to the other operand. For example, to evaluate the expression 1 + "2", the program would promote the string value "2" to a double precision floating-point value. It would then promote the integer value 1 to a double precision floating-point value, add the 2, and get the double precision floating-point result 3.0.

C# takes a different approach. If one operand is a string and the other is numeric, C# assumes that it cannot convert the string into a number, so it converts the number into a string and then concatenates the result. For the expression 1 + "2", a C# program converts the 1 into "1" and concatenates it with the "2" to get "12".

The & operator in Visual Basic always concatenates strings even if some of the operands are not strings. For example, to evaluate the expression 1 & 2, the program converts both values to strings, concatenates them, and produces the result "12", much as C# does with its + operator.

To avoid confusion in Visual Basic programs, you should use the & operator when you want to concatenate strings and the + operator when you want to add numeric values.

# Operator Overloading

Modern programming languages such as Visual Basic and C# allow a program to overload routines by creating multiple routines with the same name but different signatures. A routine's signature includes its parameters and their data types. (Parameters are values that you pass to a routine to give it information. For example, you might pass to the *PrintInvoice* routine the name of the customer whose invoice the routine should print. Chapter 9, "Routines," covers routines and their parameters in detail.)

For example, a program could create multiple versions of the *PrintInvoice* routine so long as no two versions took exactly the same types of parameters. Three different versions might take as parameters a customer ID (an integer), a customer name (a string), or a *Customer* object (an object).

You couldn't make a fourth version that took an order number (an integer) as a parameter because the program couldn't tell the difference between that version and the one that takes a customer ID as a parameter. If the code tried to call *PrintInvoice* and pass it an integer, the program wouldn't know which version to use.

In addition to overloading routines, a program can overload operators to make them work with data types for which they are not already defined. For example, you could overload the + operator so that the program could use it to combine an *Order* object and an *OrderItem* object, where *Order* and *OrderItem* are two classes that the program defines. In this example, the + operator might add the *OrderItem* to the *Order*, effectively adding a new item to an existing order.

**Note** You cannot overload an operator to make it work differently on data types for which it is already defined. For example, you cannot redefine how the + operator combines a string and an integer. That would probably lead to confusion anyway.

## Operator Overloading Overload

Just because you *can* overload an operator doesn't mean you *should*. For example, it might make sense to overload the + operator to allow a program to add an *OrderItem* object to an *Order* object because the meaning of that operation is reasonably intuitive. Someone who sees code adding an object to an order will probably have no trouble figuring out what that means, at least if they ever knew about the overloaded operator. For example, the following statement shows how a C# program might add an *OrderItem* object named *pencils* to an *Order* object named new*Order:*

```
newOrder += pencils;
```

Alternatively, you could give the *Order* class an *AddItem* method and make the code *really* obvious. The following code shows this approach:

```
newOrder.AddItem(pencils);
```

In any case, it probably doesn't make sense to define the / operator so it operates on *OrderItem* and *Order* objects. What would such an operator do? It's unlikely that the program could actually divide the *Order* object by the *OrderItem* object.

In cases where it's not intuitively obvious what an operator would mean, it is usually better to make a method instead so that the method's name can spell out its purpose.

## Conversion Operators

One type of operator overload that is often overlooked is the conversion operator, which converts one data type to another. For example, many languages can implicitly convert a value from an integer to a floating-point value (if necessary) to perform a calculation.

Similarly, you can define conversion operators to convert from one class to another. For example, you could define a conversion operator to convert a *Person* object into a *Student* object. Then the program could take any *Person* object and convert it into a *Student* object.

As another example, consider one of the classic examples in operator overloading: the *ComplexNumber* class. This class represents a complex number of the form $A + B * i$, where $i$ is the irrational number representing the square root of -1. Using simple mathematics, you can define the +, –, *, and / operators for combining two *ComplexNumber* objects.

However, the real number $R$ is also a complex number of the form $R + 0 * i$, so those operators should be able to combine floating-point numbers and *ComplexNumbers*. Unfortunately, if you want a program to be able to do that, you must overload the operators again to work with floating-point numbers and *ComplexNumbers*. Worse still, you would need to overload the operators a third time to work with *ComplexNumbers* and floating-point numbers (where the *ComplexNumber* is on the left side of the operator). You would need to overload each operator three times.

The situation is much simpler if you define a conversion operator that can convert a floating-point number to a *ComplexNumber*. Now, if the program encounters an expression that uses a floating-point number and a *ComplexNumber*, it can promote the floating-point number to a *ComplexNumber* automatically and then use the original overloaded operators.

# Summary

This chapter explained precedence, operators, and operator overloading.

In an expression, a program uses precedence rules to determine the order in which operations are evaluated. For example, * has a higher precedence than + and –, so the expression 1 + 2 * 3 - 4 equals 3 rather than 5, -3, or some other value.

The operator tables in this chapter summarized the most common operators available in C# and Visual Basic and listed them in order of precedence. By using those tables, you can determine exactly how any expression will be evaluated by a program.

You can use parentheses to change an expression's evaluation order and make the program perform operations in a different order than the one dictated by the precedence rules. You also can use parentheses to make it easier to understand how an expression will be evaluated, even if it does follow the normal rules. Although parentheses don't help the program understand how to follow the precedence rules, they can make it much easier for programmers to understand exactly what an expression means.

The final section in this chapter described operator overloading. It explained how you can give new meaning to existing operators.

You can perform complex calculations by using operators, but what if you need to perform the same calculations for a large number of similar items? For example, suppose you need to calculate the monthly bills for hundreds or thousands of customers. You might be able to perform those calculations in one of the loops described in Chapter 7, "Control Statements," but what if you need to perform similar calculations in many different parts of the program?

*Routines* let you package a piece of code such as a calculation so that you can use it from any number of other code locations. The next chapter describes routines. It explains what they are and what benefits they provide. It also discusses how you can pass values into routines to give them some context, so they don't need to perform *exactly* the same operations every time.

# Chapter 9

# Routines

**In this chapter:**

- ▪ Different types of routines

- ▪ Advantages and disadvantages of routines

- ▪ How the call stack works

- ▪ Writing good routines

- ▪ How parameters work

- ▪ Passing values by value or by reference

- ▪ Understanding value types and reference types

OFTEN, A PROGRAM MUST PERFORM THE same task in several different places. For example, a point-of-sale application might print a customer invoice as soon as a sale is complete. Each week, it might reprint invoices that are more than 30 days overdue. It might also allow you to select a customer and reprint that customer's past invoices. In all three cases, the program does the same thing: it prints an invoice.

You could duplicate the code needed to print an invoice in all three places, but that would require you to write, debug, and maintain three different copies of essentially the same code.

To avoid this kind of duplication, programming languages allow you to define *routines*. A routine is a named piece of code that other pieces of code can invoke to perform a useful task.

This chapter discusses routines. It explains their benefits, details what happens when a program calls a routine, and describes different kinds of routines. It also explains parameters and the ways a program can pass parameters to a routine, a topic that can often cause confusion for beginning programmers.

# Types of Routines

I've defined the term *routine* as "any named piece of code that other pieces of code can invoke," but routines are often called *subroutines*, *procedures*, *subprocedures*, and sometimes *subprograms*.

A routine provided by a class is often called a *method*. In C#, every routine must be part of a class or structure, so many C# programmers always call routines *methods*. In contrast, a Microsoft Visual Basic program can define routines that are not part of any class. These are usually called *subroutines* or *functions,* depending on whether they return a value.

Some routines return a value to the calling code. A routine that returns a value in this way is often called a *function.* For example, suppose a program defines a *Factorial* function that takes an integer parameter and returns the parameter's factorial. (If the number is *N,* then its factorial is written mathematically as *N!* and is given by 1 * 2 * 3 * ... * *N*.) In that case, the following C# statement sets the variable *value* equal to 6!:

```
value = Factorial(6);
```

In this example, the *Factorial* function takes the value 6 as a parameter and returns 6!. The section "Parameters," later in this chapter, explains how to pass parameters to routines.

> **Note** To simplify the terminology, this book uses the term *routine* most of the time, but it uses the term *method* to emphasize routines provided by a class. Finally, this book uses the term *function* when a routine returns a value.

# Advantages of Routines

The following list summarizes some of the advantages of using routines:

- Reducing duplicated code
- Reusing code
- Simplifying complex code
- Hiding implementation details
- Dividing tasks among programmers
- Making debugging easier

The only major disadvantage to using routines is that doing so adds some overhead to the program. When a piece of code invokes a routine, the program must prepare the routine for execution, and it must store some information so that it can return to the correct location in the code that called the routine after the routine finishes. This overhead is usually small, so it doesn't cause much of a problem unless a program calls a routine a very large number of times.

For example, suppose that a program contains a loop that calls a routine to perform a simple calculation several million times. In that case, the program may run somewhat faster if you copy the calculation into the loop to avoid the overhead of making the routine call. Usually this isn't a problem, however, so you are better off using routines to gain their advantages and then removing them later if you discover that calling the routine is truly causing problems.

The following sections explain the advantages of using routines in greater detail.

## Reducing Duplicated Code

Avoiding code duplication is probably the most obvious advantage to using routines. When a program contains the same (or similar) code in several places, programmers must write and debug the code several times, which requires duplicated effort. In contrast, when you move the duplicated code into a routine, you need to write and debug it only once, and then the program can use it in as many places as you like.

This not only saves you time when testing the code, but it also allows you to invest some of the saved time in testing the routine more thoroughly. The result is less code, and the code that is there is more reliable.

Reduced duplication also makes maintaining the program easier. If you later decide you need to change how this code works, you typically need to modify only the routine itself, not all the places that call it. This not only saves you work, but it also helps you avoid mistakes. In contrast, when you need to update duplicated code in several places, you must be sure to change it in every place that it occurs and debug each instance of the code. If you change it in one place but forget to change it in another, the program may produce inconsistent results, resulting in bugs that can be very hard to track down.

## Reusing Code

If you write a robust, well-tested routine in one program, you can reuse it in other programs without having to rewrite the routine again from scratch.

Of course, if you simply copy the code into a new program, you have created duplicate code in multiple programs, and you get all the drawbacks of duplicated code. To solve that problem, programming environments let you compile routines into libraries that you can then share among multiple programs. If you modify the code in the library, all the programs sharing it get the benefits of the change. (Note, however, that you may need to recompile the programs before they can use the new version of the code.)

## Simplifying Complex Code

A person can keep only so many ideas in mind at the same time. As code becomes more complex, it also becomes more difficult to keep track of all the details simultaneously. When a piece of code is very long, you won't be able to see it all on your computer's screen at one time, which makes it harder to understand the code's flow.

If you break the code into routines, each routine can perform a well-defined part of the total task. The main program can then call each of the routines instead of including all the code in one big pile. In this case, routines don't necessarily reduce or eliminate duplication; they simply give the code extra structure to make it easier to understand.

Breaking the code into pieces in this way may also let you debug the pieces separately. It is often easier to debug a series of self-contained routines than a long chunk of code.

## Hiding Implementation Details

To get the greatest benefit, each routine should hide its implementation details from outside code. If a routine doesn't hide the details about how it works, then a programmer trying to use the routine needs to keep track of those extra details, and that can make programming and debugging harder.

For example, suppose that a piece of code must perform three tasks:

- Determine whether a customer's service should be disconnected for lack of payment

- Disconnect the customer

- Send the customer a letter explaining the disconnection

Ideally, the code calling the three routines that perform these tasks shouldn't need to know how they work. When you write that code, you can simply call the routines and not worry about the details.

In C#, this code might look like the following, where *customerId* is a variable holding a customer's ID:

```
if (CustomerShouldBeDisconnected(customerId))
{
    DisconnectCustomer(customerId);
    PrintDisconnectLetter(customerId);
}
```

At this level, the code is quite easy to understand. All the complexity is hidden in the three routines *CustomerShouldBeDisconnected*, *DisconnectCustomer*, and *PrintDisconnectLetter*.

## Dividing Tasks Among Programmers

If you break a complex piece of code into several routines, different programmers can write them. Sometimes the programmers can write and debug their routines at the same time, allowing you to finish the project sooner.

Dividing routines among programmers also lets you assign trickier pieces of code to the more experienced programmers and simpler routines to the less experienced programmers. In contrast, if you kept all the code in a single piece, you would need to assign it to a programmer experienced enough to handle the trickiest parts. Splitting the code apart lets you take better advantage of everyone's skill levels.

## Making Debugging Easier

When a program contains duplicated code and there's a problem with that code, you won't always know which piece of code is causing the problem. But if the code is in a single routine, then you know exactly where to look.

For example, suppose that a program uses several pieces of code to search for a particular employee. If the program sometimes finds the wrong employee, you won't know which piece of code is causing the problem. However, if the program uses a single *FindEmployee* routine, you only need to look in that routine for the problem.

Many programming environments, such as Microsoft Visual Studio, include a debugger that lets you set breakpoints in the code and step through the code as it executes so that you can see what it's doing. If the problem code is in a single routine, you can simply set a breakpoint there to see what's going wrong.

## Calling Routines

When a program invokes a routine, execution jumps from the calling code into the routine. The routine performs its task, and then execution returns to the point where the routine was called. Often, execution resumes with the calling code's next statement, but sometimes, if the call to a routine is part of a complex statement, the same statement may continue to perform more tasks.

For example, if a program has defined the *Factorial* function described previously, then the following statement calculates 5! times 6!:

```
value = Factorial(5) * Factorial(6);
```

In this example, execution passes to the *Factorial* function to calculate 5!. When that function call returns, the code calls the function again to calculate 6!. When the second call returns, the statement multiplies the two results and saves the result in the variable *value*.

Programs use a call stack to manage these routine calls. The *call stack* is a chunk of memory where the program can store information about each routine call.

When a routine call begins, the program creates a stack frame on the call stack to represent the call. The *stack frame* contains information about the routine call, including the routine's local variables and the program location where execution should resume after the routine finishes.

After a routine finishes executing, the program sets a return value if the routine is a function, prepares to resume execution at the routine's return point (as given by the stack frame), and then removes the routine's stack frame from the call stack.

Development environments, such as Visual Studio, provide a call stack window that lets you see the series of routine calls that lead to a particular execution point. Figure 9-1 shows the state of execution in a simple program.

**FIGURE 9-1** The Call Stack window shows you the series of routine calls that lead to a point of execution.

The call stack window in Figure 9-1 shows the most recent routine calls at the top. The program began execution in code that is external to the program, shown at the bottom in Figure 9-1. That external code is what started the main program.

The second-to-last line in Figure 9-1 shows that the external code called the program's *Main* routine. The parts of this line provide the program (ChooseSomeObjects.exe), the namespace containing the routine (*ChooseSomeObjects*), the class that defines the routine (*Program*), and the routine (*Main*). This line indicates that the program is paused at line 18 of the *Main* routine.

In a C# program, this line is actually in code that was automatically generated by the development environment and not in the code that I wrote for this example. It calls other external code that displays the main form. The next line up in Figure 9-1 shows that call to the external code.

The fourth line up in Figure 9-1 indicates that a *Form1* object's *Form1_Load* routine is executing. This routine is an event handler that automatically fires when the program's main form is loaded. This line indicates that the routine's parameters are named *sender* and *e* (parameters are described in the section "Parameters," later in this chapter), and that the routine paused while executing line 48.

That line of code (line 48) in *Form1_Load* called the routine *SelectObjects*. Its execution paused on line 52, which is where the *SelectObjects* routine called the *Choose* routine, passing it the parameters $n$ = 4 and $m$ = 5. The *Choose* routine paused at line 132 because it called the *Factorial* routine, passing it the value $n$ = 4. The program is currently paused in that routine at line 122.

In Visual Studio, you can double-click one of the lines in the Call Stack window to make the code editor go to that line and show you the code that is currently executing. Using the Call Stack window is an excellent way to help you figure out how a program got into its current state.

# Writing Good Routines

The following list summarizes some of the rules you should follow to make routines as useful as possible:

- Perform a single, well-defined task

- Avoid side effects

- Use descriptive names

- Keep it short

- Use comments

The following sections describe these concepts.

## Perform a Single, Well-Defined Task

If a routine performs a single, well-defined task, it is easy for programmers to understand what it does and use it correctly. If a routine performs more than one task, programmers may be unable to perform one of the tasks without performing the other. They also may confuse the tasks and not use them properly.

If a piece of code performs multiple unrelated tasks, break it into separate routines, each of which will perform a single task. The code can then call each of the pieces separately.

For example, suppose that a program performs the following bookkeeping chores at the end of each day:

- Print new order summaries for the day.

- Check inventory levels and reorder if necessary.

- Check for overdue accounts and email reminders to customers.

- Move orders that are more than one year old into a long-term storage database.

You could write a single piece of code to perform all these tasks, but the code would be long and poorly focused. While writing and debugging the code, a programmer would need to keep track of lots of unrelated ideas at the same time.

A better approach would be to write an *EndOfDayCloseout* routine to orchestrate all these activities. That routine performs a single logical task: taking all the actions necessary at the end of the day. At a high level, that's all a programmer needs to know about that routine.

The *EndOfDayCloseout* routine would simply call several other routines to do the real work. It would contain little if any nontrivial code, so it would be easy to read and understand.

Other routines named *PrintDailyOrderSummaries*, *CheckInventoryLevels*, *CheckForOverdueAccounts*, and *ArchiveOldOrders* would do all the real work. Each of those routines has a simple, well-defined purpose.

# Avoid Side Effects

As discussed in Chapter 8, "Operators," a side effect occurs when a routine does something that isn't obvious and that affects code outside the routine.

For example, suppose that the *InitializeData* routine looks up some data in a database to get a program ready to run. That's its main purpose, but it also leaves a connection to the database open for later use. This is a side effect. It's not obvious from the routine's name that it leaves a database connection open, and that could cause problems later. A programmer who doesn't realize that there's an open connection might create other connections instead of reusing the open one. That wastes the system's resources, which could be a problem if the number of allowed connections is limited.

To make routines safer and easier to use, you should avoid side effects whenever possible. If a routine must perform a task that has a long-lasting effect, such as leaving a database connection open, make the routine's name indicate what it is doing.

Part of the problem in this example is that the routine doesn't perform a single, well-defined task because fetching data and opening the database are two related but different tasks. A better solution might be to break the code into two routines named *OpenDatabase* and *LoadInitialData* that will perform the tasks separately. Then, the *OpenDatabase* routine would open the database as its only function, not as a side effect.

# Use Descriptive Names

Giving a routine a descriptive name makes it easier for programmers to understand its purpose and to use it correctly. If a routine has a vague name such as *DoStuff*, programmers will need to look at it more closely to figure out what it does. A programmer who doesn't correctly figure out the routine's true purpose may use it incorrectly, creating a bug.

# Keep It Short

If a routine is too long, it is hard to see all its code at once and to keep all the routine's key ideas in mind at the same time. If a routine is long, consider breaking it into several smaller routines that the main routine can call.

Different developers use different rules of thumb for deciding when to break a routine into smaller pieces, but many recommend 100 to 200 lines as a maximum length. Other developers recommend keeping routines to no more than 20 or 30 lines. I prefer to keep routines short enough that I can see all the code and comments in a routine at the same time on the screen.

In general, use as many lines as it takes to perform the routine's single, well-defined task. If a complex algorithm takes 200 lines to implement and you can't break it into self-contained parts in a reasonable way, make the routine 200 lines long. It is better to have a slightly longer routine than to break it into pieces that don't really make sense independently.

## Use Comments

Short routines with descriptive names tend to be easy to understand, but if there's any chance of confusion, use comments to make the code easy to understand. The compiler ignores comments, so you can use them to give the reader extra information to make understanding the code easier.

The C#, C++, C, and Java languages use // to indicate the beginning of a single-line comment. Any text after the // to the end of the current line is a comment. Visual Basic uses the ' character for the same purpose.

Many languages, including C#, C++, C, and Java (but not Visual Basic), also have multi-line comments. In C#, C++, C, and Java, a multi-line comment begins with /* and ends with */.

The following C# code contains multi-line and single-line comments:

```
/* Sort the array by using the radixsort algorithm.
 * For information on bucketsort, see ...
 */
public void Bucketsort(int[] items, int numBuckets)
{
    // Create the buckets.
    ...
}
```

 **Note** Programmers often begin the second and subsequent lines in a multi-line comment with the * character to make it obvious that those lines are part of a comment.

Many languages also have a special comment syntax that indicates the comment is intended for documentation purposes. You can extract those comments to build help files or other documentation to describe the program. In C#, documentation comments begin with ///. In Visual Basic, they begin with '''.

Use a comment before the routine to describe its purpose, inputs, and outputs. Use comments within the routine to explain what the routine is doing.

If the code is easy to understand, it will be easy to debug and modify in the future. If the code is hard to understand, changes will probably break the code and require extensive debugging.

Some developers recommend that you use comments only when absolutely necessary and that you should not use comments if you can figure out what the code does. Unfortunately, what may seem obvious today (or to you) may not seem obvious tomorrow (or to another programmer).

I've read thousands of lines of code that probably seemed obvious to the programmers who wrote it, but a year later, it was very difficult to figure out how the code worked. I worked on one project where making even the smallest change could take a week or more because the code was so confusing.

I even worked on one project that failed because the developers had removed comments that they thought were unnecessary and then later couldn't figure out how the code worked.

The goal is to make it easy to debug and modify the code, not to make understanding the code an IQ test. There is a limit to how many comments you can reasonably add to the code, however. Don't add side issues and unnecessary commentary that makes it hard to keep the code's main purpose and method in mind. Also, try not to add so many comments that viewing the code is a chore. If a routine contains 10 lines of code, don't add so many comments that you can't see them all on the screen at the same time.

If you need to add a lot of really long comments (perhaps a description of a particularly tricky algorithm), put the information in a separate document. Then, include a reference to that document in the code so that programmers who read the code later can refer to it if necessary.

# Parameters

To make a routine more flexible, you can pass parameters to the routine to give it extra information that it can use to perform its task. For example, suppose that you write a routine to print a student's course schedule. You could make the routine receive a parameter that gives the ID of the student whose schedule it should print.

Giving the routine a parameter makes it much more flexible. In this example, it allows one routine to print the schedule for any number of students instead of just one.

Exactly how you define a routine's parameters depends on the language you are using, but the idea is the same in every language. The routine's declaration includes declarations for any parameters that it will take.

For example, the following code shows a *Factorial* function written in Visual Basic:

```
' Calculate N!.
Public Function Factorial(ByVal N As Long) As Long
    Dim result As Long = 1
    For i As Long = 2 To N
        result *= i
    Next i

    Return result
End Function
```

This function takes as a parameter a long integer. Inside the function, the parameter's name is *N*.

The function creates a variable named *result* and initializes it to 1. It then uses a loop to multiply *result* by each of the integers between 2 and *N*. It finishes by returning the final value of *result*.

The following code shows how a program might call the *Factorial* function:

```
Dim input As Long = 13
Dim total As Long = Factorial(input)
```

This code declares a variable named *input* and initializes it to the value 13. It then declares another variable named *total* and sets it equal to the result returned by the *Factorial* function when its parameter is set to *input*.

The value that is passed into the function, in this case *input*, is called an *argument*. (However, many programmers use the terms *parameter* and *argument* interchangeably.)

Notice that the function's declaration creates a local name for the value in the parameter that has nothing to do with whatever value is passed into the function. The function's code calls the value *N* whether the calling code passes in the value of the variable *input*, a variable with some other name, a constant such as 12, or even the result of an expression such as 3 + 5.

A routine can take more than one parameter. For example, the following C# function calculates the greatest common divisor (GCD) of its two parameters *a* and *b:*

```csharp
// Return the greatest common divisor (GCD) of a and b.
public long Gcd(long a, long b)
{
    while (true)
    {
        long remainder = a % b;
        if (remainder == 0) return b;
        a = b;
        b = remainder;
    }
}
```

This code calculates the remainder after dividing *a* by *b*. If the remainder is zero, the GCD is *b,* so the function returns it. If the remainder is not zero, the function sets *a* equal to *b* and *b* equal to the remainder, and then repeats. The loop repeats until the remainder is zero. (This clever algorithm is called the Euclidean algorithm or Euclid's algorithm. For more information, including a proof that the loop eventually stops and that the code actually works, see *http://en.wikipedia.org/wiki/Euclidean_algorithm*.)

In theory, a routine could take any number of parameters, but in practice, routines that take too many parameters are confusing to use.

Different languages may support additional parameter passing features, such as optional parameters. The following sections describe some of the most common of these features.

## Optional Parameters

Some languages allow you to declare a parameter as optional. In Visual Basic, optional parameters must come last in the parameter list and must specify a default value that the parameter takes if it is omitted in the calling code. The following routine takes the required parameters *cx, cy,* and *radius* and the optional parameter *filled*. If the code that calls this routine omits the final parameter, *filled* takes the default value false.

```
' Draw a circle centered at (cx, cy) with
' radius given by paramete radius.
' If filled is true, fill the circle.
```

```
Public Sub DrawCircle(ByVal cx As Integer, ByVal cy As Integer,
 ByVal radius As Integer, Optional ByVal filled As Boolean = False)
    ...
End Sub
```

In this example, the method would draw the circle and then fill it if the parameter *filled* is true. If the calling code omits the final argument, the *filled* parameter takes the default value *false* and the routine does not fill the circle.

Some languages, including C#, do not support optional parameters, although C# does allow you to declare nullable parameters (or variables). *Nullable* parameters can take the special value *null*, which essentially means it has no value. (Visual Basic also supports nullable parameters, but optional parameters make the code simpler and easier to read.)

## Parameter Arrays

Some languages allow a routine to take a variable number of arguments. In C# and Visual Basic, the routine's final parameter can be an array holding the variable number of arguments passed into the routine by the calling code.

For example, the following C# code shows a *SendEmails* routine. It takes two required parameters named *subject* and *body*. It also takes a parameter array named *recipients*.

```
// Send an email message to the indicated recipients.
public void SendEmails(string subject, string body, params string[] recipients)
{
    foreach (string recipient in recipients)
    {
        SendEmail(subject, body, recipient);
    }
}
```

This routine loops through the values in the *recipients* array, calling the *SendEmails* routine for each.

The following code shows how the program could call this routine, passing it two email addresses:

```
SendEmails("School closed Friday",
    "Note that the school will be closed this Friday.",
    "RodStephens@CSharpHelper.com",
    "RodStephens@vb-helper.com");
```

Note that the program could pass no arguments for the parameter array.

## Parameter-Passing Methods

There are two ways you can pass an argument to a routine: by value and by reference. These two methods determine how the parameter relates to the argument that you pass into the routine. You can pass an argument by value or by reference.

The syntax for indicating that a variable should be passed by value or reference varies by language. In Visual Basic, you use the keywords *ByVal* and *ByRef*. In C#, you use the keyword *ref* to pass a value by reference. (In C#, you also can use the *out* keyword, which will be described shortly.)

When you pass a value by value, the parameter receives a *copy* of the argument so that if the routine changes the value of the parameter, the argument does not change.

For example, the following Visual Basic code shows a new version of the *Factorial* function shown previously:

```
' Calculate N!.
Public Function Factorial(ByVal N As Long) As Long
    Dim result As Long = 1
    Do While N > 1
        result *= N
        N -= 1
    Loop

    Return result
End Function
```

This version initializes the variable *result* to 1. Then as long as the parameter *N* is greater than 1, it multiplies *result* by *N* and subtracts 1 from *N*. When the loop finishes, *result* has been multiplied by *N*, *N – 1*, *N – 2*, and so on down to 2, giving the factorial.

Because this code declares the parameter *N* using the *ByVal* keyword, the argument is passed by value. Even though the routine modifies *N* and leaves it holding the value 2, the argument used by the calling code remains unchanged.

For example, the following code initializes the variable *input* to 10 and then calls the *Factorial* function, passing it the variable *input*. Because the argument is passed by value, the value of the variable *input* is still 13 when the call to *Factorial* returns:

```
Dim input As Long = 13
Dim total As Long = Factorial(input)
```

When you pass a value by reference, the routine receives the address in memory of the argument and makes the parameter refer to that address. Inside the routine, the parameter looks just like any other variable, but it actually refers to the same value used for the argument. The result is that any changes that the routine makes to the parameter also affect the argument in the calling code.

The *SwapValues* routine shown in the following Visual Basic code takes two parameters passed by reference and swaps their values:

```
' Swap the two values.
Public Sub SwapValues(ByRef value1 As Integer, ByRef value2 As Integer)
    Dim temp As Integer = value1
    value1 = value2
    value2 = temp
End Sub
```

Because these parameters are declared using the *ByRef* keyword, the changes made to the values in the routine are reflected in the arguments passed into the routine.

The C# language also provides the keyword *out* to indicate that an argument should be passed by reference and that its initial value is not used by the routine. In other words, this is an output variable only. The argument is treated like a normal argument passed by reference except the compiler won't raise a warning if the calling code doesn't initialize the argument before passing it into the routine.

Passing arguments by reference can be confusing, so you should pass arguments by value whenever possible. If you need a routine to return a result, it's better to make the routine a function and have it return the result through its return value instead of using an argument passed by reference.

> **Note** In Visual Basic, the calling code gives no indication that a variable is passed by reference, so a programmer calling a routine might not even know that the arguments will be modified.
>
> In C#, the calling code must use the *ref* or *out* keyword to make it clear that an argument is being passed by reference.

## Reference and Value Types

Chapter 6, "Variables," discusses the difference between value types and reference types. Briefly, value types contain their data, while reference types contain a reference to the data stored elsewhere. Most simple data types such as integer, floating-point, and dates, are value types. Instances of classes are reference types.

Whether a routine's parameter is a value type or a reference type plays an important role in how changes to the parameter affect the corresponding argument.

If a parameter is a value type, then changes to the parameter are reflected in the argument only if the argument is passed by reference.

If a parameter is a reference type, then changes to the parameter's data are always reflected in the argument's data. Changes to the parameter itself are reflected in the argument only if the parameter is passed by reference.

For example, consider the following C# routine:

```
// Set the Student's Name equal to the current user's name.
public void SetStudentUserName(Student student)
{
    student.Name = Environment.UserName;
}
```

This routine takes a *Student* object as a parameter passed by value. The *Student* class is a reference type, so changes to the parameter's data (the student's *Name* property, in this example) are reflected in the argument.

The following code shows how a program might call the *SetStudentUserName* routine:

```
Student rod = new Student();
SetStudentUserName(rod);
```

After the call to *SetStudentUserName* returns, the *rod* object's *Name* property has been set to the current user's name.

If you pass a reference type argument into a routine by reference, then the routine not only can update the argument's data, but it also can update the argument itself. For example, the following routine takes a *Student* object as a parameter passed by reference:

```
// Create a new Student.
public void InitializeStudent(ref Student student)
{
    student = new Student();
    student.Name = Environment.UserName;
}
```

This routine sets the parameter equal to a new *Student* object. Because the argument is passed by reference, the argument in the calling code is updated to refer to the new object. The code then sets the new object's *Name* property as before.

Structures are an odd case because they are similar to classes in most respects, but they are value types rather than reference types. That means, for example, that if you set one structure variable equal to another, the first contains a *copy* of the second. In contrast, if you set a class variable equal to another, both then point to the same object. (If this is a bit unclear, you may want to review the section "Value and Reference Types" in Chapter 6.)

The fact that structures are value types affects how they act as arguments to routines. If you pass a structure into a routine by value, the parameter receives a *completely new copy* of the structure, so any changes to its data are not reflected in the argument.

For example, the following routine is similar to the *SetStudentUserName* routine shown previously, except that it takes a structure as a parameter instead of a class instance:

```
// Set the Person's Name equal to the current user's name.
public void SetPersonUserName(Person person)
{
    person.Name = Environment.UserName;
}
```

Because this routine's structure parameter is passed by value, the parameter contains a separate copy of the data, so changes to its data are not reflected in the argument. In this example, that means the routine doesn't work as expected because it does not update the *Name* property in the calling code's *Person* structure.

**Note** Passing a structure by value also has a slight performance penalty because the program must make a new copy of the structure. This usually isn't much of an issue unless the structure is quite large.

The following version of the routine passes its structure by reference:

```
// Set the Person's Name equal to the current user's name.
public void SetPersonUserName(ref Person person)
{
    person = new Person();
    person.Name = Environment.UserName;
}
```

In this example, the parameter contains a reference to the *Person* argument, so changes to it and its data are reflected in the argument. The code sets the parameter equal to a new *Person* structure and then sets its *Name* property. Both of those changes are reflected in the calling code's argument.

## Arrays

Like classes, arrays are reference types. That means if you pass an array into a routine by value, the routine can change the array's elements but cannot make the corresponding argument point to a completely new array.

The following routine fills an existing array with squares:

```
// Fill the array with squares.
public void FillArrayWithSquares(int[] squares)
{
    for (int i = 0; i < squares.Length; i++)
    {
        squares[i] = i * i;
    }
}
```

This code loops through the entries in the array, placing the value *i* * *i* in entry *i*. The array is passed by value, so the routine can change its entries but cannot make the argument point to a new array.

The following routine makes a new array that holds 100 items and sets their values to the first 100 squares. Because the parameter is passed by reference, the calling code's argument refers to the new array after the routine returns.

```
// Fill the array with 100 squares.
public void FillArrayWith100Squares(out int[] squares)
{
    squares = new int[100];
    for (int i = 0; i < squares.Length; i++)
    {
        squares[i] = i * i;
    }
}
```

# Routine Overloading

Chapter 8 explained how to overload operators such as * and / so they can work with new data types, such as program-defined classes. Similarly, you can overload routines to create more than one version of the same routine.

The only restriction is that each version of the routine must have a different signature, meaning that the number and types of the routines' parameter lists must be different so that the program can tell them apart. For example, if you create two routines named *FindEmployee* that both take an integer as a parameter—one that takes an employee's ID and one that takes the employee's phone extension—the program wouldn't know which version to use.

> **Tip** The parameter lists of different versions of a routine must have different numbers or types of parameters. They cannot simply differ in parameter name. For example, a program could not define two versions of the *FindEmployee* routine, both taking a single integer as a parameter but with one calling its parameter *employeeId* and the other calling its parameter *employeeExtension*.

For example, the following two Visual Basic routines search for an employee. The first takes as parameters the employee's first and last names, whereas the second takes employee ID as a parameter. Because they have different parameter lists, the program can define both versions of the routine.

```
' Find an employee by first and last name.
Public Function FindEmployee(ByVal firstName As String, ByVal lastName As String)
  As Employee
    ...
End Function

' Find an employee by ID.
Public Function FindEmployee(ByVal id As Integer) As Employee
    ...
End Function
```

Visual Basic will not let you make two versions of a routine that differ only in optional parameters. For example, if one version of a routine takes an integer as a parameter, and a second version takes an integer and an optional string as parameters, Visual Basic will display an error message because it cannot tell which version to use if you omit the optional parameter. (On the other hand, C# doesn't allow optional parameters at all.)

However, both Visual Basic and C# will allow a program to define multiple versions of a routine that differ only in a parameter array. For example, a Visual Basic program can define the following versions of the *InitializeValues* routine:

```
Public Function InitializeValues() As Integer
    ...
End Function
```

```
Public Function InitializeValues(ByVal values As Integer) As Integer
    ...
End Function

Public Function InitializeValues(ByVal ParamArray values() As Integer) As Integer
    ...
End Function
```

Versions of the routine that do not use the parameter array have priority, so if the program calls *InitializeValues* and passes it no arguments, the program uses the first version of the routine instead of the third. Similarly, if the program calls *InitializeValues* and passes it one argument, the program uses the second version of the routine instead of the third. If the first and second versions didn't exist, the program would call the third version in both cases.

Making routines that differ only by parameter arrays could be confusing, so you shouldn't do it even if the language will let you.

## Routine Accessibility

The section "Scope, Accessibility, and Lifetime," in Chapter 6, discussed when a variable exists and what pieces of code can access it. Similar concepts apply to routines.

For example, if a class defines a routine and gives it the *private* accessibility keyword, then it is visible only to code within the class.

Table 9-1 summarizes the accessibility keywords used by C# and Visual Basic.

**TABLE 9-1** Accessibility Keywords

| C# Keyword | Visual Basic Keyword | Meaning |
|---|---|---|
| *public* | *Public* | The routine is usable by any code. |
| *private* | *Private* | The routine is usable only by code in the same structure, class, or code module. |
| *protected* | *Protected* | The routine is usable only by code in the same structure or class, or in a derived class. (Chapter 10, "Object-Oriented Programming," explains derived classes.) |
| *internal* | *Friend* | The routine is usable only by code in the same assembly. |
| *protected internal* | *Protected Friend* | Both *protected* and *internal/Friend* (the routine is usable only by code in the same structure or class or in a derived class, and only in the same assembly). |

The *internal* (or *Protected*) keyword makes an item usable only to code in the same assembly. In .NET applications, an assembly is the smallest self-contained unit of compiled code. An assembly can be a complete application or a library that can be called by other applications.

# Recursion

*Recursion* occurs when a routine calls itself. Recursion can be a confusing topic because people don't normally think recursively, but some problems are naturally recursive, and in those cases, it can be useful to design routines that match the problem's recursive structure.

For example, earlier in this chapter, I defined the factorial of the number *N*, written as *N!* and given by $1 * 2 * 3 * ... * N$. You can also define the factorial function recursively as $N! = N * (N - 1)!$. The following C# code shows a recursive implementation of this function:

```
// Calculate n! recursively.
public long Factorial(long n)
{
    if (n <= 1) return 1;
    return n * Factorial(n - 1);
}
```

If the parameter is 1 or less, the function simply returns 1. (The value 0! is 1 by definition.) If the parameter is greater than 1, the function returns *n* times the factorial of $n - 1$.

Like the *Do*, *While*, and *Until* loops described in Chapter 7, "Control Statements," it is very important that a recursive routine has a stopping condition. If the routine doesn't eventually stop, it will continue calling itself forever, or at least until it uses up all the program's stack space and crashes. The previous version of the *Factorial* function stops recursion when its parameter has the value of 1 or smaller.

Roughly speaking, a fractal is a geometric shape or curve that is self-similar, having pieces that look somewhat like the whole. For example, the binary tree shown in Figure 9-2 begins with a single vertical branch at its root. At each level of recursion, it turns left and right and draws a smaller version of the tree.

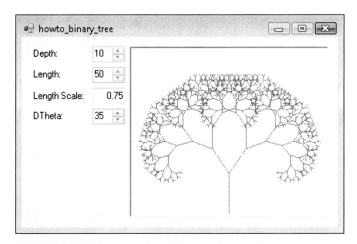

**FIGURE 9-2** This binary tree fractal is naturally recursive.

Many kinds of fractals are naturally recursive. The routine that draws a branch in a binary tree calls itself recursively to draw smaller trees sticking off the end of the current branch.

The program shown in Figure 9-2 lets the user set parameters that determine the number of levels of recursion, the length of the root branch, the factor by which each branch is shorter than the previous one, and the angles between the branches.

Other fractals also use recursion. The Sierpinski curve shown in Figure 9-3 starts by drawing the shape on the left. For each level of recursion, it replaces the horizontal and vertical line segments with combinations of other line segments.

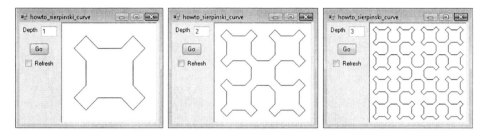

**FIGURE 9-3** This Sierpinski curve is naturally recursive.

Figure 9-4 shows how the Sierpinski curve replaces upper horizontal line segments to get from the first level of recursion to the second. It replaces the upper horizontal line segment on the left in Figure 9-3 with the series of curves A, B, D, and A (shown in Figure 9-4) to get the middle picture in Figure 9-3.

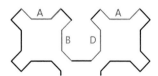

**FIGURE 9-4** The Sierpinski curve replaces upper horizontal segments with the connected series of curves A, B, D, and A.

The Sierpinski curve uses other combinations of curves to replace lower horizontal, left vertical, and right vertical segments when it moves to deeper levels of recursion.

**More Info** You can find C# programs that draw these and other fractals on my website, *http://www.CSharpHelper.com*. You can find Visual Basic versions at *http://www.vb-helper.com*.

# Summary

This chapter explained routines, which are named pieces of code that other pieces of code can invoke to perform specific tasks. Routines make programming easier and less error-prone by:

- Reducing duplicated code

- Reusing code

- Simplifying complex code

- Hiding implementation details

- Dividing tasks among programmers

- Making debugging easier

The only real drawback to routines is that a routine call requires some overhead. Because they have many advantages and only one small disadvantage, routines are part of most programs.

Writing and using routines is relatively easy. The only really complicated part is understanding how value and reference types behave when you pass them to a routine by value or by reference. Table 9-2 summarizes the combinations.

**TABLE 9-2** Value and Reference Type Behavior

| Data Type | Passing Type | The routine . . . |
|---|---|---|
| Value type | By value | . . . cannot modify the argument |
| Value type | By reference | . . . can modify the argument |
| Reference type | By value | . . . can modify the argument's properties, but not the argument itself |
| Reference type | By reference | . . . can modify the argument's properties and the argument itself |

Be sure to remember that arrays are reference types and structures are value types.

So far, this book has dealt with classes only in passing, as constructs that contain fields and routines. There's actually more to classes than just variables and code. For example, inheritance hierarchies allow classes to reuse each other's code and provide simple logical models of different kinds of related objects.

The next chapter discusses object-oriented programming. It explains classes in greater detail and covers some of their most important features, such as inheritance, constructors, and destructors.

# Chapter 10

# Object-Oriented Programming

**In this chapter:**

- The benefits of classes
- Polymorphism
- Properties, methods, and events
- Shared and instance members
- Inheritance
- Overriding and shadowing members
- Abstraction and refinement
- Multiple inheritance and interfaces
- Constructors and destructors

IN A MODERN OBJECT-ORIENTED LANGUAGE, A program consists of a group of objects working together to perform a task. One object interacts with the others by reading and setting the other objects' properties, calling the other objects' methods, and responding to the other objects' events.

In a well-defined program, the objects represent more-or-less intuitive entities, and their behaviors are easy to understand. For example, a *Customer* object would provide customer-related properties such as *Name*, *PhoneNumber*, *Adddress*, and *CustomerId*. It would provide methods such as *PrintAccountHistory* and *DisconnectFromService*. It would also provide events such as *NewOrderPlaced* and *PaymentReceived* to let other parts of the program know when something significant happened to the object.

This chapter provides an overview of object-oriented programming (OOP). It explains classes, their benefits, and the features that most programming languages provide for object-oriented development.

# Classes

In essence, a class is a very special kind of data type. Like other data types, after you define a class, you can use it to create any number of instances of it. A program can make any number of strings or integers. Similarly, if a program defines a *Vehicle* class, then it can make any number of *Vehicle* objects.

An object of a class's type is called an *instance* of the class, and the act of creating the object in code at run time is called *instantiating* it.

Because you can use a class to make any number of instances, some programmers think of a class as a blueprint for making instances. After you define the blueprint, you can use it to make as many copies as you like.

All the instances of a class have the same basic configuration. They all have the same properties, methods, and events (which will be described in detail shortly), although the properties may have different values. For example, cars all share certain properties such as color, estimated mileage, and number of cup holders. All cars have those properties, but different cars may have different values for the properties. (For example, some are red and some are blue; some have cup holders, and some do not.)

# Class Benefits

The biggest benefit of classes is *encapsulation*, the ability to group the class's properties and methods in a convenient package. A class groups the features that define a single object or concept, such as *Customer*, *Student*, or *AnnualReport*.

A well-designed class encapsulates the features needed to control its main concept and nothing else. For example, a *Student* class should store information about a student. Although it should provide a way to see what courses the student is taking, it should not store detailed information about those courses—that would be the job of a *Course* class.

Strong encapsulation hides the details of how the class works from outside code. It isolates the rest of the program from those details, so a programmer working on another part of the program can use the class's properties and methods without needing to know exactly how they work. This feature of classes is sometimes called *information hiding* or *abstraction*.

Classes promote code reuse by allowing every instance of a class to use the class's code. They also allow code reuse through inheritance. If a child class inherits from a parent class, then the child class also inherits the parent's code. (Inheritance is covered in detail shortly.)

A final benefit to classes is polymorphism. This concept, which is described in more detail later in this chapter, means that a program can treat an object as if it were from another class if it inherits from that class.

For example, suppose the *Student* class inherits from the *Person* class. Then, the program should be able to treat a *Student* as if it were a *Person* because a student is a person.

Polymorphism allows code reuse because it lets a single routine work with multiple classes. For example, suppose that the *AddressEnvelope* method prints an address on an envelope for a *Person* object. Then the same method should work for *Student*, *Instructor*, and *Administrator* objects (assuming that those classes also inherit from *Person*) because those are all different kinds of people.

The sections that follow describe some of the most important characteristics of classes in greater detail.

# Properties, Methods, and Events

A class's data and behaviors are determined by three features: properties, methods, and events. These features allow objects to interact with other parts of the program.

Together, properties, methods, and events are referred to as the class's *members*.

## Properties

Properties are data values associated with the class. For example, a *Person* class might have properties such as *FirstName*, *LastName*, *Street*, *City*, *State*, and *Zip*.

Different properties can have different accessibility levels. For example, some properties could be private (available only to code inside the class) and others could be public (available to all the code in the program).

Different languages may provide properties in different ways. The simplest method is to give the class a public variable. Then, any code can read and set the value. A property implemented in this way is often called a *field*.

Unfortunately, this technique allows any piece of code to modify the value in completely unrestricted ways. For example, suppose that an *OrderItem* class represents a single item in a customer's order. It might provide a *Quantity* property to specify the number of items that the customer wants to order. If you implement this value as a field, other pieces of code could set *Quantity* to a nonsensical value, such as -1 or 1 billion.

A generally better approach is to use special methods to let other pieces of code get and set the property's value. Many programming languages provide standard approaches for making these methods.

In Microsoft Visual Basic, the two methods are called the *property get* method and the *property set* method. In C# and some other languages, these methods are sometimes called the *getter* and *setter*. In several languages, these methods are called *accessors*.

If you use these accessor methods, then the methods can perform validation, conversion, and other tasks. For example, the *Quantity* property's setter could verify that the new value is between 1 and some reasonable upper limit and flag an error if the code tried to set the value to 1 billion.

One common technique for building properties is to store the property's value in a private field and then provide accessors to let code outside of the class modify it. In this case, the field is sometimes called the *backing field*.

The following C# code shows one way that you could implement a *Quantity* property:

```csharp
// Implement a Quantity property.
private int _Quantity;
public int Quantity
{
    set
    {
        if (value < 0 || value > 1000)
        {
            throw new ArgumentOutOfRangeException(
                "Quantity",
                "Quantity must be between 1 and 1000");
        }
        _Quantity = value;
    }
    get
    {
        return _Quantity;
    }
}
```

The code starts by declaring the backing field *_Quantity*.

In C#, the setter receives the property's new value through a special variable named *value*. In this example, the setter validates the new value and throws an exception if it is out of range so that the programmer can fix the code that is trying to set the property or provide a notification if the property can be set through user input. Otherwise, when the new value is within the allowed range, the setter saves it in the backing field.

The getter simply returns the value of the backing field.

Using accessor methods has a couple of advantages in addition to allowing you to add validation code. First, if the way the value is stored must be changed, you can modify the getter and setter to handle the change without modifying the rest of the program. For example, if you decided to store item quantities in dozens instead of single units, you could modify the getter and setter to convert between dozens and units. (I can't imagine actually needing to make that change, but you never know.)

Another benefit of accessors is that they give you a place to set breakpoints. If you know that an object's *Quantity* value is getting messed up somewhere, but you don't know which piece of code is at fault, you can set a breakpoint in the debugger to stop execution in the setter. Then, anytime the program modifies a *Quantity*, you can use the debugger to see what's happening. If you used a public field instead of accessors, you would need to find every place where other code changed the *Quantity* property to hunt down the problem.

> **Tip** The most recent versions of Visual Basic and C# provide *auto-implemented properties*, where the development environment creates a backing field for you. This makes the syntax a little easier if you don't need to add code to the accessors. If you decide to add code later, you can convert the property to one that is not auto-implemented.

# Methods

A *method* is a routine that makes an object do something. It could make the object generate a printout, reset the object's properties, connect to a database, or just about anything else.

Like any other routine, a method can take parameters. The method can return values to the calling code through parameters passed by reference, although it's generally better to make the method a function and return information to the calling code through its return value.

Different object-oriented languages provide different methods for referring to the object that is currently executing the code. For example, suppose the *Customer* class has a *PrintInvoice* method. If you invoke a particular *Customer* object's *PrintInvoice* method, that object can access its own properties and methods directly, but sometimes it might like to know which of the many *Customer* objects it is. Visual Basic calls the currently executing object *Me*. C++ and C# call the currently executing object *this*.

For example, the following Visual Basic code executes when the user clicks a button named *btnClose*:

```
' Close the form.
Private Sub btnClose_Click() Handles btnClose.Click
    Me.Close()
End Sub
```

The code uses *Me* to refer to the form that is currently running the code and calls that form's *Close* method, making the form close.

If an object refers to one of the properties or methods defined by its class and it doesn't specify an object, the program assumes that it should use the current object. That means the following code is equivalent to the preceding version:

```
' Close the form.
Private Sub btnClose_Click() Handles btnClose.Click
    Close()
End Sub
```

# Events

An object *raises* an event to notify other objects that something significant has happened. Other objects that care about the event can *catch* or *handle* it and take some action in response. The code that handles the event is called an *event handler*. Zero, one, or more objects can handle the same event as necessary.

A class may define many events, many of which are not handled by the program because they are uninteresting. For example, in Windows Forms, the *Button* control defines more than 50 events, such as *DragDrop*, *HelpRequested*, *KeyPress*, *MouseMove*, and *Resize*. Despite the availability of all these events, the only *Button* event of any real interest in the vast majority of programs is the *Click* event, which occurs when a user clicks the *Button*. When a user clicks the *Button*, an event handler catches it and does whatever is appropriate for that particular *Button*.

# Shared Versus Instance Members

Normally, a class's members apply to a particular instance of the class. For example, a *Student* object's *EmailSchedule* method emails that student's course schedule to that particular student. It does not email one student's schedule to another student.

Sometimes, however, it's convenient to make a property or method that all instances of the class can share. As an example of a shared method, consider a common design pattern called a *factory method*. A factory method is a class method that returns an instance of the class. Factory methods usually take parameters that help determine how to create the object.

Suppose that the *Student* class's *CreateStudent* method takes a student ID as a parameter, looks up the student's record in a database, and creates a *Student* object using the information retrieved from the database. If *CreateStudent* were a normal instance method, the program would first need to create an instance of the class; only then could it call *CreateStudent*. It seems silly to create an instance of the class just to be able to call the method designed to create instances of the class. However, if you make *CreateStudent* a shared method, then the program can call it without creating an instance of the class first.

The syntax for making and using shared members is different in different languages. The following code shows how you can define a simple shared method in Visual Basic:

```
Public Class Student
    Public Shared Function CreateStudent(ByVal id As String) As Student
        Return New Student()
    End Function
End Class
```

The *Shared* keyword indicates that this is a shared method. (In this example, the *CreateStudent* method shown here doesn't look up the student in a database. It simply returns a new *Student* object.)

The following code shows how a Visual Basic program could invoke this shared method:

```
Dim newStudent As Student = Student.CreateStudent("12345")
```

Notice how in its call to *CreateStudent*, the code uses the class's name instead of an instance.

The following code shows how a C# program could define a shared method:

```
public class Student
{
    public static Student CreateStudent(string id)
    {
        return new Student();
    }
}
```

In C#, the code uses the *static* keyword to indicate a shared method.

The following code shows how a C# program can invoke the shared *CreateStudent* method:

```
Student newStudent = Student.CreateStudent("1234");
```

As in the C# example, the code uses the class's name instead of an instance in its call to *CreateStudent*.

> **Note** If you access a shared member from an instance variable in Visual Basic, for example in *newStudent = newStudent.CreateStudent("12345")*, Microsoft Visual Studio warns you at compile time, does not evaluate the instance variable, and calls the class's shared method anyway.
>
> If you access a shared member from an instance variable in C#, Visual Studio flags the statement as an error and refuses to run the program.

In addition to shared members, you can define shared fields, properties, and events. Code using these items can access them by using the class's name, just as the previous examples used the *Student* class's name to access the *CreateStudent* method.

# Inheritance

Inheritance is a method for allowing one class to reuse the properties, methods, and events of another. The first class is called the *parent*, *base*, or *super* class. The class that inherits from the parent class is called the *child class*, *derived class*, or *subclass*. The act of making a new class that inherits from an existing class is called *subclassing* or *deriving*.

When one class inherits from another, the child class gains the benefits of the parent's properties, methods, and events. (You can place restrictions on how a child class can inherit the parent's members. You'll learn more about that shortly.)

For example, suppose the *Person* class has *FirstName*, *LastName*, *Street*, *City*, *State*, and *Zip* properties, and you derive the *Student* class from *Person*. Immediately, the *Student* class automatically inherits the *FirstName*, *LastName*, *Street*, *City*, *State*, and *Zip* properties defined for the *Person* class, all without requiring you to add any new code.

> **Note** Inheriting members from the parent class is a form of code reuse. It lets more than one class use the same code.

In addition to the inherited properties, methods, and events, the child class can add new features. For example, the *Student* class might add a *StudentId* property and an *EmailSchedule* method. Those items would be available to *Student* objects, but not to *Person* objects.

The syntax for deriving one class from another varies widely in different languages. The following code shows how a Visual Basic program can derive the *Student* class from the *Person* class:

```
Public Class Student
    Inherits Person

    Public StudentId As Integer
End Class
```

In this code, the *Inherits* keyword indicates that *Student* inherits from *Person*.

The following code shows how a C# program can derive the *Student* class from the *Person* class:

```
public class Student : Person
{
    public int StudentId;
}
```

Here, the code : Person indicates that *Student* inherits from *Person*.

# Polymorphism

Polymorphism is the ability for an object to act as if it were a parent class. For example, suppose that you have an *Employee* class derived from a *Person*. In that case, the program should be able to treat an *Employee* object as if it were a *Person*. That makes intuitive sense because an employee is a kind of person.

If a program has a routine that takes a *Person* as a parameter, the code should be able to pass that routine an *Employee* object. An *Employee* object has all the properties, methods, and events that a *Person* object does (plus possibly more), so the routine should be able to use the *Employee* object in the same way that it would use a *Person* object.

As a specific example, suppose that the *Person* class defines the *FirstName*, *LastName*, *Street*, *City*, *State*, and *Zip* properties, and the *PrintEnvelope* routine uses those properties to print an address on an envelope for a person object. Because the *Employee* class inherits those properties, the *PrintEnvelope* routine can still use them to print an address for an *Employee* object.

Polymorphism is another form of code reuse because it lets one piece of code handle multiple kinds of objects so long as their classes can provide the necessary support.

This simple example of polymorphism is useful, but polymorphism becomes truly amazing when you override class members, as will be discussed next.

# Overriding Members

When a child class *overrides* a member, it defines a new version for a member that is already defined in the parent class.

For example, suppose that you have defined the *Person* and *Employee* classes described in the previous section, and that the *Person* class defines the *AddressEnvelope* method. Now, suppose that you add a new *MailStop* property to the *Employee* class. In that case, you can override the *AddressEnvelope* method in the *Employee* class so that it prints the address with the *MailStop* added.

Now, if the code calls *AddressEnvelope* for a *Person* object, the original version of the method executes. If the code calls *AddressEnvelope* for an *Employee* object, the new version of the method executes.

The really amazing thing about overridden members is that the object knows which version of the method to call, even if the program's code is using polymorphism to refer to the object using a parent class. For example, suppose that you create an *Employee* object. Because an *Employee* is a kind of *Person*, polymorphism lets the program store a reference to the object in a variable of type *Person*. If the code calls the object's *AddressEnvelope* method, the program will use the version of the method defined in the *Employee* class, even if you use the *Person* variable.

The following Visual Basic code demonstrates this:

```
Dim anEmployee As Employee = New Employee()
Dim aPerson As Person = anEmployee

aPerson.AddressEnvelope()
```

The code first creates an *Employee* object. It then makes a *Person* variable and sets it equal to the *Employee* object. Polymorphism allows this because an *Employee* is a type of *Person*.

The code then calls the *Person* object's *AddressEnvelope* method. Even though the program uses a *Person* variable to refer to the object, the object knows that it is really an *Employee,* so it calls the *Employee* class's version of *AddressEnvelope*.

The syntax for overriding a member varies from language to language. In C#, the parent class must declare the parent class member with the *virtual* keyword, as in the following code. (Some languages, such as C# and C++, call a method that can be overridden *virtual*.)

```
public class Person
{
    string FirstName, LastName, Street, City, State, Zip;

    public virtual void AddressEnvelope()
    {
        MessageBox.Show("Person");
    }
}
```

In C#, the child class must declare the member with the *override* keyword, as in the following code:

```
public class Employee : Person
{
    public string MailStop;

    public override void AddressEnvelope()
    {
        MessageBox.Show("Employee");
    }
}
```

 **Note** In this example, the *AddressEnvelope* methods display message boxes rather than print envelopes, so you can tell which version of the method is executing.

In Visual Basic, the parent class must declare the member with the *Overridable* keyword, as in the following code:

```
Public Class Person
    Public FirstName, LastName, Street, City, State, Zip As String

    Public Overridable Sub AddressEnvelope()
        MessageBox.Show("Person.AddressEnvelope")
    End Sub
End Class
```

In Visual Basic, the child class must declare the new version of the member with the *Overrides* keyword, as in the following code:

```
Public Class Employee
    Inherits Person

    Public MailStop As String

    Public Overrides Sub AddressEnvelope()
        MessageBox.Show("Employee.AddressEnvelope")
    End Sub
End Class
```

**Tip** Programming languages provide syntax for accessing specific versions of an overridden method. For example, the code for an *Employee* object could access the *Person* class's version of the *AddressEnvelope* method if necessary. A Visual Basic program would use the syntax *MyBase.AddressEnvelope()*, and a C# program would use the syntax *base.AddressEnvelope()*.

Sometimes it is useful for a class to declare a member but not provide an implementation, forcing child classes to override the member. This lets the class define the syntax of a member without providing a specific implementation. This kind of member is called *abstract*.

Because the class doesn't include an implementation for the abstract member, the program cannot make an instance of the class. Otherwise, what would the program do if the code tried to call the abstract member for an object? Because the code cannot make an instance of the class, the class itself is also abstract. Any class that is not abstract is called *concrete*.

**Tip** You also can mark a class abstract if you don't want to allow the program to instantiate it directly, even if it doesn't contain any abstract members.

In C#, you declare a member or class to be abstract by using the *abstract* keyword, as shown in the following code:

```
public abstract class Person
{
    string FirstName, LastName, Street, City, State, Zip;

    public abstract void AddressEnvelope();
}
```

In Visual Basic, you use the *MustOverride* and *MustInherit* keywords to declare members and classes as abstract, as shown in the following code:

```
Public MustInherit Class Person
    Public FirstName, LastName, Street, City, State, Zip As String

    Public MustOverride Sub AddressEnvelope()
End Class
```

# Shadowing Members

A member can *shadow* another member in a parent class if it has the same signature (name and parameters, if any). In that case, the new member supersedes the old version. This is very similar to the way a class can override a parent class member, but shadowing changes the way polymorphism works. When a member shadows another version, a variable of the parent class that refers to an object of a subclass does not use the subclass's version of the member.

**Note** Overriding is more common than shadowing.

In C#, you use the *new* keyword to indicate that a new version of a member shadows another. For example, consider the following *Employee* class:

```
public class Employee : Person
{
    public string MailStop;

    public new void AddressEnvelope()
    {
        MessageBox.Show("Employee");
    }
}
```

This version of the *AddressEnvelope* method shadows the version defined by the *Person* class.

Suppose that two variables, a *Person* and an *Employee*, both refer to the same *Employee* object.

If the program calls the *Employee* object's *AddressEnvelope* method, the *Employee* class's version of that method executes. However, if the program calls the *Person* object's *AddressEnvelope* method, the *Person* class's version executes.

A Visual Basic program uses the *Shadows* keyword to indicate that a new version of a member shadows an existing version, as shown in the following code:

```
Public Class Employee
    Inherits Person

    Public MailStop As String

    Public Shadows Sub AddressEnvelope()
        MessageBox.Show("Employee")
    End Sub
End Class
```

 **Tip** In addition to overriding and shadowing methods, you can overload methods by creating new versions with different parameters.

## Inheritance Diagrams

An *inheritance diagram* is a drawing that makes it easy to visualize the inheritance relationships among classes. The normal convention uses rectangles to represent classes. A line ending in an arrowhead, with the arrowhead pointing to the parent class, indicates an inheritance relationship. If space permits, child classes are usually drawn below parent classes to make the direction of the inheritance clearer.

Figure 10-1 shows a simple inheritance diagram. In this example, the *CheckingAccount* and *SavingsAccount* classes both inherit from the *BankAccount* parent class. The *OverdraftAccount* class inherits from *CheckingAccount*.

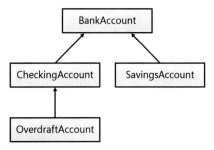

**FIGURE 10-1** Inheritance diagrams, such as this one, show the inheritance relationships among classes.

This simple inheritance diagram is easy to draw and easy to understand, so it's quite useful.

Sometimes people place additional information inside the class rectangles to give more information about the classes, such as their properties, methods, and events. Figure 10-2 shows the previous inheritance hierarchy with some additional detail.

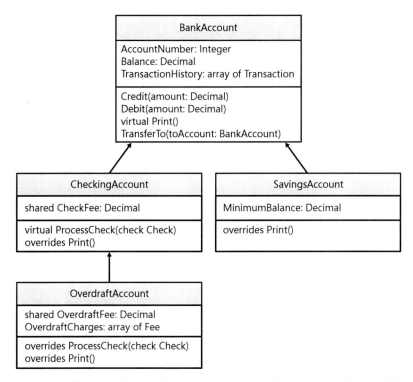

**FIGURE 10-2** You can add extra detail to an inheritance diagram to provide more information about the classes.

In this diagram, I've tried to include useful information without cluttering the result too much and without relying on special symbols. (Also, note that I've probably omitted a lot of information that a real banking application would need to include.) For example, this diagram uses keywords such as *shared*, *virtual*, and *overrides* as needed.

You can use many styles when drawing inheritance diagrams. A widely used standard for object-oriented design is the Universal Modeling Language (UML), which defines more than a dozen different kinds of diagrams for modeling object-oriented systems. You can use UML's class diagram to model inheritance, in addition to many other relationships among classes.

UML class diagrams use many special symbols for representing classes and their relationships. For example, they can use the symbols +, #, -, and ~ to flag members as public, protected, private, and package. Hollow arrowheads indicate inheritance, and other kinds of arrowheads indicate other relationships such as aggregation (one object is part of another, as in a *Wheel* is part of a *Car*). Other symbols indicate the number of objects in a relationship (1 car can be associated with 4 or 5 tires, counting an optional spare tire).

UML in general, and even class diagrams in particular, are too complicated to cover in detail here. For a brief introduction to UML, see *http://en.wikipedia.org/wiki/Unified_Modeling_Language*. UML was created and is managed by the Object Management Group (OMG). You can find more information about OMG at *www.omg.org*, and you can see their introduction to UML at *http://www.omg.org/gettingstarted/what_is_uml.htm*.

# Abstraction and Refinement

Abstraction and refinement are two ways to think about building inheritance hierarchies. Abstraction lets you build a hierarchy from the bottom up, using concrete classes to build parent classes. Refinement lets you build a hierarchy from the top down, using more general classes to build more specific classes.

## Abstraction

In *abstraction*, or *generalization*, you analyze two or more related classes and extract their common features into a parent class.

For example, suppose that you are writing a role-playing game and you know you want a *Dragon* class and a *Goblin* class. You want the *Dragon* class to have properties *HitsToKill* and *Speed*, and you want it to have methods *Bite* and *BreathFire*. You want the *Goblin* class to have *HitsToKill* and *Movement* properties and an *Attack* method.

**Note** This is a simplified model. To write a real role-playing game, you would probably need a lot more information.

It takes only a moment to realize that both classes have a *HitsToKill* property. You can avoid writing code to handle this property twice if you generalize the two classes to make a parent class, such as *Monster*. The *Monster* class can implement *HitsToKill*, and the *Dragon* and *Goblin* classes can inherit from it.

With a little more thought, you might decide that the *Dragon* class's *Speed* property is really the same as the *Goblin* class's *Movement* property, but with a different name. Similarly, the *Dragon* class's *Bite* method is the same as the *Goblin* class's *Attack* method. To save more code, you can move the *Bite* property and *Attack* method into the *Monster* class and let the other classes inherit them.

Figure 10-3 shows the inheritance hierarchy for the revised classes.

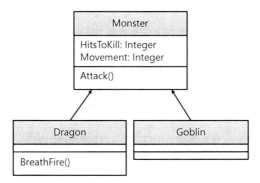

**FIGURE 10-3** The *Monster* class is an abstraction of the *Dragon* and *Goblin* classes.

Abstraction is a good technique for reducing code, but it has one danger: *overabstraction* or (*overgeneralization*). In overabstraction, you abstract more features from existing classes to create classes that aren't necessary for the program.

In this example, you might look at the *Dragon* and *Goblin* classes and, realizing that they are both animals, abstract them to form an *Animal* class. You could then move the *HitsToKill* and *Movement* properties into the new class, resulting in the inheritance diagram shown in Figure 10-4.

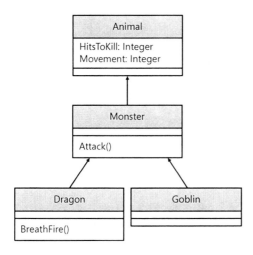

**FIGURE 10-4** Overabstraction leads to tall, thin inheritance hierarchies.

Although the model shown in Figure 10-4 can be considered a more accurate representation, the extra *Animal* class isn't really useful. It provides an extra level of detail, but the model worked just fine when the members of the *Animal* and *Monster* classes were contained in a single *Monster* class.

One clue that the new class is unnecessary is the fact that adding the class didn't add any new properties or methods, and that all the classes that you actually instantiate (*Dragon* and *Goblin*) have the same properties and methods they did before the change. Functionally, nothing has changed.

Unless the program needs to distinguish between animals and monsters (for example, if you add non-monster animals such as horses and kittens to the game), the *Animal* class complicates things unnecessarily.

In general, you should avoid tall, thin inheritance hierarchies. Short, wide hierarchies are usually simpler and more effective. If you notice a class that has only one child, such as the *Animal* class in Figure 10-4, you should ask yourself whether that class is really necessary.

## Refinement

In *refinement*, you look at a class and think of different variations of that class. You then make child classes to represent the different behaviors.

To continue the role-playing example, you might decide that you want to create two kinds of dragons: red dragons that cast spells, and spiny dragons that use their spiked tails to carry out an extra attack. In that case, you could add *RedDragon* and *SpinyDragon* classes as children of the *Dragon* class, as shown in Figure 10-5.

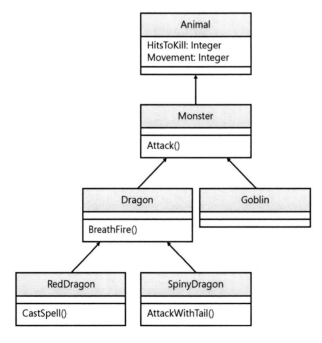

**FIGURE 10-5** Refinement adds new child classes to a model.

Just as you can use too much abstraction in a model, you also can use too much refinement. For example, suppose that you decide you want to break the *Goblin* class into *MountainGoblin* and *SwampGoblin* classes to get the hierarchy shown in Figure 10-6.

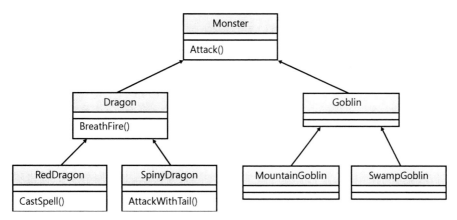

**FIGURE 10-6** Classes such as *MountainGoblin* and *SwampGoblin*, which are functionally the same, may be unnecessary.

If you look at Figure 10-6, you can see that the *MountainGoblin* and *SwampGoblin* classes don't add any new properties or methods, so they are functionally the same as their parent class. The only reason to create them is so the program can tell them apart and provide more detail for the user. For example, the program can add variety by telling the user "The mountain goblin attacks."

Because the two new classes don't add any real functionality, they are probably unnecessary. In this example, it would probably be better to add a new *Name* property somewhere in the hierarchy, perhaps in the *Monster* class, to provide this extra information. Then, the program can use the *Name* property to tell the user what kind of monster is attacking.

As another example, suppose that you wanted to add white dragons to the game, which are similar to red dragons except they breathe ice instead of fire. You could add a new *SpellCastingDragon* class that inherits from the *Dragon* class, and then make the *RedDragon* and *WhiteDragon* classes inherit from the new class.

As is the case with the *MountainGoblin* and *SwampGoblin* classes, however, the *RedDragon* and *WhiteDragon* classes would be virtually identical. A better solution would be to add a new *BreathType* property to the *Dragon* class. Then, the program could look up the monster's name and the breath weapon's name to give the user information such as "The white dragon breathes ice at you."

Note that the different inheritance hierarchies, with various combinations of the *Animal*, *MountainGoblin*, *SwampGoblin*, *SpellCastingDragon*, and *WhiteDragon* classes, do work; they just contain more classes than necessary. In most cases, if some classes are present only so that the program can differentiate among different kinds of objects, you probably can merge the classes and use a property to differentiate the objects instead. That makes the object model smaller and makes it easier to write one set of methods to handle all the different cases. In general, there may be many models that will work for a given application, however, so there aren't always right and wrong answers.

## "Is-A" Versus "Has-A"

Two common concepts in object-oriented design are "Is-A" and "Has-A."

An Is-A relationship, more formally called a *subclass* or *parent-child* relationship, is when one kind of object *is a* type of some other kind of object. For example, a *Customer* is a *Person*.

You can model Is-A relationships by using subclassing. For example, you can derive the *Customer* class from the *Person* class. The *Person* class includes all the properties and methods that are generally applicable to persons, and the *Customer* class adds those that apply only to customers. (Note that using two classes would be overrefinement if *Person* has no other child classes, such as *Employee*.)

A Has-A relationship, more formally called *composition*, is when one kind of object contains or is composed of another kind of object. For example, a *CustomerOrder* is (partly) composed of *OrderItems*.

You can model a Has-A relationship by giving one class a property that has the type of the other class. For example, the *CustomerOrder* class could have an *OrderItems* property that has an array of *OrderItem* objects.

## Multiple Inheritance and Interface Implementation

Some programming languages allow *multiple inheritance*, where a class can inherit from more than one parent class. For example, suppose that you have a *Domicile* class and a *Vehicle* class. You might want a *HouseBoat* class or a *MotorHome* class to inherit from both those classes.

Unfortunately neither Visual Basic nor C# allows multiple inheritance. In fact, most object-oriented languages support only single inheritance. You can, however, gain some of the benefits of inheritance from multiple parent classes by using interfaces and composition.

In Visual Basic and C#, you can define an interface. An *interface* defines a set of members that a class can provide. A class that *implements* the interface must provide those members.

In some ways, an interface acts as a parent class. In particular, a program can use interfaces polymorphically. For example, suppose you create an *IVehicle* interface (by convention, interface names begin with *I*) that defines the *SeatingCapacity* and *MaxSpeed* properties. Several classes, such as *Car*, *Truck*, and *MotorHome*, implement the interface. Then, a routine could take as a parameter an *IVehicle* object. No matter which class the object actually is (*Car*, *Truck*, or *MotorHome*), the routine knows that the object will provide *SeatingCapacity* and *MaxSpeed* properties so that the routine can use them. This makes the code easier to read and lets the development environment perform type checking (however, it would not allow a generic untyped *object* to use those properties).

Interface implementation provides half the solution to the *HouseBoat/MotorHome* problem. Instead of making these classes inherit from the *Domicile* and *Vehicle* classes, you can make them inherit from the *Domicile* class and then implement the *IVehicle* interface.

That provides the polymorphism; now, the classes can act as either *Domiciles* or *Vehicles*. Unfortunately, interface implementation does not provide code reuse the way inheritance does. In this example, if the *Domicile* class defines a *SquareFeet* property, both the *HouseBoat* and *MotorHome* classes inherit that property, but if the *IVehicle* interface defines a *MaxSpeed* property, each of the two classes must implement that property separately.

One solution to this problem is to create a separate *Vehicle* class in addition to the *IVehicle* interface. This class would implement the *IVehicle* interface and provide code to handle the *MaxSpeed* and whatever other properties are defined in the interface.

Now, the *HouseBoat* and *MotorBoat* classes can include a property that is an instance of the *Vehicle* class. To implement the members defined by the *IVehicle* interface, they invoke the members of their *Vehicle* objects.

The following Visual Basic code shows a simple *IVehicle* interface that defines the *MaxSpeed* property:

```
Public Interface IVehicle
    Property MaxSpeed() As Integer
End Interface
```

The following Visual Basic code shows a *Vehicle* class that implements the *IVehicle* interface:

```
Public Class Vehicle
    Implements IVehicle

    ' Implement IVehicle.
    Private _MaxSpeed As Integer
    Public Property MaxSpeed() As Integer Implements IVehicle.MaxSpeed
        Get
            Return _MaxSpeed
        End Get
        Set(ByVal value As Integer)
            _MaxSpeed = value
        End Set
    End Property
End Class
```

Notice the *Implements* statement that indicates that *Vehicle* implements *IVehicle*. Also, notice the *Implements IVehicle.MaxSpeed* syntax that indicates that the *MaxSpeed* method implements the *IVehicle* interface's *MaxSpeed* property.

The following code shows a simple *Domicile* class that provides the single field *SquareFeet*. (You could implement *SquareFeet* as a property instead of a field, but this code is slightly shorter and works just as well for this example.)

```
Public Class Domicile
    Public SquareFeet As Integer
End Class
```

Finally, the following code shows the *HouseBoat* class that inherits from *Domicile* and implements *IVehicle*:

```
Public Class HouseBoat
    Inherits Domicile
    Implements IVehicle

    ' Delegate IVehicle members.
    Private MyVehicle As New Vehicle()
    Public Property MaxSpeed() As Integer Implements IVehicle.MaxSpeed
        Get
            Return MyVehicle.MaxSpeed
        End Get
        Set(ByVal value As Integer)
            MyVehicle.MaxSpeed = value
        End Set
    End Property
End Class
```

This may seem a bit roundabout. The class includes a private *Vehicle* object named *MyVehicle* and then delegates the *IVehicle* members to that object, when the *HouseBoat* class could have just implemented them directly. In this example, adding the extra layer doesn't save any code and even makes things a bit more complex. However, this approach lets other classes that "inherit" from both the *Domicile* and *Vehicle* classes, such as *MotorHome* and *Camper*, use the same *Vehicle* class. They would each need to provide code to delegate to a *Vehicle* object, but if you needed to make changes to the *Vehicle* code, you could make those changes in the *Vehicle* class and the *HouseBoat*, *MotorHome*, and *Camper* classes would "inherit" the changes automatically.

The following code shows how a Visual Basic program could treat a *HouseBoat* object as a *Vehicle* and as a *Domicile*:

```
Dim houseBoat As New HouseBoat()
houseBoat.MaxSpeed = 10
houseBoat.SquareFeet = 150
```

The first statement declares and instantiates a *HouseBoat* object. The next statement sets the object's *MaxSpeed* property as defined by the *IVehicle* interface, and the last statement sets the *SquareFeet* field as inherited from the *Domicile* class.

The *HouseBoat* class doesn't really inherit from two parent classes, but in many ways, it acts like it does.

**Note** The code needed to build these classes and the interface in C# is a bit more cumbersome than the Visual Basic version because of the syntax that C# uses for interfaces, but the basic idea still works.

# Constructors and Destructors

You can define all sorts of methods for a class, but there are two kinds of methods that have a very special place in an object's lifetime: constructors and destructors.

## Constructors

A *constructor* is a method that is called automatically when the program creates a new instance of a class. When part of the program creates a new instance of the class, the system calls the appropriate constructor before it returns the new object to the code that created it.

You can use a constructor to initialize the object's properties and fields, get data for the object from a database, open resources, such as files, that the object will use, and generally prepare the object for use.

The syntax for constructors differs from language to language. In Visual Basic, a constructor is a subroutine (that returns no value) with the special name *New*. You can overload the constructor to create several versions, all named *New*, with different parameter lists.

> **Note** A constructor that takes no parameters is called a *parameterless constructor* or sometimes an *empty constructor*.

The following Visual Basic code shows a simple *Person* class with two constructors—one that takes no parameters and one that takes two:

```
Public Class Person
    Public FirstName, LastName As String

    ' Initialize the Person.
    Public Sub New()
        FirstName = ""
        LastName = ""
    End Sub

    ' Initialize the Person with the indicated values.
    Public Sub New(ByVal newFirstName As String, ByVal newLastName As String)
        FirstName = newFirstName
        LastName = newLastName
    End Sub
End Class
```

A constructor that uses its parameters to initialize the new object's fields, as the second constructor shown here does, is sometimes called an *initializing constructor*.

In C#, a constructor is a method that has the same name as the class, but which has no return type (not even *void*). The following code shows a C# version of this class:

```
public class Person
{
    public string FirstName, LastName;
```

```
    // Initialize the Person.
    public Person()
    {
        FirstName = "";
        LastName = "";
    }

    // Initialize the Person with the indicated values.
    public Person(string firstName, string lastName)
    {
        FirstName = firstName;
        LastName = lastName;
    }
}
```

Both Visual Basic and C# provide syntax that lets a child class's constructor invoke a constructor in the parent class or to invoke another constructor in the same class.

**Note** Neither Visual Basic nor C# allows a constructor to invoke more than one other constructor.

## Constructors in the Same Class

In Visual Basic, a constructor can use the *MyClass* keyword to invoke another constructor in the same class. The following code shows how a constructor that takes no parameters can invoke a constructor that takes first and last names as parameters:

```
' Initialize the Person.
Public Sub New()
    MyClass.New("", "")
End Sub
```

**Tip** Making one constructor call another in this way lets you reuse the code in the called constructor.

In C#, you can use the *this* keyword to invoke another constructor in the same class. The following code shows a C# version of the previous Visual Basic code:

```
// Initialize the Person.
public Person()
    : this("", "")
{
}
```

## Constructors in the Parent Class

In Visual Basic, a constructor can use the *MyBase* keyword to invoke a constructor in the parent class. The following code shows how a *Student* class constructor can invoke a constructor in the *Person* parent class:

```
' Initialize the Student with the indicated values.
Public Sub New(ByVal newFirstName As String, ByVal newLastName As String)
    ' Invoke the parent class's constructor.
    MyBase.New(newFirstName, newLastName)
End Sub
```

In C#, you can use the *base* keyword to invoke a parent class constructor. The following code shows a C# version of the previous Visual Basic code:

```
// Initialize the Student with the indicated values.
public Student(string firstName, string lastName)
    : base(firstName, lastName)
{
}
```

# Destructors

Constructors are executed when a new object is created. Destructors are executed when a new object is destroyed.

An object can be destroyed when the last referring variable stops referring to it. For example, a routine might create an *Invoice* object and work with it for a while. When the routine ends, the variable referring to the object no longer exists, so no variable points to the object. At that point, the object could be destroyed, and its destructor would execute.

Because the code that you write doesn't explicitly call the destructor, there's no way to pass parameters to it, so the destructor cannot take parameters. That also means you cannot overload the destructor for a class because any two destructors would need to have the same parameter list containing no parameters.

In Visual Basic, a destructor is a special routine named *Finalize*. It overrides a protected method that is predefined for the class, so you need to use the keyword *Protected Overrides* in the declaration. The following code shows a destructor that displays a message in the output window:

```
' Free resources.
Protected Overrides Sub Finalize()
    MessageBox.Show("Person destroyed")
End Sub
```

In C#, the destructor is a method named after the class with a tilde character (~) in front of it. The following code shows a destructor similar to the previous Visual Basic version:

```
~Person()
{
    Console.WriteLine("Person destroyed");
}
```

You may have noticed that earlier in the chapter, I said, "An object *can* be destroyed when the last referring variable stops referring to it," I didn't say that the object *would* be destroyed. An object with no variables referring to it is destroyed immediately in some languages, but in .NET, it's not clear when the object is actually destroyed because .NET uses a garbage collection scheme.

## Garbage Collection

When a program creates an object and then releases the variables pointing to it, the program loses the ability to refer to the memory that the object occupied. That memory becomes lost, and in .NET, the program cannot reuse that memory.

After a while, the program may have lost a lot of memory in this way and may have trouble allocating memory for new objects. When the available memory becomes low enough, the garbage collector (GC) runs to reclaim the lost memory.

The GC first marks all the memory that could be available for use, including the "lost" memory, as not in use. It then examines all the variables currently accessible to the program and marks their memory as in use. When the GC finishes this process, any memory that is still marked as not in use really is not in use, so the GC *reclaims it* (that is, makes it available again so that the program can use it to create new objects).

Because you can't predict when garbage collection will occur, you don't know exactly when unused objects will be destroyed. The idea that you don't know when objects will truly be destroyed or finalized is called *non-deterministic finalization*.

## IDisposable

For many objects, non-deterministic finalization isn't a problem. The program loses access to an object, and the object's memory sits around "lost" until garbage collection eventually occurs. This can cause problems, however, if the object allocates scarce resources that must be freed. For example, if an object opens a file and keeps it open, other processes may have trouble writing into the file or deleting it.

You might try to free the resources in the class's destructor. Unfortunately, due to non-deterministic finalization, you don't know when the object will really be destroyed and its destructor executed. If the program doesn't use a lot of memory, the object may not be destroyed until the program ends.

To work around this problem, you can make a class implement the *IDisposable* interface. This interface requires the class to implement one method, *Dispose*, that should free the object's resources.

Calling *Dispose* isn't automatic, however. The program should call an object's *Dispose* method before losing access to the object. If the program doesn't call *Dispose*, it's not the end of the world. It just means that the object's resources aren't freed until it is finally destroyed.

That raises one final complication: the destructor must be able to release the object's resources if *Dispose* wasn't called, but it should not release the resources a second time if *Dispose* already released them.

To summarize:

- When memory runs low, the GC runs to reclaim lost memory.

- You don't know when the GC will run (non-deterministic finalization).

- An object's destructor isn't called until it is finally destroyed. Due to non-deterministic finalization, you don't know when that will be, so you cannot rely on the destructor alone to free resources.

- To allow the program to free resources, you should make the class implement the *IDisposable* interface. The *Dispose* method should free the resources.

- The destructor should free resources if and only if the *Dispose* method did not.

Of course, none of this is an issue if the class doesn't control scarce resources that must be freed.

 **More Info** For more information on the IDisposable interface, see *http://msdn.microsoft .com/library/system.idisposable.aspx.*

# Summary

This chapter explained the basics of classes and OOP. It listed some of the benefits of OOP, such as encapsulation, code reuse, and polymorphism, and described the members of classes, properties, methods, and events. The chapter covered how inheritance allows a child class to inherit members from a parent class. It also explained how a child class can modify inherited members by overriding or shadowing them.

Although most object-oriented languages, including C# and Visual Basic, do not allow multiple inheritance, this chapter showed how you can gain many of the same benefits by using interfaces and composition. Finally, this chapter covered constructors that execute when an object is created and destructors that execute when an object is destroyed.

OOP is a big topic, and this chapter covers only the basics. However, with a little study, this should be enough information to get you started and to give you the background you need to understand other books and online information about object-oriented design and programming.

Classes and objects provide some important benefits, such as code reuse and inheritance, but there are other, non-object-oriented techniques that also can make programs easier to write, debug, and maintain. The next chapter describes some of those techniques, such as using comments effectively, following naming conventions, and building generic classes.

# Chapter 11

# Development Techniques

**In this chapter:**

- The benefits of comments

- Extensible Markup Language (XML) comments in .NET and IntelliSense support

- Naming conventions

- Development techniques

- Agile, extreme, and test-driven development

**MANY FACTORS DETERMINE THE QUALITY OF** a finished application. These include everything from the quality of the development environment to the quality of the programmers. Some of these factors are out of your control. For example, the development platform and staff are often assumed before the project really gets started.

However, you do have some control over other factors, such as the quality of the comments you write and what development approach you use.

This chapter discusses some of these issues. It explains good commenting and naming conventions and some popular development approaches that you can use to increase the quality of your programs.

## Comments

Ironically, one of the most important programming statements is a statement that doesn't make the computer do anything: the comment.

This makes perfect sense if you think about programs as written for programmers rather than for the computer. The computer doesn't care whether you write a program using nicely formatted *for* loops and well-defined classes or a tangled mess of *go to* statements. In fact, the computer can't really execute a program the way you write it anyway. The computer first must convert the program into machine code before executing it. If the goal were to make programs easy for the computer to execute, you would write in machine code.

High-level programming languages, such as C++, C#, and Microsoft Visual Basic, are designed to make it easy for programmers to understand a program. They include elements such as *for each* loops, routines, and classes that make it easier to write code that a programmer can understand.

When you write a particular piece of code, it is essential that you understand how it is supposed to work. When you debug or modify code later (or someone else does), understanding the code is even more critical. If you don't completely understand the code, you are much more likely to introduce new bugs as you modify it.

Studies have shown that a programmer is more likely to introduce a bug while editing old code than while writing new code. That old code was once new code, so why should it suddenly have become more fragile? That isn't it, actually; it's that the programmer doesn't have the same rich understanding of the code that the original author had. Even if you're modifying code that you originally wrote, you probably don't have the full picture in mind when you're editing the code. It's very common to move right to a piece of code that contains a bug or that needs modification and not bother to rediscover all the intricacies of the rest of the surrounding code.

You can help later programmers (even if it turns out to be you) understand the code more completely by using explanatory comments. If you use good, descriptive names for objects and variables, code can be relatively self-documenting, but you can make it a lot easier to understand the code if you add instructive comments.

Comments should not simply repeat the code. For example, the comment for the statement x  += 1 should not simply say "Increment x." That is obvious from the statement itself. Instead, the comment should explain why the statement is incrementing *x*. For example, a better comment might say "Move to the next *X* position in the data to plot the next point on the graph."

Some developers believe you should include a comment only if it is absolutely necessary to understand the code. I disagree with this philosophy. The idea is to make it as easy as possible for programmers to understand the code, not to conserve space. This idea also encourages programmers to use fewer comments than they should. While you are writing a piece of code, you have a good understanding of it, so naturally you don't need many comments to know how it works. When another programmer looks at the code, or when you look at it much later, you don't have all this background knowledge in your head, and it's much harder to figure out what the code is doing.

Instead of including comments only where absolutely necessary, I include comments unless they are absolutely *un*necessary. You shouldn't fill the code with so many comments that it's hard to read, but you should include enough information so a less-experienced programmer can figure out quickly what the code does.

In my many years of programming, I have never worked on a project where too many comments hurt the project, but I have worked on several where too few comments caused a lot of harm.

On one C project, our team wrote an algorithm containing several thousand lines of code. We used a first tier of comments in the code to explain in general what the program was doing. Off to the right of the code, we included even more comments explaining what individual lines of code were doing. You didn't even see those comments unless you wanted to and scrolled to the right. After we finished the project, we transferred it to another part of the company for maintenance. The people in this area had a policy that comments were prohibited unless they were absolutely essential, so they removed most of our comments. A few months later, though, they couldn't maintain the code because they couldn't figure out how it worked.

In a second project, I helped maintain a Visual Basic program containing more than 50,000 lines of code and around 500 comments. The comments were so sparse that they could give only a general idea of what the routines did and couldn't give any help in understanding how they worked. On that project, it was common for a developer to spend a week or more trying to understand how a piece of code worked before making a simple change in one or two lines of code. Often, what seemed like a simple change in one piece of code would cause unexpected consequences in another piece of code so the programmer would need to study other routines to figure out what they did and how they worked. Much of that extra work could have been avoided if the code had contained more comments.

# Types of Comments

There are several levels at which you might need to understand a piece of code, and there are comments appropriate for each of those levels. To decide whether you need to use a class and to understand how the classes work together, you need only a high-level overview of the class. For example, to use the *Obstacle* class in a puzzle program, you need to know generally what an *Obstacle* represents.

The same applies to code modules, libraries, and any other high-level grouping of routines. To use the *Crypt* library, you need to know that it contains classes and routines for performing cryptography.

To make it easy to understand classes, code modules, and libraries, each should begin with a block comment explaining the purpose and general ideas behind it. For example, the *Crypt* library's comment should explain that it is a cryptography library and give an overview of how to use it. If this requires a lengthy explanation, you can move it into an external document and then refer to it in the comment.

To use a routine or class member effectively, you need an overview of that item. You need to know what parameters to pass into the routine, what the routine does, and what value it returns, if any.

To provide this information, begin each routine or class member with a brief comment explaining what it does and describing parameters and return values. If the code makes assumptions, such as an input array already being sorted or a parameter being greater than zero, spell that out in the comment.

To debug or modify a routine or class member, you need a much more in-depth understanding of what the routine does and how it works. Add comments within the code to explain what the code is doing. Also, explain why the code does what it does. A good programmer can eventually figure out what the code does, but figuring out why it does what it does can be a difficult, time-consuming, and sometimes frustrating process.

# XML Comments

Microsoft Visual Studio allows you to add a special kind of comment to code: Extensible Markup Language (XML) comments. These are special comments that contain XML tokens indicating the meaning of various parts of the comments. The comments are indicated by three comment characters: ''' in Visual Basic or /// in C#.

For example, the following code shows the declaration for a simple factory method that uses a student's first and last names to create a new *Student* object:

```
/// <summary>
/// Returns a Student object populated from the database.
/// </summary>
/// <param name="firstName">The first name of the student to find.</param>
/// <param name="lastName">The last name of the student to find.</param>
/// <returns>A Person object initialized from the database.</returns>
public static Student FindStudent(string firstName, string lastName)
{
    ...
}
```

(Note that the comments shown here aren't particularly informative. I kept them short mostly so that the tooltips shown in Figures 11-1 and 11-2 wouldn't be too long and would fit reasonably well in the book.)

XML comments have two benefits: they support IntelliSense and they support automatic documentation.

## IntelliSense Support

The first benefit of XML comments is that they allow the IntelliSense feature in Visual Studio to give programmers extra information when writing code that uses a method. For example, when you highlight a method in the code editor, IntelliSense displays the text in a *summary* XML comment, as shown in Figure 11-1.

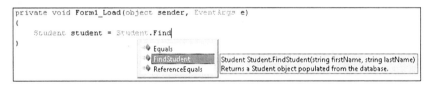

**FIGURE 11-1** IntelliSense describes a method by displaying the text in a *summary* XML comment.

When you need to enter parameters, IntelliSense displays the text in the corresponding *param* XML comment, as shown in Figure 11-2.

```
private void Form1_Load(object sender, EventArgs e)
{
    Student student = Student.FindStudent(|
```
Student Student.FindStudent (**string firstName**, string lastName)
**firstName:**
The first name of the student to find.

**FIGURE 11-2** IntelliSense describes parameters by displaying the text in *param* XML comments.

IntelliSense tooltips such as these can be extremely helpful to programmers who are using classes and routines that they didn't write.

## Automatic Documentation

The second benefit to XML comments is that you can extract them to create documentation. Visual Studio can extract the comments automatically for you if you set it up correctly.

To make Visual Studio extract comments, right-click the project in Solution Explorer and select Properties. Select the Build tab and scroll down until you can see the XML Documentation File check box. Select that box and enter the name and path for the resulting XML file, as shown in Figure 11-3.

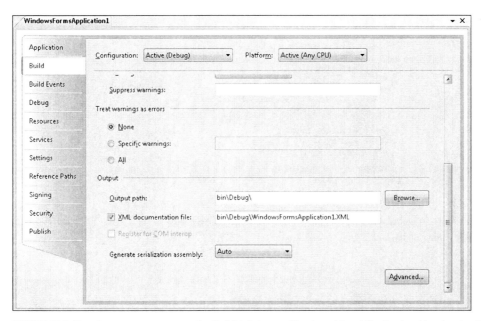

**FIGURE 11-3** Use the property page on the Build tab to specify where Visual Studio should put extracted XML comments.

The resulting XML file contains your comments, along with information about other automatically generated symbols defined by the program. Now, you can use other programs to pull the information that you want from this file and turn it into documentation. For example, you could use an Extensible Stylesheet Language Transformation (XSLT) program to convert the XML file into a formatted document. XML and XSLT are outside the scope of this book. For more information on them, search online or look for books about XML.

## Creating XML Comments

To create XML comments in Visual Studio, create the method's declaration and then place three comment characters on a blank line before the method. When you add the third character, Visual Studio creates an XML comment with places where you can fill in summary, parameter, and return information.

The comment includes only sections that are relevant to the declaration that you have written. This example includes two parameters, so the comment initially included two *param* tags to describe the parameters. (Visual Basic also includes a *remarks* tag, which isn't included in C#.)

## Supported XML Comments

XML comments include two types of tags: primary tags and supporting tags.

Primary tags can sit by themselves and cannot be contained by other tags. Table 11-1 summarizes the primary tags supported by Visual Studio.

**TABLE 11-1** Primary Tags in Visual Studio

| Tag | Purpose |
| --- | --- |
| example | Example showing usage. |
| exception | Exceptions that the code may throw. |
| include | Indicates documentation should include an external file here. |
| param | Describes a parameter. |
| permission | Permission-related information. This could be an accessibility value such as *public* or *friend,* or it could indicate necessary user permissions. |
| remarks | General clarifying remarks. |
| returns | Describes the return value. |
| seealso | A reference to more information. |
| summary | Overview of the method. |

Supporting tags provide extra formatting information within a primary tag. For example, a *list* tag could indicate that items inside a *remarks* section should be formatted as a list. The following table summarizes Visual Studio's supporting tags.

**TABLE 11-2** Supporting Tags in Visual Studio

| Tag | Purpose |
| --- | --- |
| c | Marks a piece of text as code, often inline. |
| code | Marks multiple lines of text as code. |
| description | Gives the description of a term. Must be contained within an *item* tag. |
| list | Defines a list. Uses *listheader, item,* and *term* tags to define the list's items. |
| listheader | Defines a list's header. |
| item | Defines an item in a list. May contain *term* and *description* tags. |
| para | Defines a paragraph. |
| paramref | Used to refer to a parameter defined by a *param* tag. |

| | |
|---|---|
| *see* | Specifies a hyperlink. |
| *term* | Gives the name of a term. Must be contained within an *item* tag. |
| *value* | Describes the meaning of a property. |

 **More Info** For more information on XML comments, see *http://msdn.microsoft.com/library/ b2s063f7.aspx and http://msdn.microsoft.com/magazine/dd722812.aspx.*

# Naming Conventions

Back in the old days, some programming languages restricted variable names to no more than six characters. But modern languages let you use very long names, so it's easy nowadays to give descriptive names to classes, routines, properties, and other programming items. For example, instead of naming a variable *PCSTNO*, you can name it *PreferredCustomerNumber*.

Development environments such as Visual Studio also provide name completion features that let you enter long names quickly without a lot of extra typing. In Visual Studio, when you start typing a name, IntelliSense displays a list of possible matches. If you select the one you want and press the Tab key, IntelliSense fills in the rest for you. This kind of feature lets you use longer, more descriptive names without taking you more time to type.

Naming conventions make it easier for developers on a project to create similar names. That makes reading the code easier, which increases comprehension and decreases bugs.

Different programming groups and programmers using different languages tend to have different naming conventions, and it's impossible to say that any particular one is the best. A few general guidelines, however, are worth mentioning.

Some common naming conventions (many recommended by Microsoft) include:

- Use natural word ordering; for instance, *NextPlayer* instead of *PlayerNext*.

- Use descriptive names, not short ones.

- Do not use underscores, hyphens, or other non-alphanumeric characters.

- Do not use Hungarian notation (using a prefix to give extra information about a variable).

- Do not use names that are also keywords in widely used languages such as C, C++, C#, or Visual Basic, such as *Function*, *Sub*, or *For*.

- Do not use abbreviations or contractions.

- Only use acronyms that are widely accepted.

- Begin method names with verbs; for instance, *PrintReport* and *FindStudent*.

- Begin class, structure, module, and property names with a noun; for instance, *Student* and *ItemCost*.

- Begin interface names with *I* followed by a noun; for instance, *IVehicle* and *ISortable*.

- Begin event handler names with a noun followed by *EventHandler;* for instance, *MouseDownEventHandler.*

- Avoid using the same name in different scopes, such as creating a variable named *PlayerNum* at the class level and another variable named *PlayerNum* inside a method.

- Use forms of the verb "to be" (is, was, will be, and so on) for Boolean values; for instance, *IsDisconnected* and *WasShipped.*

- For public members, use *Pascal casing,* where every word is capitalized; for instance, *GenerateSalesReport.*

- For private members (including variables inside routines), use *camel casing,* where every word except the first is capitalized; for instance, *generateSalesReport.*

- For property backing fields, use a leading underscore, for instance, *_numEmployees.*

Not all developers follow these rules. For example, some use underscores instead of Pascal casing, as in *customer_last_overdue_bill_date* instead of *CustomerLastOverdueBillDate.*

When a program works with a value entered in a control on a form, it must have some way to distinguish between the control and the variable holding the control's value. You can't name both *FirstName.* Some developers distinguish between the two by using *control prefix notation* to give the type of a control. For example, a *TextBox* holding a customer's first name might be called *txtFirstName.* This also makes it easier to find the control in IntelliSense. (This is not quite the same as Hungarian notation, which uses prefixes to identify a variable's data type and scope to make type checking easier.)

Some purists think that it shouldn't matter whether a customer's name is typed by the user in a *TextBox,* selected from a *ListBox,* or automatically populated in a *Label* control, so the control's name should indicate that it is a control, but not what kind. Some developers use *ui* (for "User Interface") or *ux* (for "User Experience") for all control types.

Many C++ and C# developers and developers at Microsoft use a control postfix, as in *FirstNameTextBox.*

C# developers usually use Pascal and camel casing, no underscores, and control name postfixes.

Visual Basic developers, particularly with older code, often use Pascal casing for public class members, lowercase with underscores for private members, and control prefixes in all cases. This may change over time, particularly if Microsoft continues to recommend the C#-style conventions.

You should decide which conventions make the most sense to you and try to use them consistently. Using whatever naming convention you pick consistently will make your code easy to read and understand. It's more important that you pick a convention and stick to it rather than picking any particular convention.

For more detailed conventions recommended by Microsoft, see these links:

- *http://msdn.microsoft.com/library/ms229002.aspx*

- *http://msdn.microsoft.com/library/ms229045.aspx*

- *http://msdn.microsoft.com/library/0b283bse.aspx*

# Development Techniques

There are many approaches to designing and building applications. One thing they all have in common is that they put design first. Often, it is tempting to sit down and start cranking out code without first creating a well-defined plan. For very simple programs that won't be used for very long, that may be good enough. For anything but the most trivial program, however, it's a huge mistake.

A solid design can help you better understand the application and how its pieces fit together. The better you understand the code, the less likely you are to make mistakes.

This issue is compounded when many developers work together. If different developers have different ideas about how the application (or even parts of it) should work, they are likely to write code that is incompatible, resulting in bugs that often can be quite subtle and hard to track down.

Although it is tempting to just start writing code, it's worth taking the time to plan things out beforehand. Over the lifetime of a project, fixing bugs can take up a large fraction of the project's total cost, so spending some extra time up front to reduce the number of bugs in the system is always worth the expense.

The following sections describe several approaches for designing and implementing applications. Even if you don't adopt one of these, you may find some of the concepts useful.

## Data-centric Viewpoint

Most commercial applications involve data to one extent or another. In fact, many applications are little more than user interfaces for manipulating a database. For example, a customer order and inventory system might be built around a database holding customer orders and inventory data. Forms would allow users to create new orders, add and remove items from orders, and track orders through the system as they are filled, sent to customers, and billed.

For this kind of application, it is often useful to design the database first. You can think about the kinds of information that the application needs and how it should be arranged to make an efficient and robust database. My book *Beginning Database Design Solutions* (Wrox, 2008) explains how to design efficient and robust databases.

After you know what tables the database will contain, you can design forms to let the user work with the tables. One-to-one relationships between tables often indicate data that you can include on the same form. One-to-many relations often indicate that you need a scrolling control that can hold any number of items.

For example, suppose that the *Order* table contains basic information about an order, such as the *CustomerId* (linking to the *Customer* table), *OrderId*, and other fields such as *OrderedDate*, *ShippedDate*, and *PaidDate*. The *OrderItem* table contains records describing the items in an order. This table also has an *OrderId* field that links to the *Order* table. The *OrderItem* records for an *Order* are those having the same *OrderId*.

In this example, an order form could contain labels or text boxes to hold the order's dates. It also could display the customer's name, address, phone number, and other relevant information.

Because one *Order* record could correspond to any number of *OrderItem* records, the form couldn't have a single entry (or even a fixed number of entries) for order items. Instead, it can display item information in a *ListBox*, *ListView*, or other scrollable control.

## User-centric Viewpoint

An alternative to the data-centric design approach is to focus on the needs of the user, design a user interface to meet those needs, and then build a database to support the design.

In an order tracking example, the user would need a form that lets him or her enter order information (dates), customer information (contact information and addresses), and information about the items ordered. Buttons also would be needed to add and remove items and to accept or cancel the order.

Figure 11-4 shows one possible result. This form uses multiple tabs to display groups of information about the order (the dates) and the customer (contact information and various addresses).

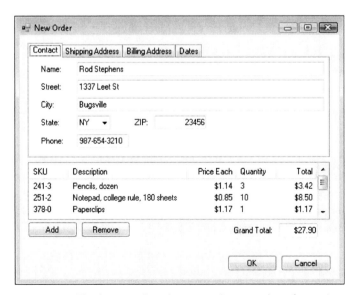

**FIGURE 11-4** The data-centric and user-centric approaches often arrive at a similar solution.

Data-centric and user-centric approaches often lead to a similar solution, but sometimes one approach picks up some detail that the other misses. In this example, taking a user-centric viewpoint might make you realize that the user needs Add and Remove buttons, while you might not think of that using a data-centric viewpoint.

Sometimes the two viewpoints can arrive at very different solutions where the user interface converts the data in a major way. For example, the user interface might display a graph or bar chart showing data stored in the database.

To get the greatest benefit, it's often useful to look at a problem from both viewpoints, at least briefly.

# Agile Development

Agile software development is an approach that focuses on building projects incrementally, using frequent builds, to ensure that the project works at some level almost continually.

The 12 principles of agile development are summarized in the following list:

1. Satisfy customers by rapidly delivering useful software with frequent incremental improvements.

2. Handle changing requirements at all stages of development.

3. Deliver working software frequently.

4. Require close daily interaction between businesspeople and developers.

5. Give motivated individuals the tools and environments they need to do the work, and then trust them to do it.

6. Communicate with face-to-face conversations.

7. Measure progress with the delivery of working software.

8. Work at a sustainable pace (no 60-hour weeks to meet deadlines).

9. Pay constant attention to technical excellence and good design.

10. Keep things simple.

11. Use self-organizing teams.

12. Regularly reflect on progress and make adjustments to improve future progress.

Many agile teams perform weekly builds so that the project can run at least once a week. Frequent builds help reveal bugs as quickly as possible so developers can't go too far down an incorrect path before being caught and corrected.

I have heard some agile developers say that you're not using agile methods unless you follow all 12 of the principles. Whether you call your development process agile or not, incorporating some of these principles can probably help increase the success of your projects. For example, performing frequent builds as the project incrementally approaches its goals will reduce bugs in any development effort.

 **More Info** For more information on agile development, see *http://en.wikipedia.org/wiki/ Agile_development* and *agilemanifesto.org*.

## Extreme Programming

Extreme programming uses some of the same general ideas as agile development. The central ideas include creating frequent small releases that gradually approach the project's goals. A representative customer must be available at all times to answer questions, programmers are highly motivated, and—if they get the tools they need—work progresses at a sustainable pace.

Some of the other techniques used by extreme programming are worth mentioning because they can benefit many projects.

For example, extreme programming encourages programmers to code to the specific problem, not a general solution. Many traditional development groups plan far ahead and try to make solutions to specific problems as general as possible. That may be useful later, but the general solution often isn't all that helpful for later projects and must be modified before it can be reused. Programmers sometimes spend far too much time perfecting extremely flexible code that is never fully used. In extreme programming, developers solve the problem at hand and nothing more. Only later, if you discover that a tool must be reused, should you generalize the software.

Another extreme programming tool is pair programming. Here, one programmer, called the "driver," writes code and explains what he is doing while another programmer watches and studies the code. Every now and then, the programmers switch roles. Having two people focused on the same piece of code often can catch mistakes and incorrect assumptions that a single programmer would miss. With some practice (and this method does require practice), two programmers working together can write almost as much code as they would separately in a given timeframe, but with much higher quality.

 **More Info** For more information on extreme programming, see *http://www .extremeprogramming.org, http://www.extremeprogramming.org/rules.html,* and *http://en.wikipedia.org/wiki/Extreme_Programming*.

One particularly useful technique used by extreme programming that has gained popularity in many other development approaches is test-driven development.

# Test-driven Development

In test-driven development, programmers write testing routines to determine whether a piece of software satisfies its requirements before writing the software itself. They then write the software and validate it against the tests. If the software doesn't pass the tests, it is improved until it does. Fixing the software may uncover other special cases that require new tests. The process repeats until the software passes all the tests.

Ideally, tests are performed on the smallest pieces of code possible. For example, before you write a new routine, you write tests for it, so when it is finished, you have a high-quality routine that has already been thoroughly tested before you plug it into the rest of the project. As larger pieces of the project are assembled, you write tests for them, too, and improve the code until it passes all its tests.

Test-driven development has several important benefits. First, frequent testing helps reveal bugs quickly, before they become deeply embedded in the system. Bugs are much easier to fix if they are found shortly after they are introduced. Ideally, test-driven development will find most bugs right after they are written so that they can't contaminate other code with incorrect assumptions.

A second benefit of test-driven development is that it requires programmers to write lots of tests, something they are often reluctant to do. After you write a piece of code, it's natural to assume that it is correct. After all, if you knew there was a problem in your code, you would fix it. Making programmers write tests before writing the code encourages them to write more tests.

Writing tests before writing code also helps programmers write the tests without preconceptions about how the code works so that they don't avoid testing cases that they "know" the code can handle. You can decrease preconceptions further if different programmers write the tests and the code being tested.

Finally, test-driven development produces a *lot* of tests. With little extra work, you can incorporate those tests into an automated testing tool so that you can rerun the tests later to see if recent changes have broken any of the older code. If you can rerun the tests easily, you are more likely to run them frequently. Doing so allows you to find and fix bugs quickly, while they are still relatively easy to find.

One particularly useful kind of test that is also easy to implement is an assertion. An *assertion* is a statement about the state of the program that the code claims to be true. If it is not true, then the program throws an error, so you can look into the code and see what's wrong.

In .NET, the *Diagnostics* namespace contains a *Debug* class, which has an *Assert* method that makes it easy to make assertions. The method's first parameter is a Boolean statement. If the statement is false at run time, the method throws an exception. Other parameters let you specify messages to display when the method throws an exception.

The following code shows part of a *SortEmployees* method that includes some input and output assertions:

```
Public Function SortEmployees(ByVal employees() As Employee) As Employee()
    ' Input assertions.
    Debug.Assert(employees IsNot Nothing, _
        "SortEmployees: Parameter employees is missing")
```

```
        Debug.Assert(employees.Length > 1, _
            "SortEmployees: Too few employees")
        Debug.Assert(employees.Length < 100, _
            "SortEmployees: Too many employees ")

        ' Sort the employees.
        Dim result(0 To employees.Length - 1) As Employee
        '...

        ' Output assertions.
        For i As Integer = 1 To employees.Length - 1
            Debug.Assert(result(i).EmployeeId > result(i - 1).EmployeeId, _
                "SortEmployees: Sorting error.")
        Next i

        ' Return the result.
        Return result
End Function
```

When the code starts, it uses *Debug.Assert* to verify that the array of *Employee* objects that it should sort is present (not *Nothing*), holds at least 2 objects, and contains fewer than 100 objects. If the first test fails, the program contains a bug that should be fixed. If one of the other two tests fails, the code calling this method might contain a bug because the number of objects is outside the expected range. After investigation, if you determine that the number of objects should be allowed, you can change the tests to be more lenient.

When you make a debug build of the program, the *Debug.Assert* statements check their conditions and throws exceptions if appropriate. When you make a release build, the *Debug.Assert* statements are removed from the project. That means that you can add as many of these as you like without hurting the performance of the final released project. It also means that you must ensure that the program can run even if an assertion fails.

In this example, if testing doesn't find a special case where the program passes *SortEmployees* an empty array, the program should be able to run anyway without crashing. The idea that code should be able to run even under unexpected conditions is called *defensive programming*.

The main ideas behind defensive programming are that it reduces bugs and that it makes the code run more consistently under unexpected conditions. Unfortunately, defensive programming actually hides bugs rather than reducing them. Making the *SortEmployees* method robust is good for that method, but if another piece of code is passing it an empty array, then that other code probably contains a bug. If you make *SortEmployees* silently continue and return a reasonable result, you hide the bug in the other code and make it harder to find. It may only be much later, in a completely different piece of code, that the incorrect result surfaces and you notice that something is wrong.

The best solution is to use the combination of assertions and robust code that can keep running even if there is an error. When you are testing the program, the assertions uncover bugs quickly. When you give the user a release build, the program won't crash even if an assertion fails.

# Summary

This chapter discussed some techniques that you can use to improve the quality of your software. It explained how to use comments and naming conventions to make reading and understanding code easier. It also provided brief introductions to several popular development approaches, including agile, extreme, and test-driven development.

Even if you don't adopt one of those approaches in its entirety, some of the ideas they use are worth adopting. For example, frequent incremental releases, focusing on immediate needs instead of overgeneralizing code, and input and output assertions can make your code more effective, reliable, and maintainable.

Design and development are huge topics, however, and this chapter barely scratched the surface, so you should spend some time looking into this topic further. Many books and websites are dedicated to different design methodologies, and the more you learn about them, the better. Even if you have no control over the methodology that your programming team uses, you may be able to pick up some useful techniques that you can add to your code.

When programmers think of bugs, they usually think of code that crashes the program or that produces incorrect results, but if you write applications used in different parts of the world, a program may produce correct results that are displayed incorrectly.

For example, suppose that a program adds up some costs and displays the value in dollars: $1,234.56. The number may be correct, but users in Germany will expect to see 1.234,56 €, and users in Great Britain will expect to see £1,234.56.

The next chapter discusses globalization: the process of making an application work correctly in multiple locales. It discusses some of the issues involved in globalization and explains how to globalize applications in .NET.

# Chapter 12

# Globalization

**In this chapter:**

* Globalization terminology

* Culture codes

* Locale-specific text and symbols

* Localizing user interfaces in Microsoft Visual Studio

* Locale-specific formats

* Culture-aware .NET functions

**IN RECENT YEARS, PARTICULARLY WITH THE** exponential growth of the Internet, the world is much smaller than it used to be. A program that you write and post online today can be in use all over the world in a matter of hours.

Some applications are really usable only locally, but for many applications, it makes sense to create versions that can run globally. Sometimes it takes only a little extra work to make a program usable in many countries. If you post such an application and there is enough demand for it in a particular region, you can spend more effort making your program available there and possibly open up a whole new market.

This chapter discusses some of the issues that you face when you try to write a program for use in other parts of the world. It explains some of the most important regional differences and ways that you can handle them, particularly in .NET applications.

# Terminology

Several terms are used to describe different aspects of globalization. Some of the terms have similar meanings, and although many developers use them interchangeably, it's useful to know the differences.

A *locale* identifies a country and region. As far as a program is concerned, it identifies the cultural conventions used in a particular area, including such things as language and fonts, and formats for such values as dates, times, numbers, and currency values.

Every computer has a defined locale that tells the operating system how to format values. For example, if your system is set up for a French locale, it will format numbers using spaces for thousands separators and commas for decimal separators, as in 1 234,45 (1,234.45 in American format).

*Localization* is the process of making a program support a single, specific locale. That includes using an appropriate font, text in the locale's language, images and icons that make sense for that locale, and appropriate formatting for times, dates, numbers, and other values.

According to Microsoft, *globalization* is the process of making a program support multiple locales. Some developers use the term *internationalization* to mean the process of making a program capable of easily supporting different locales and the term *globalization* to mean both internationalization and localization. (At this level, the difference seems like splitting hairs.)

# Culture Codes

In .NET programming, you set a program's locale by specifying a culture. A *neutral culture* is associated with a language, but not a particular country or region. A *specific culture* is a neutral culture, together with a country or region.

For example, *en-US* has the neutral culture code "en," meaning English and the country code "US," meaning the United States. So the specific culture code *en-US* means English as used in the United States. There are more than a dozen other English culture codes, including English as used in Australia (*en-AU*), Belize (*en-BZ*), Jamaica (*en-JM*), Great Britain (*en-GB*), and Trinidad and Tobago (*en-TT*).

**More Info** For a list containing more than 100 culture codes, see *http://msdn.microsoft .com/library/ee825488.aspx.*

# Locale-Specific Text and Symbols

The most obvious change needed to localize a program is its text. Any text that the program displays, either on forms or in dialog boxes, must be changed for the new locale. The program also needs to understand text typed by the user in the locale's language.

Sometimes developers overlook the fact that text doesn't always take up the same space in different languages. Something that may be easy to say in a few words in one language may take many words in another language. When you design a program to be localized, you must be sure that you leave enough room for whatever text is required in every locale that you will support. (More likely, you will go back and rearrange controls to add room where necessary as you begin localizing an application.)

In addition to text, you may need to change icons, symbols, and other graphics so that they make sense in the new locale. For example, in the United States, a picture of a dog can symbolize loyalty, playfulness, security (a guard dog), or the ability to fetch something. In many parts of the world, however, dogs are not kept as pets or service animals. They may be considered sneaky, dangerous, or vicious. If you want to localize a program for those parts of the world, you will need to pick other symbols.

Thinking of a symbol's name as representing something else with a similar name often can cause trouble when localizing an application. This is particularly true when the symbol represents a pun or play on words that doesn't translate well into other languages.

For example, suppose a program has a button that makes a bell ring. A picture of a diamond ring (the kind that goes on your finger) would probably be a bad symbol for that button. It makes some sense in English and is even mildly amusing (although many people don't like that sort of pun), but it relies on the fact that the word *ring* has multiple meanings in English, and this joke would probably make no sense in many other languages. A better symbol would be a picture of a small bell ringing. That would not be as interesting, and you might need to change it if a different kind of bell were common in a particular locale, but at least you'd have some chance that users would understand the symbol without needing to figure out a pun.

## Localizing User Interfaces in Visual Studio

Modifying the controls on a form at run time to support the user's locale can be a lot of work. For different languages, you might need to change the text displayed by the controls, change control sizes and positions, and switch graphics so that they make sense to the user. Microsoft Visual Studio provides some features to make it much easier to display different user interfaces for different locales.

To give a program multiple user interfaces for different locales, start by building the application as you usually would to create a default user interface. The program will use this interface if it doesn't have a more specific interface for the user's locale. For example, if you write a program in English and then localize it for German and Spanish, the program will default to English if the user's locale is Russian.

Next, in the Form Designer, set the form's *Localizable* property to *true,* and then set the form's *Language* property to the locale that you want to support, as shown in Figure 12-1. You can see in Figure 12-1 that Visual Studio lists five specific German locales in addition to the generic German locale. It also supports 17 Arabic locales, 7 Chinese locales, 17 English locales, 21 Spanish locales, and many others, for a total of more than 100 locales.

**FIGURE 12-1** Visual Studio lets you select many locations, including six German locales.

Now, change the properties of the form and its controls to support the new locale. Change any displayed text and rearrange controls, if necessary, to make them fit into the new language.

Start with less specific locales and then add more specific ones as necessary. For example, start with German and then add German (Austria) later if necessary.

When the program runs, it will automatically select the most specific localization that matches. If the user's computer is set for the German (Austria) locale, the program will pick that localization. If the user's computer is set for the German (Luxembourg) locale and you have not included that localization, the program will pick the more generic German locale as the next best choice. If the user's computer is set for Italian (Italy) and you have no localizations for Italian, the program will pick the default locale that you built initially.

Unfortunately, Visual Studio does not localize every property—just the ones that Microsoft thought you would be most likely to need to localize, such as *Font*, *Text*, *Size*, and *Location*. In particular, the *PictureBox* control's *Image* property is not automatically localizable, so if you want to display different images for different locales, you'll need to write some code to do so.

# Locale-Specific Formats

In addition to text and symbols, different cultures use different formats for values such as numbers, currency, percentage, date, and time.

A program must be able to both read and display values in the appropriate format.

Table 12-1 shows examples of some values for the United States (*en-US*), Great Britain (*en-GB*), Germany (*de-DE*), France (*fr-FR*), and Greece (*el-GR*).

**TABLE 12-1** Culture-Specific Values

| Item | Culture | Result |
|------|---------|--------|
| Currency | en-US | $1,234.56 |
| | en-GB | £1,234.56 |
| | de-DE | 1.234,56 € |
| | fr-FR | 1 234,56 € |
| | el-GR | 1.234,56 € |
| Percentage | en-US | 123,456.00% |
| | en-GB | 123,456.00% |
| | de-DE | 123.456,00% |
| | fr-FR | 123 456,00% |
| | el-GR | 123.456,00% |
| Short Date | en-US | 4/1/2012 |
| | en-GB | 01/04/2012 |
| | de-DE | 01.04.2012 |
| | fr-FR | 01/04/2012 |
| | el-GR | 1/4/2012 |
| Long Date | en-US | Sunday, April 01, 2012 |
| | en-GB | 01 April 2012 |
| | de-DE | Sonntag, 1. April 2012 |
| | fr-FR | dimanche 1 avril 2012 |
| | el-GR | Κυριακή, 1 Απριλίου 2012 |
| Time | en-US | 1:46 PM |
| | en-GB | 13:46 |
| | de-DE | 13:46 |
| | fr-FR | 13:46 |
| | el-GR | 1:46 μμ |

If you look closely at the table, you'll find a variety of different currency symbols, thousands separators, decimal separators, and the positioning of those symbols.

Dealing with all the possible formats for even these few cultures could be a lot of work. Fortunately, .NET provides several culture-aware functions, which will be discussed next.

# Culture-Aware Functions in .NET

To work correctly in different locales, a program must be able to parse and display values correctly for each locale. For example, if the user enters the date **4/1/12**, the program should treat the value as April 1 if it is running in Chicago, and January 4 if it is running in London.

Knowing how to parse and format values in each locale could be a lot of work. Fortunately, the Microsoft .NET Framework provides several methods that handle these differences automatically. The most important methods for reading locale-formatted values are the *Parse* methods and the *Convert* class's conversion methods. The most important methods for producing formatted output are the data types' *ToString* methods and the *String.Format* method.

Each of the standard data types has a *Parse* method that converts a string into a value of that type. For example, *DateTime.Parse* takes a date string as a parameter and returns the corresponding *DateTime* value. For example, the statement *DateTime.Parse("4/1/12")* returns a *DateTime* variable representing April 1 if the computer is running in the *en-US* locale, and January 4 is the computer is running in the *en-GB* locale.

The *Convert* class provides locale-aware shared methods for converting values from one type to another. For example, the statement *Convert.ToDateTime("4/1/12")* returns the same values as *DateTime.Parse*.

Each data type defines a *ToString* method that converts a value into a string. For example, if the variable *dueDate* holds a date, then *dueDate.ToString()* returns a string representing the date that has been formatted properly for the computer's locale.

Similarly, the *String.Format* method produces strings formatted for the computer's locale. For example, if the variable *dueDate* holds a date, then *String.Format("{0}, dueDate)* returns a string representing the date, formatted for the computer's locale.

Note that the *ToString* and *String.Format* methods can take formatting strings as parameters to indicate how a value should be formatted. For example, the statement *dueDate.ToString("M/d/yy")* returns a date in the format *month/day/year* even if that is not appropriate for the computer's locale. To prevent incorrect results, you should not use custom time, date, and numeric formats unless there's some special reason why you must. Instead, omit the format string or use standard formats such as *d* (short date), *D* (long date), *t* (short time), *T* (long time), and *C* (currency).

Some data types also provide conversion methods that convert their values into strings. For example, the *DateTime* data type has *ToShortDateString*, *ToShortTimeString*, *ToLongDateString*, and *ToLongTimeString* methods that return strings in different locale-correct formats.

To summarize:

- Do not parse strings by reading the pieces of the string and trying to interpret them in code.

- Use a data type's *Parse* method or a shared *Convert* method, such as *Convert.ToDateTime,* to convert strings into values.

- Do not use custom format strings or try to build your own formatted strings in code.

- Use locale-aware string creation methods, such as *ToString*, *String.Format*, *ToLongDateString*, and *ToShortTimeString*.

- Do not use custom formatting strings such as M/d/yy.

- Use standard formatting strings, such as *d, T,* or *C.*

**More Info** For more information on formatting characters, see:

- **Standard Date and Time Format Strings**
  *http://msdn.microsoft.com/library/az4se3k1.aspx*

- **Custom Date and Time Format Strings**
  *http://msdn.microsoft.com/library/8kb3ddd4.aspx*

- **Standard Numeric Format Strings**
  *http://msdn.microsoft.com/library/dwhawy9k.aspx*

- **Custom Numeric Format Strings**
  *http://msdn.microsoft.com/library/0c899ak8.aspx*

# Summary

This chapter discussed several issues that you should consider when you localize a program. A program may need to display different fonts, text, pictures, and symbols for different locales. In addition, it may need to rearrange controls to make everything fit in a new locale. Visual Studio makes this sort of customization for different locales relatively easy and automatic.

In addition to rearranging the user interface, a localized program needs to parse and display values in the correct formats. For example, a program should display April 1, 2012, as 4/1/12 in the United States, 01/04/12 in Great Britain, and 01.04.2012 in Greece.

The data types' *Parse* methods (such as *Integer.Parse*) and *Convert* class's conversion methods (such as *Convert.ToDateTime*) let a program parse values in different locales.

The data types' *ToString* methods and *String.Format* can convert values into strings that are properly formatted for a locale so long as you use only standard formats. Some data types also provide their own culture-aware formatting methods, such as the *DateTime* data type's *ToShortDateString* method.

If you localize the interface for different cultures and use only the locale-aware parsing and formatting methods, you'll be well on your way to making a program usable around the world.

One last thing you should do before you release your program to millions of unsuspecting users, however, is to have a native of each locale test the program to ensure that it makes sense. Instruction manuals and signs that have been poorly translated into English have been entertaining (and frustrating) English speakers for decades. Unless you want your program to be the target of local ridicule, and maybe even mocked worldwide on the web, have it checked by someone who lives in the area you are targeting.

Truly globalized applications are a relatively new but growing phenomenon. One type of application that is not at all new is the database application. The idea of relational databases is at least 40 years old, and some estimates indicate that as many as 80 percent of all Microsoft Visual Basic applications involve a database. The percentage may be lower for other programming languages, but it's clear that databases play a vital role in modern business programming.

The next chapter discusses databases and data storage more generally. It describes different methods for storing different kinds of data and explains when different techniques are appropriate.

# Chapter 13

# Data Storage

**In this chapter:**

- Files as databases

- INI and config files, and the registry

- Extensible Markup Language (XML) files and related tools such as XML Schema Definition (XSD), Extensible Stylesheet Language for Transformations (XSLT), and XML Path (XPath)

- Relational databases

- Spreadsheets, object stores, and object-relational databases

- Hierarchical and network databases

**WHEN MANY PEOPLE THINK ABOUT DATA** storage, they think about large relational databases, but there are many other ways a program can store data. It can store data in formatted text files, comma-delimited files, configuration files, the system registry, or plain old text files.

Each method has advantages and disadvantages. For example, although a relational database provides powerful searching and reporting features, it comes with significant overhead and requires a special code to access. If your program simply needs to load a set of values when it starts, a simple configuration file will be easier.

This chapter describes some of the ways a program can store and retrieve data. It explains several of the most useful methods, their strengths and weaknesses, and how you can decide which is best for your application.

# Files

One of the simplest ways to store data is in a file. The program can use file system tools to create, read, update, and delete files. The file may be a text file that you can read and edit with any text editor, or it may contain binary data that only your program can read and write correctly. You can even encrypt the file if you want to make it hard for others to read.

Although a file can contain any kind of data, standard programming tools make it easier to work with files that have standard formats. The following sections describe some kinds of files that a program might use for data storage.

## Text Files

A plain text file can store anything you want. Unless the file contains a block of text, the data is usually separated by some sort of delimiter, such as a tab, comma, semicolon, or new line.

File manipulation classes provide methods that make it easy to read and write the lines in a file and to split strings containing delimiters.

For example, suppose that you want to store student test scores. Each line might contain a student's name followed by a comma-delimited list of test scores, as in the following:

```
Able,100,90,94,97
Baker,89,92,96,100
Carter,100,98,100,96
Davis,76,79,65,72
```

A program could read this file, split it into lines, and then use the commas to split the lines into fields.

Because this kind of file contains values separated by commas, it is called a *comma-separated value* (CSV) file.

The simplest type of text file contains a single data value on each line. Although this makes the file seem very large in an editor, it doesn't really take up much more space than any other kinds of delimited file because the *newline* character occupies only a couple of bytes in the file.

These kinds of text files have the advantage that you can read and modify them in a text editor. This is very important if there is a problem in the data and you need to see what values are in the file.

These files have the disadvantage that they normally contain only text. For example, you cannot easily store an image or sound file in such a file. They also have the drawback that a program cannot modify them in the middle. The program may be able to append data to the end of the file, but to make changes in the middle, it must rewrite the entire file. This usually happens fast, so it may not be a problem unless the file is very large or multiple programs need to access and modify the file at the same time.

Although plain text files seem very low-tech, they can be very useful.

# Random Access Files

The reason that a program cannot modify the middle of a plain text file easily is that the pieces of data it contains don't necessarily have the same lengths. For example, consider the following line from the previous test scores file:

```
Baker,89,92,96,100
```

Now suppose you wanted to change Baker's second test score from 92 to 100. If the program simply overwrote the bytes at that position in the file, it would replace the following comma with 0, giving this erroneous result:

```
Baker,89,10096,100
```

A random access file allows a program to modify an arbitrary part of the file by assigning a fixed amount of space to each record that it holds. The following text shows a fixed-length record version of the original test scores file:

```
Able       100  90  94  97
Baker       89  92  96 100
Carter     100  98 100  96
Davis       76  79  65  72
```

Each record allows 10 characters for each student's name and then 4 entries for test scores, each stored in 4 characters.

To update Baker's second test score, a program would use the length of the records to calculate the position in the file where that value is stored. It would then change the value without updating the rest of the file.

Random access files have the advantage that you can find an arbitrary record in the file if you know where it is. For example, you can find the second record without reading and parsing the rest of the file. It also has the advantage that you can modify a record in the middle of the file without rewriting the whole file.

These files have the disadvantage that they take up extra space. In this example, every record must have the same length even though the students' names have different lengths. If you plan to use the file to store 10 test scores for each student, you also need to create the file initially with enough space for all the scores, even though that space won't be used right away.

These files also have the disadvantage that they are relatively complex to use. You need to figure out where the record you want is. The tools for working with these files also tend to be more primitive than those used to work with relational databases.

# INI Files

An INI file (the name comes from *initialization file*) is simply a text file with a special format. The file can contain sections delimited by section names surrounded by brackets. Each section contains item names and values separated by an equal sign. The file can contain comments started with semicolons to make reading the file easier.

The following text shows a simple INI file:

```
[User]
LastUserName=Rod Stephens
LastUsedDate=04/01/2012
[Config]
Top=100
Left=250
Width=300
Height=200
```

This file contains two sections named *User* and *Config*. The *User* section contains the name of the last user to run the program and the date it was last run. The *Config* section stores the program's position when it closed so the program can restore itself to the same position when it runs again.

Typically, a program reads an INI file to initialize itself when it starts. You can change the way that a program behaves by modifying the INI file and restarting the program.

Programming tools make reading and writing INI files reasonably easy. Like plain text files, the program must rewrite the entire file to make any changes.

In recent years, INI files have fallen out of favor. It is more common to use config files, described shortly, to hold this sort of initialization data.

# XML Files

An Extensible Markup Language (XML) file is another form of text file that has a special format. Because of its usefulness and popularity, XML and its associated technologies have grown very powerful and complicated, so there's no room to do more than briefly summarize them here. For more information, search online or see a book about using XML.

The basic rules for creating an XML file are reasonably simple, however, so this section provides a brief introduction to XML.

XML files are hierarchical, with a single root element. Each element begins with a token consisting of a name enclosed in pointy brackets (<>) and ends with a corresponding token that also includes a slash (/) character. You can make these names up as you go along. They can be just about anything that makes sense to you, but they can't contain any special characters, such as < or #.

Between the start and end token, an element can contain data, which may include text or other elements.

The following text shows a simple XML file containing the previous test score data:

```
<TestScores>
  <Student>
    <Name>Able</Name>
    <Score>100</Score>
    <Score>90</Score>
    <Score>94</Score>
    <Score>97</Score>
  </Student>
```

```
    <Student>
      <Name>Baker</Name>
      <Score>89</Score>
      <Score>92</Score>
      <Score>96</Score>
      <Score>100</Score>
    </Student>
    <Student>
      <Name>Carter</Name>
      <Score>100</Score>
      <Score>98</Score>
      <Score>100</Score>
      <Score>96</Score>
    </Student>
    <Student>
      <Name>Davis</Name>
      <Score>76</Score>
      <Score>79</Score>
      <Score>65</Score>
      <Score>72</Score>
    </Student>
  </TestScores>
```

This file's root element is named *TestScores*. It contains a series of *Student* elements, each holding a series of *Score* elements. The *Score* elements contain their values.

Figure 13-1 shows the same data graphically so that it's easy to see its hierarchical structure.

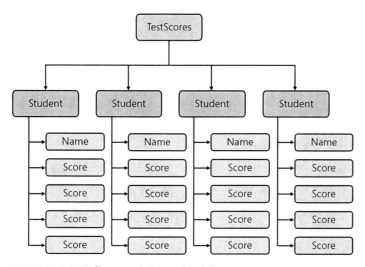

**FIGURE 13-1** XML files contain hierarchical data.

There are lots of other rules for building XML files. For example, as a shortcut, if an element contains no data, you can begin and end it with a single token that includes a slash character before the closing bracket. For example, the element *<Present></Present>* is equivalent to *<Present/>*.

You can also give an element attributes to give additional information about the element. In the previous test score example, you might decide to make *Name* be an attribute of the *Student* element instead of a separate element. You could also make a *Score* element include its value as an attribute instead of as a separate element. The following text shows the file with those changes:

```
<TestScores>
  <Student Name="Able">
    <Score Value="100"/>
    <Score Value="90"/>
    <Score Value="94"/>
    <Score Value="97"/>
  </Student>
  <Student Name="Baker">
    <Score Value="89"/>
    <Score Value="92"/>
    <Score Value="96"/>
    <Score Value="100"/>
  </Student>
  <Student Name="Carter">
    <Score Value="100"/>
    <Score Value="98"/>
    <Score Value="100"/>
    <Score Value="96"/>
  </Student>
  <Student Name="Davis">
    <Score Value="76"/>
    <Score Value="79"/>
    <Score Value="65"/>
    <Score Value="72"/>
  </Student>
</TestScores>
```

Although an XML file can hold any hierarchical data, using files that have a very irregular structure can be confusing. They often work best for holding data that is naturally hierarchical, such as a company's organizational structure or a horse's ancestry. They can also be useful for holding recordlike data, as in the previous test scores example.

Several libraries are available that make reading and writing XML files easier. *Document object model* (DOM) is used to load an XML file into an in-memory data structure that mimics the arrangement of the data. The program can manipulate the data structure's objects to change the data and then write the result back into the file.

DOM methods are reasonably intuitive but require all the data to be loaded into memory at the same time. If the XML file is extremely large, that may be impractical. In that case, you can use other methods that let the program process one element before moving to others. This method is generally more confusing, but it lets the program skip large chunks of data if they are not needed and keeps less data in memory at one time.

One disadvantage to XML files is that, like other text files, a program cannot update them in the middle. For example, if you want to change a particular test score value, you need to rewrite the entire XML file.

Binary formats for XML files are defined, but the text version is much more common. Text XML files can even use text encoding techniques to store binary data such as image, audio, or video files.

In recent years, XML has become very popular for storing and transmitting data. The following list summarizes several other kinds of files that have been defined to make XML more useful.

- **Schemas**   Document Type Definition (DTD) and XML Schema Definition (XSD) files are schema files that define the types of data that an XML file can hold. For example, they might require that the file hold a *TestScores* root element that contains a series of *Student* elements, each having a *Name* attribute and a collection of *Score* elements. A program can use schema files to validate data and learn more about the kinds of data that an XML file should hold.

- **XSLT**   eXtensible Stylesheet Language for Transformations (XSLT) is a programming language that you can use to write programs that transform XML files into a new format. For example, an XSLT program can transform XML data into a new XML file with a different arrangement of elements, a plain text file holding a report, or a CSV file containing some of the data.

- **XPath**   The XML Path (XPath) language specifies how to select elements in an XML file. For example, an XPath expression might select all *Student* elements that contain a *Score* element with *Value* attribute less than 70.

- **SOAP**   Simple Object Access Protocol (SOAP) is a protocol for exchanging information between programs and web services.

- **Web service**   A web service is a program running on a network that another program can call for service. For example, a web service might allow a program to look up product prices or place an order with a company.

## Config Files

In general, *configuration files* (also called *config files*) are files that contain information that a program can use to initialize itself when it starts. As is the case with INI files, you can change the way a program behaves by modifying the config file and restarting the program.

In .NET programming, configuration files are XML files with a specific format. Programs automatically load config file information, so it is easily available to the program.

The easiest way to work with config file settings in C# and Microsoft Visual Basic is to open the project in Microsoft Visual Studio, open the Project menu, and select Properties. Then click the Settings tab to see a settings page similar to the one shown in Figure 13-2.

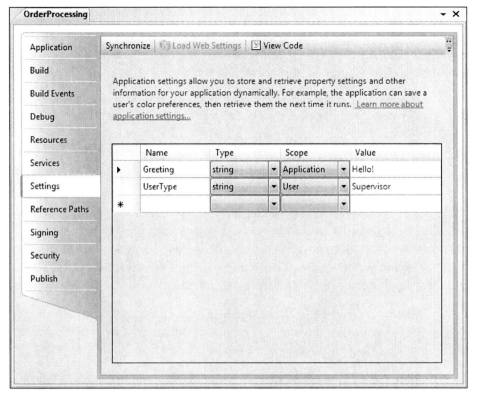

FIGURE 13-2 The project's Settings tab lets you add values to the application's config file.

On this page, you can add, modify, and remove settings. Enter a name for the setting in the left column. In the second column, either select from more than 20 predefined data types, such as *string*, *int*, *Color*, or *Point*, or browse for new data types.

You can set the scope to User, so that each user has a separate setting value, or Application, to make all users share the same value.

The intent is that application settings let you configure the program for all users. The program's code cannot modify application settings while the program is running.

The user settings let the program save configuration information such as color preferences, form layouts, and query history separately for each user. The program can update user settings.

The following code shows how a C# program could use these settings to display a greeting and the user's type in two labels:

```
private void Form1_Load(object sender, EventArgs e)
{
    greetingLabel.Text = Properties.Settings.Default.Greeting;
    userTypeLabel.Text = "You are logged in as a " +
        Properties.Settings.Default.UserType;
}
```

This code sets the *greetingLabel* control's *Text* property to the value of the *Greeting* setting. It makes the *userTypeLabel* control's *Text* property include the value of the *UserType* setting.

The following code shows comparable Visual Basic code:

```
Private Sub Form1_Load() Handles MyBase.Load
    greetingLabel.Text = My.Settings.Greeting
    userTypeLabel.Text = "You are logged in as a " & My.Settings.UserType
End Sub
```

Config files are similar to INI files in many ways, although they are easier to use and they support values with application and user scope.

# The System Registry

The system registry is a hierarchical database that Microsoft Windows uses to hold configuration information for the operating system and many of the programs installed on the system. It holds information such as the various locations of important executable programs, which programs to associate with which kinds of files, and the locations of libraries.

> **Note** The registry is extremely important for the operating system to run correctly. If you fool around in there and break something, you can do serious damage to the system, possibly making it unbootable, so make any changes carefully. Also, you may want to save a copy of the part of the registry that you're changing, just in case. For example, the File menu of the RegEdit tool contains an Export command which can copy part of the registry into a text file.

Microsoft calls the top-level branches from the root of the registry *hives*. The registry uses separate hives for classes, the current user, the local computer, all users, and the current configuration.

Many applications store shared settings in the *HKEY_LOCAL_MACHINE\Software* branch of the registry. For example, Microsoft Word stores some settings in *HKEY_LOCAL_MACHINE\SOFTWARE\ Microsoft\Office\12.0\Word\Document Inspectors\Comments And Revisions*.

The registry automatically makes a separate *HKEY_CURRENT_USER* hive for each user, so many programs store user-specific settings there. For example, Word stores a user's option settings in *HKEY_CURRENT_USER\Software\Microsoft\Office\12.0\Word\Options*.

A .NET program can use the *Microsoft.Win32.Registry* class to manipulate the registry. Visual Basic programs also can use the *GetSetting* and *SaveSetting* functions to get and save values in the *HKEY_CURRENT_USER\Software\VB and VBA Program Settings* part of the registry.

Because the registry is hierarchical, you can make branches inside other branches to store data, much as you can in an XML file. The registry isn't really intended for building complex data hierarchies or for storing huge amounts of data. It's a handy place to store small bits of information, such as user preferences and configuration data, but it's not a good place to store customer, order tracking, or student data. Those kinds of data are better kept in a relational database, which provides much better reporting features.

# Relational Databases

Without getting too technical, a *relational database* contains *tables* that hold *records*. Each record holds *fields* containing data for that record.

For example, a test scores database might have a *Student* table. Each record holds the same data about a specific student: *StudentId*, *FirstName*, and *LastName*.

Different tables are linked by using common values in their fields. For example, the *TestScore* table would contain information about test scores: *StudentId*, *TestNumber*, and *Score*. In this example, the *Student* table's *StudentId* field links to the *TestScore* table's *StudentId* field. To find the scores for a particular student, you would look up that student's *Student* record, find the *StudentId*, and then find all the *TestScore* records with the same *StudentId*.

Figure 13-3 shows these tables graphically. Arrows connect corresponding *Student* and *TestScore* records.

| Student | | | | TestScore | | |
|---|---|---|---|---|---|---|
| FirstName | LastName | StudentId | | StudentId | TestNumber | Score |
| Kim | Abercrombie | 10201 | | 10201 | 1 | 100 |
| Jay | Hamlin | 12490 | | 10201 | 2 | 97 |
| Terrence | Philip | 2910 | | 10201 | 3 | 94 |
| Sanjay | Shah | 21816 | | 10201 | 4 | 98 |
| | | | | 12490 | 1 | 86 |
| | | | | 2910 | 1 | 93 |

**FIGURE 13-3** In a relational database, tables are linked by fields holding the same values.

In this example, the *TestScore* table holds four test scores for Kim Abercrombie, one test score for Terrence Philip, and one test score for Jay Hamlin.

**Note** Figure 13-3 shows the records in the *TestScore* table in order so that they match up nicely with the records in the *Student* table, However, in general, you cannot assume that the records are stored physically in that order in the database. When you select data from the tables, you can use an *ORDER BY* clause to order the results in whatever way is most convenient at the time.

Relational databases use sophisticated indexing methods to make it fast and easy to search for particular records and to find matching records in other tables. That makes it very easy to build complex reports, such as a list of the students in each class and their test scores, or a list of students with failing average scores for each class.

These sorts of queries make relational databases powerful and flexible, so they are preferable for most applications that work with any significant amount of data. Databases in Microsoft SQL Server are particularly common in .NET applications, although .NET programs can use other databases, such as MySQL, Oracle, PostgreSQL, Sybase, and DB2.

**Note** Microsoft also offers SQL Server Express, a free edition that works just like SQL Server but with a few restrictions, such as limiting the number of CPUs and the amount of memory that the database can use, and limiting the total size of the database. Many developers start with SQL Server Express and then move to the full (non-free) version of SQL Server if the database grows enough so that the free version cannot handle it.

Relational databases have many advantages, such as the following:

■ They let you perform complex queries to select data from many tables.

■ They use index structures to make finding a particular piece of data quick and easy.

■ They let you update a piece of data without rewriting the entire database.

■ Some support multiple users simultaneously.

■ Some provide transactions to ensure that the operations in a sequence are either all performed or all canceled.

■ Some provide backup and mirroring features to protect against data loss.

■ They can enforce data constraints, such as the requirement that test scores are integers between 0 and 100.

■ They can enforce relational constraints, such as the requirement that the program cannot create a *TestScore* record without a corresponding *Student* record.

■ They allow you to associate a single piece of data (such as a *Student* record) with any number of other pieces of data (such as many *TestScore* records).

- Some support multiple views so that specified groups of users can see only some of the data in a table or query result. For example, a mailroom clerk may be able to see contact information in the *Customer* table but not see the customer's billing information.

- They are flexible enough to let you perform queries that you didn't know you would need when you built the database.

- They are very common, so there is a lot of information and a large number of books about them.

Relational databases do impose some overhead so they are not perfect for storing small amounts of information that would fit more naturally in a config file. You also will need to spend some time learning how to use a relational database before you can get the greatest benefit.

Relational databases are a big topic. For more information, search online or see one of the many books on this topic. For information about designing flexible and robust relational databases, see my book *Beginning Database Design Solutions* (Wrox, 2008).

# Other Databases

Flat files and relational databases are the most common ways that programs store large amounts of data, but sometimes other options are useful when you need to work with data that has special characteristics. The following sections describe some of these specialized databases.

## Spreadsheets

Spreadsheet programs such as Microsoft Excel hold rows and columns of data in a way that is somewhat similar to the way that tables in a relational database hold data. They allow the user to enter formulas to perform calculations on the values stored on a sheet, and they automatically update the results if any of the values change. Some spreadsheets also can display graphs and charts of the data.

More advanced formulas can refer to entries on other worksheets within the same workbook. Formulas can even select particular values if a condition is true, so they act a bit like the *select* statements supported by relational databases.

However, spreadsheets are not really relational databases, and they do not perform the same tasks. They cannot join data from multiple worksheets easily, do not automatically perform data integrity to ensure that the user doesn't enter incorrect or duplicate values, and provide only the typical, gridlike interface.

Still, spreadsheets have their place. Many users are comfortable with them, know how to enter values into them, and know how to modify their formulas. Sometimes that lets users perform additional data analysis without requiring you to write extra code.

Sometimes you also can mix a spreadsheet with normal Windows code. For example, a program could use a Windows form to take inputs, perform some calculations, and then place outputs in a spreadsheet for the user to view and analyze.

## Object Stores

An object store is a database that holds objects. It provides methods for creating, extracting, updating, and deleting objects from the database.

For example, suppose that you build an order-tracking application that uses *Customer*, *Order*, and *OrderItem* classes. In that case, the program would be able to pass the data store some search parameters, and then the database would use them to create the appropriate *Customer* object for the program to use. An object store also may provide concurrency support so that it can refuse to let two users modify the same *Customer* object at the same time.

Many applications use a relational database in the place of an object store and include routines for moving objects in and out of the database. This usually works well when done correctly, although the code must handle issues such as concurrency support.

## Object-Relational Database

An object-relational database provides several features that make creating objects from data easier. It can execute the same complicated queries that a relational database can.

A closely related concept is an *object-relational mapping system*, which provides a connecting layer between a relational database and an object-oriented program's code. This gives some separation so that developers working on the relational database and developers working on the object-oriented code can work separately.

## Hierarchical Databases

A hierarchical database stores data that naturally has levels within its structure, such as a company's organizational chart, the files on a computer's hard disk, or a list of components that are made up of other components.

Hierarchical data has a treelike structure. Each node in the tree has a single parent node (except the root node, which has no parent) and can have child nodes. A node that has no child nodes is called a *leaf node*. A node that is not a leaf node is called an *internal node*.

Figure 13-4 shows a simple organizational chart for a company. All the nodes, except the *Executive Director* root node, have a parent node. The blue nodes at the bottom of the tree are leaf nodes.

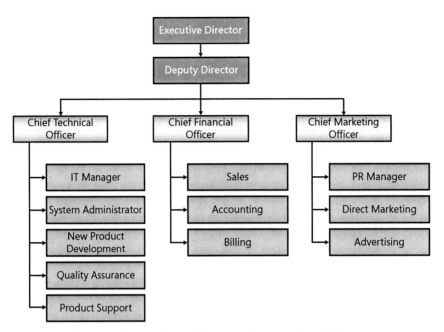

**FIGURE 13-4** A company's organizational chart contains hierarchical data.

The links between nodes in a hierarchical data structure cannot contain any loops because that would create a node that has more than one parent. For example, if the *Chief Marketing Officer* had the *Sales* department as a child, then *Sales* would have two parents: the *Chief Marketing Officer* and the *Chief Financial Officer*.

A hierarchical database provides methods for searching the data and manipulating its treelike structure. For example, it provides methods for adding, moving, and deleting branches at any point in the hierarchy. It also may provide methods for iterating through the hierarchy in different orders and for looping through the children of a node in the hierarchy. However, hierarchical databases may not provide good tools for comparing data across multiple levels of the hierarchy, an operation that is easy with a relational database.

XML files store hierarchical data, but they are simply text files; they don't provide any tools for data validation, searching, or manipulating the data. Other tools, such as schemas, XSLT, and XPath, help provide some of these capabilities, but the result isn't integrated as closely as a true hierarchical database. For more information, see the section "XML," earlier in this chapter.

You can store hierarchical data in a relational database, but a relational database is not really designed to hold hierarchical data, so manipulating the data can be slow and awkward.

**Note** I once worked on a project that stored hierarchical data in an Excel workbook. It took as long as 20 minutes to load some of the larger data sets. One test program I wrote could load similar data from an XML file in less than 80 seconds. Using a type of database that was not designed to handle hierarchical data killed the application's performance.

 **More Info** For more information on hierarchical databases, see *http://en.wikipedia.org/wiki/Hierarchical_database_model*.

## Network Databases

In a hierarchical database, each node has one parent, so the links that connect nodes cannot form loops. In a network, nodes are connected by any number of entering and editing links. Network data can represent all sorts of things, including telephone lines, computer networks, airline or bus routes, and streets.

Often, both nodes and links have associated data. For example, in a street network, the nodes might represent intersections and store latitude and longitude. The links would represent the streets connecting intersections, and they might store information about the street, such as its name, number of lanes, surface type (asphalt, concrete, gravel), and speed limit or driving time.

Figure 13-5 shows a small street network. The links are labeled with the time it takes to drive across them.

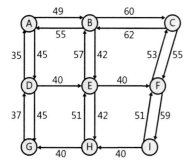

**FIGURE 13-5** A network database stores nodes and links information for building networks.

A network database provides features that make it easy to load, edit, modify, and save networks. For example, it might provide methods to add new nodes to the network and connect them to existing nodes with links.

A network database also may provide methods for performing special network calculations, such as finding the shortest path between two nodes and finding the shortest route that connects several nodes.

Some XML files can store network data, although they don't include any functionality for manipulating the data.

**More Info** Network databases are rather exotic, so they're not described further here. For more information, see *http://en.wikipedia.org/wiki/Network_database*.

## Temporal Databases

A temporal database is one that has a built-in notion of time. For example, it may store the time during which a piece of data is valid. In a sales database, that could be useful for determining a product's price as it changes over time.

It's usually not too hard to add temporal data to some other form of database. For example, in a relational database, a product's record normally holds a single price. To add temporal data, you instead could link products to a Price table that holds each product's price and the date on which that price became effective. Adding temporal data to a relational database adds extra complexity, so it's not worth the effort unless you will need that data frequently.

**More Info** Like network databases, temporal databases are rather exotic, so they're not described further here. For more information, see *http://en.wikipedia.org/wiki/Temporal_database*.

# Summary

This chapter discussed several different kinds of databases. Many applications need databases, but not all databases are suitable for all purposes. Certain types of database are appropriate for some kinds of data but not others. By picking the right database type, you can make your application faster, more efficient, and easier to program.

The following list summarizes some of the issues that you should consider when deciding what kind of database to use:

- Plain text files are suitable for storing simple values, although they do not provide concurrency features, and to update values, you need to rewrite the entire file.

- Random access files let you find and update records in the middle of the file without rewriting the entire file. Support for them is relatively weak, however, and they do not provide concurrency features.

- INI files can hold initialization values. If each user has a separate INI file in a different directory, each user can have separate settings. In .NET applications, INI files have been superseded by config files.

- XML files are good for storing hierarchical data, and they also can be useful for storing simple, tablelike data values. They are common enough that they are useful for transferring data from one application to another.

- Config files can hold shared and individual configuration settings. They are easy to use in .NET.

- The registry can hold shared and individual configuration information and small pieces of data. The registry is fairly easy to use in .NET, but viewing it requires special editors, such as the RegEdit tool, so it is not as easy to modify as config or INI files. Installing values into the registry also takes more work than simply copying a configuration file onto a computer.

The previous points summarize simpler alternatives to more powerful database solutions. These are really just data storage techniques and do not provide data integrity, searching, sorting, reporting, concurrency, or other database features.

The following list summarizes some of the more powerful database options:

- Relational databases hold tables that contain records. They can provide type checking, constraints between tables, sorting, searching, filtering, combining data from different tables, concurrency control, backups and mirroring, the ability to update only pieces of data, indexing to make queries faster, transactions, and multiple views of tables and query results. They are flexible enough to allow you to execute queries that you didn't know you would need when you built the database. This is the most common type of database used in large applications.

- Spreadsheets are useful when the data has a fairly simple, tablelike structure and you don't need a full relational database. They can perform complex analysis of the values entered and automatically update results if the values change. They can generate graphs and charts, and many users are also familiar with them, so sometimes you can avoid extra programming by giving the data to the user to study.

- Data stores and object-relational databases make it relatively easy to store and retrieve objects.

- Hierarchical databases are useful when the data has natural levels within its structure. XML files can store this kind of information, but you need other tools to provide database features.

- Network databases are useful when the data naturally forms networks. They are very specialized but extremely useful for some applications.

By carefully reviewing your data needs and comparing them to the features provided by various database options, you can pick the best solution for your application.

Up to now, the chapters in this book have been somewhat independent of .NET programming. The code examples are taken from Visual Basic and C#, but many of the general ideas apply whether you're using C# in Windows or Fortran in Unix. For example, your database options are similar no matter what language and operating system you use.

The next chapter moves away from that approach and covers a topic that applies only to .NET developers: the Microsoft .NET Framework. It summarizes the most useful parts of the enormous .NET Framework libraries to give you an idea of what's available when programming for .NET. It won't explain everything there is to know about the .NET Framework. Rather, it's intended to give you the "big picture," so when you need the advanced features the .NET Framework provides, you will remember what it contains that you can use.

# Chapter 14

# .NET Libraries

**In this chapter:**

- Namespaces for C#, Microsoft Visual Basic, and Microsoft Windows theme tools

- System namespaces containing numerous tools for collections, data, diagnostics, globalizations, input/output (IO), Language Integrated Query (LINQ), and many more

**MOST OF THE GENERAL TOPICS DISCUSSED** so far have applied to some extent to many programming environments. For example, the most commonly used programming languages today have *for* loops, *while* loops, and classes.

This chapter deals with a topic that applies only to .NET programming: the Microsoft .NET Framework libraries. These libraries provide all sorts of useful tools that can save you a huge amount of programming time and lines of code, but they are available only in .NET, so they won't do you much good if you're programming in C++ in Unix.

The .NET Framework contains hundreds (if not thousands) of classes, each with myriad properties, methods, and events that can make programming easier. Thus, there isn't enough room here to cover them all in any depth. The intent of this chapter is to familiarize you with the libraries so you have some idea of what they contain, rather than to provide a complete reference. If you later need to perform a task covered by one of the libraries, such as encrypting a file or building a multithreaded application, hopefully you will remember that the .NET Framework contains classes that can help you, and you can search online for more information.

The most useful namespaces in the .NET Framework are divided into two main categories: Microsoft namespaces and System namespaces.

# Microsoft Namespaces

The Microsoft namespaces generally contain tools that are more Microsoft-specific than the System namespaces. They deal mostly with specific languages such as C# and Microsoft Visual Basic, and the operating system.

The following list summarizes the most useful Microsoft namespaces in the .NET Framework:

- **Microsoft.CSharp**   Contains items that support the compilation of C# code. The *Microsoft.CSharp.CSharpCodeProvider* class provides access to the C# code generator and compiler that you can use to compile source code programmatically. For example, you could use this ability to make a program that lets the user write and compile code. For more information, see "How to programmatically compile code using C# compiler," at *http://support.microsoft.com/kb/304655*.

- **Microsoft.VisualBasic**   Contains items that support compilation of Visual Basic code in addition to extra Visual Basic features, such as the *My* namespace and Visual Basic 6 compatibility features. The *Microsoft.VisualBasic.VisualBasicCodeProvider* class provides access to the Visual Basic code generator and compiler that you can use to programmatically compile source code. For example, you could use this ability to make a program that lets the user write and compile code. For more information, see "How to programmatically compile code by using the Visual Basic .NET or Visual Basic 2005 compiler," at *http://support .microsoft.com/kb/304654*.

- **Microsoft.Win32**   Contains types that handle events raised by the operating system and that manipulate the registry. This namespace also defines common file dialog boxes.

- **Microsoft.Windows.Themes**   Provides access to Windows Presentation Foundation (WPF) themes, which provide default appearances for controls and other elements in a WPF application.

# System Namespaces

The System namespaces contain more basic classes that might be useful in languages other than C# and Visual Basic (if such languages were defined for .NET). They provide additional tools that would be useful for many programs, such as collection types, web tools, and globalization classes.

The following list summarizes the most useful System namespaces in the .NET Framework:

- **System**   Provides fundamental classes and data types for use by programs. Sub-namespaces provide more specialized features, such as collections, cryptography, and diagnostic tools.

- **System.CodeDom**   Provides classes that can represent various code elements. You can use the classes to model the structure of a code document in a language-independent way. For information on using *System.CodeDom* to generate and compile code, see "Dynamic Source Code Generation and Compilation," at *http://msdn .microsoft.com/library/650ax5cx.aspx*.

- **System.Collections**   Defines a variety of collection classes representing stacks, queues, lists, hash tables, dictionaries, and more. Sub-namespaces include *System. Collections.Concurrent* (for applications where multiple threads access a collection concurrently), *System.Collections.Generic* (collections that can hold any type of data while using strong typing), and *System.Collections.Specialized* (specialized collections such as *HybridDictionary*, *ListDictionary*, *NameValueCollection*, and *StringCollection*).

- **System.ComponentModel**   Defines classes that implement the behavior of components and controls. Includes classes used to implement attributes and type converters.

- **System.Configuration**   Contains classes for working with configuration data.

- **System.Data**   Contains classes for working with data using ADO.NET data access. Defines the classes that a program uses to manipulate ADO.NET data, such as *Constraint*, *DataColumn*, *DataRelation*, *DataRow*, *DataSet*, *DataTable*, *ForeignKeyConstraint*, and many others. Sub-namespaces, such as *System.Data.Odbc*, *System.Data.Oledb*, *System.Data.Sql*, and *System.Data.OracleClient,* provide classes to support different types of relational databases.

- **System.Deployment**   Provides tools for customizing installation behavior for ClickOnce applications.

- **System.Device.Location**   Provides tools to let a program determine the computer's location using various location providers.

- **System.Diagnostics**   Contains classes for working with various diagnostic tools, such as event logs and performance counters. The *System.Diagnostics.Debug* class provides some particularly useful debugging features, such as the ability to display debugging messages and make code assertions. (This namespace is included automatically in Visual Basic applications by default, but you must include it explicitly in C# programs.)

- **System.DirectoryServices**   Provides tools for working with Active Directory directory service.

- **System.Drawing**   Provides classes that support GDI+ drawing. These are the classes that you use to draw lines, ellipses, rectangles, polygons, images, and other objects in a drawing surface such as a *Bitmap*.

- **System.Globalization**   Contains classes that define culture-specific information.

- **System.IO**   Contains classes for performing input/output (IO) operations. The classes can read and write data in streams, search and manipulate files and directories, compress stream data, use pipes, and interact with serial ports.

- **System.Linq**   Contains classes that support Language Integrated Query (LINQ) extensions, which let a program perform queries on data sources such as arrays and lists.

- **System.Management**   Contains classes that provide access to system management information. This includes information about the system, devices, disks, applications, and services.

- **System.Media**   Contains classes that play sound files and system-defined sounds.

- **System.Messaging**   Contains classes for working with message queues on a network.

- **System.Net**   Contains classes that provide interfaces for several network protocols. The *WebRequest* and *WebResponse* classes let a program easily interact with websites. The *System.Net.Mail* sub-namespace contains classes that send email. The *System.Net.NetworkInformation* sub-namespace provides access to network information, such as traffic data and network address information. *System.Net.Security* provides streams for secure network communication.

- **System.Numerics**   Contains the *BigInteger* class, which represents arbitrarily large integers, and the *Complex* class, which represents complex numbers.

- **System.Printing**   Contains classes for working with print servers, queues, and jobs.

- **System.Reflection**   Contains classes that can interrogate objects and types to learn more about them. For example, given a variable of type *object*, the tools in this namespace let a program find out what methods the object has at run time and invoke them. Similarly, a program could learn about the object's properties and read or set their values. (This is a very powerful technique, but it can be rather confusing.)

- **System.Resources**   Contains tools for manipulating a program's culture-specific resources.

- **System.Runtime**   Contains tools that allow a program to interact with the common language runtime to affect caching, serialization and deserialization, advanced exception handling, and distributed applications.

- **System.Security**   Contains tools for working with application security, permissions, authentication, and cryptography.

- **System.ServiceProcess**   Contains types that let you install and control Windows services.

- **System.Speech**   Contains classes for generating and recognizing speech.

- **System.Text**   Contains tools for working with text. It includes encoders and decoders for moving characters in and out of sequences of bytes. The *System.Text.RegularExpressions* namespace contains classes for performing regular expression matching and replacements.

- **System.Threading**   Contains classes for working with threads and tasks. It includes classes for working with timers, semaphores, mutexes, threads, and thread pools. The *System.Threading.Thread.CurrentThread* property gives access to the currently running thread. The *System.Threading.Thread.Sleep* method makes the current thread sleep for a specified amount of time.

- **System.Timers**   Contains the *Timer* component.

- **System.Transactions**   Contains classes that support transactions, which lets multiple distributed programs participate in transactions so that either all operations in a transaction occur or they are all canceled.

- **System.Web**   Contains classes that support browser and server communication.

- **System.Windows**   Contains classes used by WPF and Windows Forms applications. The *System.Windows.Controls* sub-namespace contains WPF controls. The *System.Windows. Forms* sub-namespace contains Windows Forms controls.

- **System.Xaml**   Contains classes used to read and write Extensible Application Markup Language (XAML) code for WPF applications.

- **System.Xml**   Contains classes for programming Extensible Markup Language (XML). This includes classes for LINQ to XML, XML serialization, XML Path (XPath), and Extensible Stylesheet Language for Transformations (XSLT). See the section "XML Files," in Chapter 13, "Data Storage," for more information about XML, XPath, and XSLT.

 **More Info**  For more information on the .NET Framework class library namespaces, see the article ".NET Framework Class Library," at *http://msdn.microsoft.com/library/gg145045.aspx*.

# Summary

This chapter briefly summarized almost three dozen .NET Framework namespaces, and it should illustrate how you might approach further learning about the .NET Framework. Most of these tools contain many classes, each of which may have numerous properties, methods, and events, so there's no room in this book to describe any of them in much depth.

Some of these classes are so specialized that you may never need them; however, if you do find that you need to use the features provided by one of these namespaces, I hope you'll remember that these tools are available and search online for more information about them. Using some of these namespaces can save you many hours of work.

# Glossary

## A

**abstract class**  A class that cannot be instantiated directly. You can only instantiate concrete child classes. A class that contains an abstract member is abstract. You also can mark a class as abstract even if it contains no abstract members. In contrast, a *concrete class* is any class that is not abstract.

**abstract member**  A parent class member that must be overridden in a child class.

**abstraction**  The process of moving common members from two or more classes into a new parent class. *See also* information hiding.

**accelerator**  A key that a user can press with the Alt key to navigate through the menu hierarchy. For example, Alt+F typically opens the File menu.

**accept button**  In a modal dialog box, the button that fires when the user presses the Enter key.

**accessibility**  A modifier that determines what code (if any) outside an item's scope can use the item. For example, a public method inside a class can be called by code outside the class.

**accessor**  A method that gets or sets a property or other value.

**agile development**  A development approach that focuses on building projects incrementally using frequent builds.

**all-in-one**  A desktop computer where the computer is integrated into the monitor.

**argument**  The value passed into a routine through a parameter.

**array**  A variable that holds a series of values with the same data type. An *index* into the array lets the program select a particular value.

**assembler**  A program that converts assembly mnemonic code into machine language for execution.

**assembly**  In .NET applications, the smallest self-contained unit of compiled code. An assembly can be a complete application, or a library that can be called by other applications.

**assertion**  A statement about a program that the code claims to be true.

**attached property**  In Windows Presentation Foundation (WPF), a property that is provided by the parent of a control. For example, a *Grid* control provides the *Grid.Row* property for the controls that it contains.

## B

**base class**  *See* parent class.

**bit**  A single 0 or 1 value.

**block scope**  A scope that is limited to a block of code within a routine, such as a *for* loop.

**Blu-ray**  A system that stores data on removable discs with a typical capacity of 50 GB.

**ByRef**  *See* pass by reference.

**byte**  A group of 8 bits.

**ByVal**  See pass by value.

# C

**cache**  *v.* To store information or a program in memory for quick use later. *n.* A location where a program saves information for quicker use later.

**CAD**  See computer-aided design (CAD).

**call stack**  A chunk of memory where a program stores information about routine calls. See also stack frame.

**camel case**  A naming convention where each word is capitalized, as in *generateSalesReport*.

**cancel button**  In a modal dialog box, the button that fires when the user presses the Esc key.

**CD**  See compact disc (CD).

**central processing unit (CPU)**  The computer's main processor, which performs normal programming commands. Other processing units include the graphics processing unit and floating-point unit.

**child class**  A class that is derived from a parent class. Also called a *sub class* or *derived class*.

**CIL**  See Common Intermediate Language (CIL).

**class**  A program-defined data type that stores data and methods to represent a type of object. In many ways, a class is similar to a structure, but classes are reference types, whereas structures are value types.

**class scope**  The scope for items defined inside a class but not inside any of its methods.

**cloud computing**  A business model where programs, data storage, collaboration services, and other key business tools are stored on a centralized server that users access remotely, often through a browser.

**CLR**  See Common Language Runtime (CLR).

**code module scope**  The scope for items defined inside a code module but not inside any of its routines.

**coercion**  Converting a value explicitly from one data type to another.

**comma-separated value (CSV) file**  A text file where records are written on separate lines and the fields within a record are separated by commas.

**comment**  A line of source code that doesn't make the computer do anything placed there to help programmers understand the code.

**Common Intermediate Language (CIL)**  Formerly called Microsoft Intermediate Language (MSIL), this is a pseudo-assembly language into which Microsoft Visual Studio programs are compiled. They are then compiled into machine code during execution.

**Common Language Runtime (CLR)**  The run-time component that converts a .NET program's Common Intermediate Language (CIL) into machine code and executes it.

**communication protocol**  A formal description of the formats and rules for passing information across a network.

**compact disc  (CD)**  A system that stores data on removable CD discs with a typical capacity of 700 MB.

**compiler**  A program that converts high-level language code into a lower-level language. It may convert directly to machine language for execution, or it may convert the high-level program into an intermediate language, such as Common Intermediate Language (CIL) or Java bytecode instructions for running on a virtual machine.

**component**  A program object similar to a control, but without a visible presence on the form at run time.

**composition**  When one object contains another kind of object. For example, a *CustomerOrder* is (partly) composed of *OrderItems*.

**computer-aided design (CAD)**  Using a program to assist in designing something, such as an architectural drawing.

**concrete class**  A class that is not abstract. See also abstract class.

**conditional operator**  An operator that evaluates its first operand and returns either its second or third operand, depending on whether the first operand is true or false.

**config file**  *See* configuration file.

**configuration file (config file)**  A file containing information that a program can use to initialize itself when it starts. In .NET programs, config files are Extensible Markup Language (XML) files that programs can load automatically, making the values easy for the program to use.

**constructor**  A method that is called automatically when the program creates a new instance of a class.

**context menu**  A menu that pops up when the user right-clicks a particular part of the user interface.

**control**  A program object that represents a visible feature in a Microsoft Windows program.

**control prefix notation**  Using a prefix to identify control types or the fact that a variable is a control.

**control run time**  The time when a control's code runs in the development environment to provide feedback. This is different from just run time, when the program containing the control executes and the control's code also runs.

**control variable**  A variable used to control a *for* loop.

**core**  The part of a processor that actually executes instructions. Multi-core processors have more than one core, so they can execute multiple instructions at the same time.

**CPU**  *See* central processing unit (CPU).

**CSV file**  *See* comma-separated value (CSV) file.

# D

**data-centric viewpoint**  A project design that focuses on the data that the user must process and how to support it in the user interface.

**datagram**  A basic unit of data transfer consisting of a header that includes addressing information and a data area.

**defensive programming**  The idea that code should be able to run even under unexpected conditions.

**derive**  To make a new class that inherits from another.

**derived class**  *See* child class.

**design time**  The time when you build a program in a development environment.

**desktop**  A computer intended to sit on or near your desk and not be portable.

**destructor**  A method that is called when an object is destroyed.

**dialog**  *See* dialog box.

**dialog box**  A (usually modal) form that lets the user make selections before performing an action.

**distributed computing**  When multiple computers connected by a network work to solve a single problem. The large communication overhead means that distributed computing is usually effective only when the problem is embarrassingly parallel.

**document object model (DOM)**  An in-memory representation of a document such as an XML file.

**Document Type Definition (DTD) file**  A type of schema definition file. *See also* schema.

**DOM**  *See* document object model (DOM).

**DTD**  *See* Document Type Definition (DTD) file.

**DVD**  Stands for "digital versatile disc" or "digital video disc," a system that stores data on removable discs with a typical capacity of 4.7 GB.

# E

**embarrassingly parallel**  A problem that has a naturally parallel solution, such as displaying fractals or 3-D ray tracing.

**empty constructor** *See* parameterless constructor.

**encapsulation** The ability of a class to group properties and methods in a well-defined package.

**enterprise server** Another term for mainframe.

**Ethernet** A set of technologies for connecting devices using wires or cables.

**event** A mechanism that lets a control tell the program that something interesting has occurred.

**event handler** Code that catches or handles an event.

**explicit type conversion** When code includes statements that convert from one data type to another. *See also* implicit type conversion.

**Extensible Application Markup Language (XAML)** The window-definition language used to define a Windows Presentation Foundation (WPF) application's user interface.

**Extensible Markup Language (XML)** A specification for creating text files that contain hierarchical data.

**Extensible Stylesheet Language Transformations (XSLT)** A programming language that allows a program to translate an Extensible Markup Language (XML) file into a file with some other format, such as an XML file with a different structure, a plain text file, or a comma-separated value (CSV) file.

**extreme programming** A development approach that focuses on building projects incrementally using frequent builds. It includes techniques such as coding to the specific problem rather than a general one, paired programming, and test-driven development.

# F

**factory method** A class method that returns an instance of the class.

**flash drive** A device that stores data in nonvolatile, solid-state memory.

**floating-point unit (FPU)** A processor designed for performing mathematical operations. Also known as a *math coprocessor*.

**flops** Stands for "floating-point operations." For example, a 1-megaflop computer can execute 1 million floating-point operations per second.

**FPU** *See* floating-point unit (FPU).

**function** A routine that returns a value.

# G

**garbage collection** A task performed periodically to reclaim lost memory so the program can use it again.

**garbage collector (GC)** The process that performs garbage collection.

**GB** *See* gigabyte (GB).

**GC** *See* garbage collector (GC).

**generalization** *See* abstraction.

**getter** A method that returns a property's value.

**gigabyte (GB)** A unit of measure equal to 1,024 MB.

**globalization** The process of making a program support multiple locales. Sometimes used to mean the combination of internationalization and localization.

**GPU** *See* graphics processing unit (GPU).

**graphical user interface (GUI)** An interface characterized by the windows, menus, and controls typical in a Microsoft Windows application. GUIs usually are easiest to use with a mouse or other pointing device, although sometimes they include shortcuts for mouse-free use that are particularly useful for the visually impaired.

**graphics processing unit** A processor specialized for executing graphical commands such as managing the screen and generating 3-D graphics.

**GUI** *See* graphical user interface (GUI).

# H

**handheld computer**  A programmable device that is small enough for you to carry in your hand.

**handle**  To take action when the event occurs.

**Has-A relationship**  *See* composition.

**hierarchical database**  A database that stores data that is naturally structured, such as a company's organizational chart or the files on a computer's disk.

**Hungarian notation**  Using a prefix to give information, such as a variable's data type and scope.

# I

**IDE**  *See* integrated development environment (IDE).

**immutable**  A variable whose value does not change after it is assigned. (For example, strings are immutable.)

**implement**  To implement an interface, a class must provide the members that the interface defines.

**implicit type conversion**  When a programming language automatically converts a value from one data type to another. *See also* explicit type conversion.

**index**  Determines which entry in an array is to be manipulated by the code.

**information hiding**  The ability of a class to hide the details about how it works from outside code.

**inheritance diagram**  A drawing that makes it easy to visualize the inheritance relationships among classes.

**INI file**  *See* initialization (INI) file.

**initialization (INI) file**  A file containing sections given by names surrounded by brackets, each containing name and value pairs.

**initializing constructor**  A constructor that takes as parameters values to assign to the new object's fields and properties.

**instance**  A specific object that is of a class type. For example, *RodStephens* is an instance of the class *Author*.

**instance member**  A class member that applies to instances of the class as opposed to the class as a whole. Instance members are referred to by using an instance of the class, as in *newStudent. EmailSchedule()* where *newStudent* is an instance of the class. *See also* shared member.

**instantiation**  The process of creating an instance of a class.

**integrated development environment (IDE)**  A single large application that includes programming tools that let you write, build, run, test, and debug programs.

**interface**  Defines a set of members that a class can provide.

**Intermediate Language (IL)**  *See* Common Intermediate Language (CIL).

**intern pool**  A pool of memory where string values are stored. Strings that contain the same textual value share the same buffer in the intern pool.

**internationalization**  The process of making a program capable of easily supporting multiple locales.

**Internet**  A global system of connected computer networks. The Internet uses the Internet Protocol Suite to define how traffic should work.

**Internet Protocol (IP)**  A set of procedures that provides addressing to let a network route data packets called *datagrams* to the appropriate destination.

**Internet Protocol Suite**  The suite of protocols used by the Internet. Also called TCP/IP for the two most important protocols that it contains: Transmission Control Protocol (TCP) and Internet Protocol (IP).

**Is-A relationship** Subclassing or a parent-child relationship; when one kind of object is a type of some other kind of object. For example, an *Employee* is a *Person*.

# J

**Java Virtual Machine (JVM)** The run-time component that converts a Java program's bytecode into machine code and executes it.

**JIT** *See* just-in-time (JIT).

**just-in-time (JIT)** JIT compilers convert bytecode into machine code just before it is executed.

**JVM** *See* Java Virtual Machine (JVM).

# K

**KB** *See* kilobyte (KB).

**kilobyte (KB)** A unit of measure equal to 1,024 bytes.

# L

**laptop** A computer with an integrated screen and keyboard that is intended to be carried around easily and used just about anywhere.

**latency** A period of time that the computer must wait while a disk drive is positioning itself to read a particular block of data.

**lifetime** The time during which a variable is available for use.

**locale** An identification of a country and region and the cultural conventions used there, including such things as font, language, and formats for dates, times, currency, and other values.

**localization** The process of making a program support a specific locale.

**lock** A mechanism that grants exclusive access to a resource for one thread in a multithreaded application. Locks can prevent race conditions.

**looping variable** *See* control variable.

# M

**mainframe** A large centralized computer that can serve hundreds or even thousands of users simultaneously.

**MB** *See* megabyte (MB).

*Me* In Visual Basic, a keyword that refers to the object currently executing code.

**megabyte (MB)** A unit of measure equal to 1,024 KB.

**member** A property, method, or event belonging to a class.

**method** (1) A piece of code provided by an object, such as a control, that a program can call to make the object do something.
(2) A routine (that may or may not return a value) provided by a class.

**Microsoft Intermediate Language (MSIL)** *See* Common Intermediate Language (CIL).

**millions of instructions per second (MIPS)** A measurement of a computer's speed.

**MIPS** *See* millions of instructions per second (MIPS).

**modal** A dialog box is modal if it keeps the application's focus so that the user cannot interact with other parts of the application until it is closed.

**modeless** A dialog box is modeless if it allows the user to interact with other parts of the application while it is still visible.

**modulus** The operator, represented by the symbol %, that returns the remainder after division. For example, 20 % 3 is 2 because 20 divided by 3 is 6 with a remainder of 2.

**multiple inheritance** When a child class inherits from more than one parent class. Neither Microsoft Visual Basic nor C# allows multiple inheritance.

**multitasking** Executing multiple processes quickly in turn to make them appear to all be running simultaneously.

**multithreading** Executing multiple threads within a single process, either multitasking on a single central processing unit (CPU) or simultaneously on multiple cores.

# N

**narrowing conversion** When a value is converted from one data type to another that may not be able to hold the value without losing precision.

**netbook** A laptop that's even more stripped down than a notebook. They often are intended for using network applications such as web browsers where most of the processing occurs on a remote server. *See also* laptop *and* notebook.

**neutral culture** A culture such as *en* or *fr* that is associated with a language, but not a particular country or region. *See also* specific culture.

**non-deterministic finalization** The idea that you can't predict when garbage collection will occur, and thus when unused objects will be destroyed or finalized.

**non-volatile** Not requiring power to retain data.

**notebook** A stripped-down laptop that trades power for portability. These typically don't include external devices such as DVD or CD drives. *See also* laptop.

**nullable** Indicates that a parameter or variable can take the special value *null*, which means it has no meaningful value.

# O

**object store** A database designed to store and retrieve objects.

**object-oriented programming (OOP)** Writing programs that use classes and objects as a major part of their design.

**object-relational database** A database that provides extra features to make storing and retrieving objects easier.

**object-relational mapping** Provides a layer between a relational database and a program's object-oriented code. This gives a separation

between developers working on the two pieces of the application so they can work more efficiently.

**OOP** *See* object-oriented programming (OOP).

**operand** One of the values combined by an operator.

**operator** A symbol, such as + or /, that a program uses to tell the computer how to combine values to produce a result.

**overabstraction** Using abstraction too much, resulting in very abstract classes that are not necessary for the program.

**overgeneralization** *See* overabstraction.

**overridable** In Microsoft Visual Basic, refers to a class member that a child class can replace with new functionality.

**override** A child class can override a member defined by the parent class by defining a new version.

# P

**paging** When the computer moves data between random access memory (RAM) and the hard disk to free up memory. Paging can greatly reduce a program's execution speed.

**pair programming** A coding technique where one programmer (the driver) writes code and explains what he or she is doing, while another watches and looks for problems.

**palmtop** A handheld computer with limited graphics and computing power typically used to store simple information, such as contact information and phone numbers.

**parameter** A value that can be passed to a routine to give it information that it can use in performing its task.

**parameterless constructor** A constructor that takes no parameters.

**parent class** A class from which other classes are derived.

**Pascal case** A naming convention where each word is capitalized, as in *GenerateSalesReport*.

**pass by reference** A reference to an argument is passed into a routine's parameter. Changes to the parameter are reflected as changes to the argument. In Visual Basic, arguments passed by reference use the *ByRef* keyword.

**pass by value** A copy of an argument's value is passed into a routine's parameter. Changes to the parameter are not reflected as changes to the argument. In Visual Basic, arguments passed by value use the *ByVal* keyword.

**PC** *See* personal computer (PC).

**PDA** *See* personal digital assistant (PDA).

**personal computer (PC)** A computer intended to be used by a single person at one time.

**personal digital assistant (PDA)** A handheld computer similar to a palmtop. Most of these use a stylus for input. Some of the more powerful of these include networking capabilities.

**pocket computer** *See* palmtop.

**polymorphism** The ability of a program to treat an object as if it were from a parent class.

**pop-up menu** *See* context menu.

**precedence** Used to define the order in which operators are evaluated in an expression. For example, * and / have higher precedence than (and are therefore performed before) + and −.

**procedure** *See* routine.

**process** An executing instance of a program.

**programming environment** A set of tools that help you design, write, build, run, test, and debug programs.

**property** A value associated with an object.

**property** *get* **method** A method that returns a property's value.

**property** *set* **method** A method that sets a property's value.

**pseudocode** A method that uses statements similar to a programming language for describing computer algorithms.

# R

**race condition** A problem in parallel computing where the result depends on the exact sequence or timing of the processes.

**raise** An object raises an event.

**RAM** *See* random access memory (RAM).

**random access file** A file with fixed-length records so that a program can jump to a particular record and update one record without rewriting the entire file.

**random access memory (RAM)** A memory device where data is stored while a program is using it. Ideally, all variables are stored in RAM while the program is running, but if all the RAM is full, the program may need to use paging to free some memory. When the computer is turned off, RAM loses its data.

**read-only memory (ROM)** Similar to RAM, except that the computer can only read the memory and cannot change the data it contains. Unlike RAM, ROM retains its data when the computer is turned off. *See also* random access memory (RAM).

**reference type** A data type where a variable contains a reference to the value stored elsewhere in memory. Classes are reference types.

**registry** A hierarchical database used by Microsoft Windows to store configuration information for the operating system and many of the programs installed on the system.

**regression testing** Testing a program to see if recent changes to the code have broken any existing features.

**relational database** A database where tables hold records containing fields. Fields holding the same values link related tables.

**ROM** *See* read-only memory (ROM).

**routine** A named piece of code that other pieces of code can invoke to perform some useful task. Routines are also called *subroutines, procedures, subprocedures, subprograms, functions,* or *methods.*

**routine scope** A scope limited to the code within a routine after a variable's declaration.

**run time** The time when the compiled program is executing.

# S

**schema** A file that determines the kinds of values allowed in an Extensible Markup Language (XML) file. For example, it might require that the file have a *TestScores* root element containing a series of *Student* elements. Types of schema files include Document Type Definition (DTD) and XML Schema Definition (XSD) files.

**semicolon-delimited file** A text file where records are written on separate lines and the fields within a record are separated by semicolons.

**server** A generic term for a computer that serves multiple users or client applications simultaneously.

**setter** A method that sets a property's value.

**shared member** A class member that is shared by all instances of the class. Shared members are referred to using the class itself, as in *Student.CreateStudent()*. *See also* instance member.

**short-circuit operator** *See* conditional operator.

**shortcut** A key sequence that immediately invokes a command. For example, Ctrl+S might save the file that a program is editing.

**shortcut operator** *See* conditional operator.

**side effect** An unexpected effect that occurs outside a routine. For example, if a function that returns a value also leaves a database connection open. Side effects can be confusing, so they often lead to bugs.

**spaghetti code** Code that's so convoluted that it's extremely difficult to figure out how it works. The unrestrained use of *Go To* statements can lead to spaghetti code.

**specific culture** A neutral culture plus a particular country or region, as in *en-US* or *de-DE*. *See also* neutral culture.

**spreadsheet** A program that stores data in gridlike pages. Typically, spreadsheets allow the user to enter formulas and display charts and graphs.

**stack frame** A piece of memory allocated on the call stack to hold information about a routine call, such as its local variables and the program location where execution should resume when the routine exits. *See also* call stack.

**structure** A program-defined data type that keeps related fields together. In C# and Microsoft Visual Basic, a structure also may contain methods.

**structure scope** The scope for items defined inside a structure but not inside any of its methods.

**subclass** The act of making a subclass from a parent class. *See also* child class.

**subprocedure** *See* routine.

**subprogram** *See* routine.

**subroutine** *See* routine.

**super class** *See* parent class.

# T

**tab-delimited file** A text file where records are written on separate lines and the fields within a record are separated by tab characters.

**Task Parallel Library (TPL)** A library in the Microsoft .NET Framework containing tools for executing multithreaded tasks in parallel relatively easily.

**TB** *See* terabyte (TB).

**TCP** *See* Transmission Control Protocol (TCP).

**TCP/IP** *See* Internet Protocol Suite.

**terabyte (TB)** A unit of measure equal to 1,024 gigabytes.

**ternary operator** *See* conditional operator.

**test-driven development** A development approach where programmers build tests to evaluate software before writing the software. After the software is written, the developers use the tests to evaluate it.

***this*** In C# or C++, a keyword that refers to the object currently executing code.

**thrashing** When a program causes frequent paging.

**thread** A sequence of executing instructions within a process that may execute in parallel with other threads.

**tower** A desktop computer with a larger case, making it easier to add new hardware but making it hard to fit on a desk (so it often sits on the floor).

**TPL** *See* Task Parallel Library (TPL).

**Transmission Control Protocol (TCP)** A protocol that provides reliable delivery of a stream of bytes from one computer to another. TCP provides reliable delivery of a stream of bytes from one computer to another.

**type conversion** Transforming a value from one data type to another.

# U

**user-centric viewpoint** A project design that focuses on the tasks that the user must perform and building a user interface that supports those tasks.

# V

**value type** A data type where a variable contains the value itself. Examples include the *Integer*, *Decimal* types, enumerations, and structures.

**variable** A named piece of memory that can hold data of a specific type so that the program can manipulate it.

**virtual** In C#, refers to a class member that a child class can replace with new functionality.

# W

**web service** A program running on a network that another program can call for service.

**Wi-Fi** A standard for connecting devices wirelessly.

**widening conversion** When a value is converted from one data type to another that is guaranteed to be able to hold the value without losing any precision.

**Windows Forms** A development technology used in building Microsoft Windows applications that uses Windows Forms controls. *See also* Windows Presentation Foundation (WPF).

**Windows Presentation Foundation (WPF)** A development technology used in building Microsoft Windows applications. WPF controls use graphics hardware more directly than Windows Forms controls, so they provide better graphic performance and additional features, such as control transformations. *See also* Windows Forms.

**word** A group of bytes. The number of bytes in a word is chosen so a particular computer and operating system can manipulate words efficiently. For example, there may be 8 or 16 bytes in a word.

**workstation** A powerful desktop or tower that has extra hardware features, such as multiple screens or more powerful graphics processors.

**WPF** *See* Windows Presentation Foundation (WPF).

# X

**XAML** *See* Extensible Application Markup Language (XAML).

**XML** *See* Extensible Markup Language (XML).

**XML comment** A special comment containing Extensible Markup Language (XML) code that the code editor in Microsoft Visual Studio can understand. These can also be extracted to use in making documentation.

**XML Path (XPath) language**  A language for specifying how to select elements in an XML file.

**XML Schema Definition (XSD) file**  A type of schema definition file. *See* schema.

**XPath**  *See* XML Path (XPath) language.

**XSD**  *See* XML Schema Definition (XSD) file.

**XSLT**  *See* Extensible Stylesheet Language Transformations (XSLT).

# Index

## Symbols

^ operator, 107, 109, 111
^= operator, 110
- operator, 108
-= operator, 110
! operator, 108
!= operator, 109
? operator, 113
?: operator, 109
* operator, 108
*= operator, 110
/ operator, 108
/= operator, 110
\ operator, 108
\= operator, 110
& operator, 109, 112
&& operator, 109
&= operator, 110
% operator, 108
%= operator, 110
+ operator, 108
+= operator, 110
< operator, 109
<< operator, 109, 112
<<= operator, 110
<= operator, 109
<> operator, 109
= operator, 109
== operator, 109
> operator, 109
>= operator, 109
>> operator, 109, 112
>>= operator, 110
| operator, 109, 112
|= operator, 110
|| operator, 109

~ operator, 108, 111
--x operator, 108, 111
++x operator, 108, 111

## A

A.B operator, 108
About command, 38
abstract classes, 151
abstraction, 154–156
accelerators (with menus), 34–35
Accept button, 43
accessibility, 87–89
    of routines, 136
accessors, 144
addition, 106
additive operators, 109
agile development, 177–178
A(i) operator, 108
A[i] operator, 108
AL register, 25
Alt key, 34
Anchor property, 61, 62
AndAlso operator, 109
And operator, 109
AppendText method, 66
arrays, 75
arrays, parameter, 130, 134
artificial intelligence, 21
assemblers, 26
assembly language, 26
Assert method, 179
Assignment operators, 110
auto-hiding windows, 30
automatic documentation from, 171
AutoSize property, 61

# X

# About the Author

**Rod Stephens** started out as a mathematician, but while studying at MIT, he discovered the joys of algorithms and has been programming professionally ever since. During his career, he has worked on an eclectic assortment of applications in such diverse fields as telephone switching, billing, repair dispatching, tax processing, wastewater treatment, photographic processing, vision diagnostics, cartography, and training for professional football players. Rod has spoken at programming conferences and user's group meetings, and is an experienced instructor.

A Visual Basic Microsoft Most Valuable Professional (MVP), Rod has written 24 books that have been translated into half a dozen different languages, and more than 250 magazine articles covering C#, Visual Basic, Visual Basic for Applications, Delphi, and Java. Rod's popular VB Helper website (*http://www.vb-helper.com*) receives several million hits per month and contains thousands of pages of tips, tricks, and example code for Visual Basic programmers. His new C# Helper website (*http://www.csharphelper.com*) contains similar tips, tricks, and examples for C# developers.

Sign up for his Visual Basic newsletters at *http://www.vb-helper.com/newsletter.html*, visit his blog at *http://blog.csharphelper.com*, or contact him at *RodStephens@vb-helper.com* or *RodStephens@csharphelper.com*.

# What do you think of this book?

We want to hear from you!
To participate in a brief online survey, please visit:

**microsoft.com/learning/booksurvey**

Tell us how well this book meets your needs—what works effectively, and what we can do better. Your feedback will help us continually improve our books and learning resources for you.

Thank you in advance for your input!

nformation can be obtained at www.ICGtesting.com
the USA
0936241011
IBV00002B/1/P